RED RIVER RISING

BOREALIS
BOOKS

Red River

The Anatomy of a Flood and the Survival

Rising

of an American City

Ashley Shelby

Borealis Books is an imprint of the Minnesota Historical Society Press.

The Minnesota Historical Society Press is a member of the Association of American University Presses.

www.borealisbooks.org

Manufactured in the United States of America

10 9 8 7 6 5 4 3 2 1

∞ The paper used in this publication meets the minimum requirements of the American National Standard for Information Sciences—Permanence for Printed Library materials, ANSI Z39.48-1984.

International Standard Book Number 0-87351-500-5 (cloth)

Library of Congress Cataloging-in-Publication Data
Shelby, Ashley, 1977–
    Red River rising : the anatomy of a flood and the survival of an American city / Ashley Shelby.
        p.   cm.
    Includes bibliographical references.
    ISBN 0-87351-500-5 (alk. paper)
    1. Floods—North Dakota—Grand Forks Region.
    2. Floods—Red River of the North.
    3. Disaster relief—North Dakota—Grand Forks Region.
    I. Title.
GB1399.4.N9S54 2003
978.4'16—dc22

                                                2003025177

Title page photograph: Looking west across the Sorlie Bridge from East Grand Forks, Minnesota, to Grand Forks, North Dakota, on April 21, 1997, the day the Red River of the North reached its highest recorded flow. Photo by Steven W. Norbeck, United States Geological Survey.

For my father

RED RIVER RISING

Introduction

It's late June 2000 and I am driving northwest on I-94, that lonely trucker's passage into the big bad West. The hand-painted signs for buffalo meat begin showing up in fallow soybean fields around Fergus Falls, Minnesota. Crumbling silos stand like tired sentries over farms that have fallen into disuse or been reduced to hobbies. At the turnoff to I-29, the city of Fargo is inundated with American consumer culture—Old Navy, Hooters, Wal-Mart. Interstate 29 is flat and lonely, offering an uninterrupted vista to the Canadian border. And somewhere, out of my sight but not far from the highway, the Red River of the North is heading to the same place I am.

I knew Grand Forks, North Dakota from photographs burned on my brain: a city under water, a river becoming an inland sea, an old downtown submerged while being consumed by fire. The Red River of the North had burst through the dikes, destroying first the working-class neighborhoods crouched on the banks, then the historic downtown. As the overfed Red River swept through the streets of old Grand Forks, eleven of the city's oldest and best loved landmark buildings were consumed in a spectacular electrical fire.

These images are familiar to me because my father, a television journalist in Minneapolis, spent weeks in Grand Forks in April of 1997, floating down its main street in a motorboat. In the tapes of his reports, he looks haggard and cold, sitting in a boat that rocks gently in the current moving down DeMers Avenue. One tape shows him floating down North Fourth Street, and in the old downtown buildings some distance behind him, an angry, orange fire slides its tongue in and out of the windows. That's what I knew about Grand Forks. An old river town, submerged in its river, and fifty-two thousand people leaving their homes, some for the last time, retreating to the outskirts of their city to watch it go under, to watch it burn. And though a city's fate was still undecided, to everyone except those personally affected by the flood, what had just transpired was only a fleeting news story.

In Grand Forks, it is simply called "the flood." It has affected this town like a war. Here, time is measured against it. *Before the flood. After the flood.* And in a town that has been battered by severe floods for over a century, including five low-grade catastrophic events in the last twenty years, the fact that "the flood" means the same flood to everyone is a testament to the events of the spring of 1997.

Farther upstream that spring, little towns all along the Red's course found themselves underwater, as they had in other years. Cows and hogs, trapped in shallow oxbows, drowned as the river rose. When the temperature dropped, their carcasses froze solid, stones in the iced-over river. Levees failed. Some didn't. It was a bad flood year—in some towns, the worst ever. But when the Red reached Grand Forks, high up on the North Dakota–Minnesota border, it performed an act of revenge, it seemed. The original offense was never disclosed, or it had simply gone unnamed. Few in Grand Forks could remember what they had done that could have warranted the punishment they received. But they weren't innocent. No one was.

According to some estimates, the U.S. government spends an average of nearly $54 billion a year to help communities crushed by natural disasters. In any year, it is likely that nearly three-quarters of all federally declared disasters are due to flooding. Each year, some community will suffer a staggering catastrophe. It will be showered with federal dollars, infiltrated by federal employees, then left to build itself again. In 2001, Tropical Storm Allison resulted in nearly $5 billion in damage. The year before, the horrific fire season in the American West caused $4 billion in losses. Hurricane Floyd in 1999 and Hurricane Georges in '98 cost a combined $12 billion. And for each community devastated by such events, a complex narrative ensues, one in which the concepts of fairness, community, and accountability are major themes.

I've chosen to tell the story of the 1997 Grand Forks flood not because it was the nation's worst disaster—although it ranks as one of the most expensive in U.S. history—but because the story of the town's demise and recovery could be the story of any American community unexpectedly destroyed and then left to pick up the pieces and rebuild. There are no villains—although many who lived through the '97 flood would argue that the National Weather Service's failure to accurately predict the Red's flood crest was an act of villainy. There are only real, complicated human beings—a mayor, two gifted engineers (one civic, one federal), two dedicated National Weather Service hydrologists, and a number of heroic Grand Forks residents—who struggled to save a town.

On my first visit to Grand Forks I snapped a photograph that seems to hold all the contradictions within its frame. It shows a house in the floodplain that used to be Lincoln Drive, a riverside neighborhood now reduced to an empty meadow. It was, then, the only structure still standing: a pretty little yellow box house with blue shutters and a red door. As in all the neighborhoods that had been smudged out, the grass in Lincoln Drive was overgrown and brown, and the sidewalks—where there were still sidewalks—were chunks of displaced cement. Everywhere, cracked steps and wedges of driveway marked home sites like gravestones. The little yellow house was empty, but it was not abandoned. Right under the west window, in black spray paint, someone had warned the city "Do Not Tear Down. Die If You Do," and added a smiley face.

When I took that photograph, I did not yet know the woman who used to live in that house, who refused to leave it for years after the flood, who insisted on living in it despite having no electricity, water, or heat. Meanwhile, her neighbors had sold their ruined homes to the city and moved on. But then as now, that photograph tells me what is claimed, what is taken anyway, and what is left when all is said and done—if all can ever be said and done here.

It is, of course, important to note that Grand Forks was not the only city devastated by the 1997 Red River flood. Fargo, North Dakota, lost neighborhoods and a good percentage of its downtown; Breckenridge and Ada, both Minnesota towns, were heavily damaged; and countless small towns up and down the course of the Red suffered immeasurable losses. The story of the 1997 Red River valley flood cannot be told in one tidy narrative. This book is, instead, about the anatomy of a flood in one city along the river, and that city's ultimate survival. The story of Grand Forks differs from the stories of the other cities, too, in that it is a story of the failure of a federal agency to protect an American city and the efforts of countless other agencies to rebuild that city.

It's also important to acknowledge that a disaster affects each victim in a different and complex way. Memory can warp. Interpretation may become "fact." This account of the 1997 Red River flood in Grand Forks is by no means the definitive history of the disaster. One could argue that a disaster can have no true definition. We do have facts and numbers and documents and recollection and memory and photographs, though, and somehow we cobble these things together and come up with an account. And still, it will always remain incomplete, will always be contrary to someone's remembered experience.

Perhaps what is most significant about the photograph I took of the house in Lincoln Drive is what is not there. The empty space that surrounds the house seems to be an invisible neighborhood. Even as a blank floodplain, it is still infused with very great, very palpable grief. This photograph, most importantly, speaks of all the stories not yet told, and the stories which, even after the last page of this book is turned, will remain untold.

One

1 *The Way Winter Ends*

On either side of any highway, the land of the Red River valley unfolds across the earth in what seems, in places, like an endless repetition of the same acre. In the dark, cold mornings of a northern winter, the grain elevators slowly materialize from the shadows as hulking, sluggish monsters. The sky is big, and sunrise first appears there as slender ribbons of pale purple cirrus clouds, seemingly as taut and crisp as taffeta. The land on both sides of the Red River of the North is naked, the topographic equivalent of a confession.

The people of North Dakota take the land on its own terms. The grain elevators stand full or they stand empty—depending on the year's wheat crop; farmers raise barley and ranch Hereford cattle and don't complain about a bad year and don't celebrate a good one; the American Crystal Sugar plant in Grand Forks turns tons of sugar beets into sugar cubes and hardly anyone who buys them at the giant supermarkets in Fargo knows or even cares where they come from. It's not that there is nothing to complain of in North Dakota; it's just that this is life, not a tourism campaign. North Dakota is a state that has little to brag about; and, in general, very little bragging goes on here. There is one thing, however, that its people will boast of: the weather. Plains weather summons merciless droughts that so chap the land that the soil splits and swallows crop seed, and any hope of harvest. Plains weather reacts so angrily to the collision of a frosty Alberta clipper and a warm Gulf jet stream that it spits out twenty or thirty inches of snow on fifty-mile-per-hour winds. Plains weather may be mild and salubrious in the morning, then arctic and saturnine in the afternoon. People in North Dakota are on intimate terms with weather, dependent upon it, sensitive to its subtle shiftings, and proud of its random ferocity.

The only thing more impressive than the weather is the good fight the people of North Dakota put up against it each year. In Grand Forks, when the Red River swells during spring thaw, people worry little and sandbag a lot. This is the way winter ends. Nature is not romantic here—it is stark and present. Although North Dakota raises churches and monasteries in much the same way it raises Scotch Fife and Velvet Chaff wheat, even the monks know better than to ascribe the whims of nature to God. Nature is an independent force. And Nature hit North Dakota hard as 1996 ended and through that winter and spring. The Red River of the North at Grand Forks, high up on the North Dakota–Minnesota border, did more damage that year than it had anywhere else along its course, than it ever had.

The author of the 1997 Grand Forks flood has been in dispute for years. Some in Grand Forks believed it was simply winter, a familiar guest who always overstayed his welcome. Winter has always been tough on North Dakota. Back when men used horse and sleigh to get around town in the winter, snow banks could grow so high and so dense that a man could ride his horse and cart over the drifts and never break the crust. When Grand Forks was a frontier town, farmers strung wire or rope between their barns and their farmhouses in late fall so they could feel their way between them during winter's blinding blizzards.

Despite an illustrious history of demon winters and successful adaptation to a frozen land, there are many people in Grand Forks who believe that if Nature gets the credit for the 1997 flood, then the National Weather Service should be considered its ghostwriter.

Hydrologists identify at least five factors that can predetermine spring flood conditions: a wet fall, an unusually cold winter, heavy snow accumulation, a cool spring followed quickly by a warming trend, and heavy rainfall during the thaw. The Red River valley had already been dealt a very rainy fall; by November 1996, the autumn moisture level in Grand Forks was more than twice the average amount. Then came an early cold snap and three blizzards. By December the people of Grand Forks had already dug out of enough blizzards to feel as fatigued as they normally did in late April. The head of the University of North Dakota's Regional Weather Information Center, professor Leon Osborne, Jr., told the local newspaper in mid-December, "We've already had a month of January weather, and January isn't even here yet."

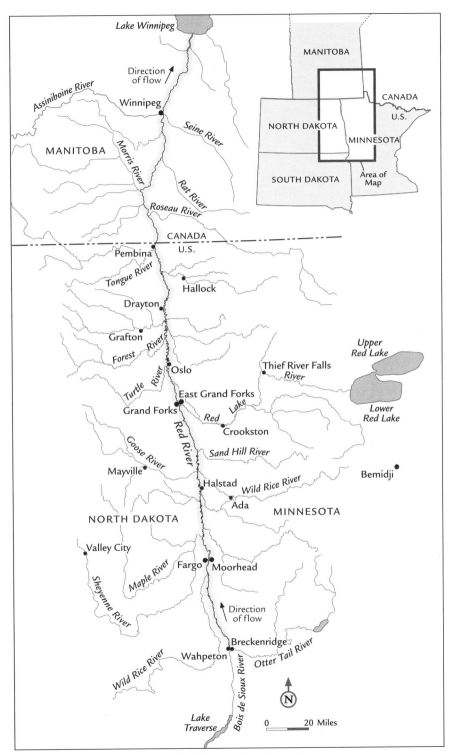

The Red River of the North and its Tributaries

January weather consists first of unobstructed prairie winds blasting across the plains in startling gusts and often bearing fifty-below-zero wind chills. It then delivers blizzards that stretch their frozen arms across the coteaus and prairies and drop inch after inch of snow, paralyzing whole cities in their embrace.

The threshold between accident and disaster is slender, yet the landscape on either side is manifestly different. To this day in Grand Forks, there is a difference of opinion regarding the fundamental character of the 1997 flood. Some consider it simply a natural disaster, dealt to Grand Forks by the same hand that delivered the blizzards of the previous winter. To consider it simply another act of Nature's hand is comforting—it implies history, regular promises to be kept. Others, however, consider what happened in the spring of 1997 a man-made calamity.

The fall had been cold and wet, and the winter composed of ice-rinsed winds and blizzards. Grand Forks had been buried under eight blizzards that season, each one so ruthless that it became a distinct personality with its own character traits. The *Grand Forks Herald* named them like hurricanes: Andy, Betty, Christopher, Doris, Elmo, Franzi, Gust, and Hannah.

In its new Grand Forks office—just a year old—the National Weather Service was performing well. Its meteorological forecasts were nearly flawless during that fall and winter. It issued blizzard warnings promptly, providing users ample time to prepare, and although its employees were themselves snowed in during several blizzards and worked with little or no staff relief for consecutive shifts, operations continued without interruption. Moreover, the agency's precipitation forecasts were uncannily precise. It was as if the weather events of that winter were not composed by Nature, but were instead dictated by the National Weather Service; if an NWS meteorologist had pointed to the sky and said, "Snow ten inches in Grand Forks," you half-believed it would.

"You say it's going to snow on that square piece of land, by God it's going to happen," Gregory Gust, a meteorologist at the Grand Forks National Weather Service office said. "We try to do it that way."

The agency's predictive skills with blizzards seemed to extend to river forecasting. For the Upper Midwest, those predictions are made at the North Central River Forecast Center (NCRFC), an NWS regional office in

Chanhassen, Minnesota, near Minneapolis. Here, scientists formulate river forecasts and relay them to local NWS offices throughout the region; those offices interpret the results to the public. The coverage area includes the Red River of the North, among 850 other basins. In 1996 the NCRFC had predicted a crest of 44.5 feet for the Red at Grand Forks. The river ultimately crested at 45.8 feet—very accurate, as river forecasts go. However, in the early 1990s, the NCRFC had displayed a tendency to overshoot the mark. In 1994 it forecasted a crest of 42 feet. When the river finally crested, it was ten feet lower than the widely publicized forecast.

It might seem of little consequence if the National Weather Service overestimates a flood stage; how much harm could there be, some might ask, in giving a city some room to breathe? A lot. Overestimating a flood crest can be as grave a mistake in terms of financial impact as underestimating can be in terms of human impact. Small cities all along the Red's course rely heavily on the NWS, designing costly flood protection plans around its forecast crest number. Reinforcing a dike with clay and sandbags—adding even only a couple of feet of protection—can cost a town millions of dollars. Small towns on the Red often exhaust their meager financial resources paying for flood protection supplies and machinery.

The National Weather Service, then, is under immense pressure to produce accurate flood crest numbers that will neither underestimate nor overestimate the actual flood crest level. Either way, a city on the Red could lose millions of dollars and blame the loss on the National Weather Service. In Chanhassen, the NCRFC hydrologists in charge of forecasting the Red River regularly field phone calls during flood season from frantic local emergency managers who tell them that if the crest prediction rises one more foot, their cities will go bankrupt. Those hydrologists often hear the emergency managers' questions echoing in their heads as they close their eyes to sleep: *Are you sure?* Since the 1994 ten-foot overshoot, NCRFC hydrologists were intent on avoiding another costly overestimate.

On January 23, 1997, the St. Paul district of the U.S. Army Corps of Engineers hosted an interagency "Winter Planning Meeting" to discuss flood potential in the Upper Mississippi River, Red River, and Great Lakes Basins. Representatives from the Corps, the National Weather Service, the United States Geological Survey, and the Federal Emergency Management Agency attended, along with local officials. Each representative presented data thought to be relevant to the task at hand—preventing a catastrophic flood. The buzz about this year's flood potential had grown louder at the agencies with each blizzard that descended upon the Red River valley. Few in the Corps' or National Weather Service's delegations had seen so much snow on the ground this early in the season.

Another interagency meeting was held a few days later, this time in Fargo. Both meetings conveyed one overriding message: this was going to be a rough flood season. Fargo weather office warning coordination officer Lou Bennett and service hydrologist Wendy Pearson began making the rounds to small communities along the Red, trying to relay the message the National Weather Service had adopted as its temporary mantra: expect to see more water this spring than you've ever seen in your life. At area shopping malls, Bennett manned booths under the slogan "Flooding: When, Where and How High." He participated in television and radio interviews about the flood potential, and attended, with Pearson, town meetings in small North Dakota towns like Harwood and Kindred.

"We've never seen this much water in the snow before," Pearson told them. "We're expecting a serious situation."

People in Grand Forks noticed an unsettling influx of strangers during the first days of February. Federal disaster officials had arrived to begin reconnaissance work and to initiate flood mitigation activities. At the same time, the Federal Emergency Management Agency (FEMA) and National Flood Insurance Program (NFIP) began issuing press releases, television public service announcements, and newspaper appeals urging Grand Forks residents to purchase low-cost federal flood insurance. On February 5, FEMA announced that it was providing an emergency enrollment plan for North Dakota towns on the Red River, cutting the required sign-up time for local and county governments by more than half. The public service spots ranged from outright pleas to slickly produced scare tactics filled with images of past catastrophes—people clinging to treetops while water raged around them. But by the middle of February virtually no one in Grand Forks had purchased flood insurance.

On February 13, the National Weather Service issued a flood outlook for the Red River valley, nearly a month earlier than usual: "Above normal soil moisture and high snowpack water equivalent represent a high spring snowmelt flood potential for the tributaries to the Red River, and a *severe* spring snowmelt flood potential for the Red River from Wahpeton, North Dakota to the Canadian border."

Later, some people in Grand Forks would criticize this first narrative outlook as wordy and imprecise. Employees of the National Weather Service, on the other hand, would wonder, "What part of 'record flooding' did they not understand?" In fact, the agency had attached a kind of glossary, titled "Terminology," to the outlook. There, "Severe Snowmelt Flood Potential" was defined as "crests from near record levels to exceeding record levels . . . assuming normal future precipitation for the remainder of the snow season." Buried in the sixth page of the seven-page outlook was this caveat: "Additional above normal precipitation and a rapid melt, combined with spring rains would increase the flood threat." For anyone without a degree in hydrology, however, this was eye-glazing verbiage.

On February 26, the NCRFC hosted an interagency flood coordination meeting at its offices in Chanhassen. It was the third held in just over a month, and the flood season hadn't even officially begun. The hydrologists assigned to the Red River announced to representatives from the U.S. Army Corps of Engineers and the United States Geological Survey (USGS), among others, that they would be issuing their first numerical flood outlook in two days. This was a big event in this circle of scientists, forecasters, and engineers. But would it catch the attention of the public?

The next day, the Red River hydrologists traveled from their Chanhassen offices to Fargo for yet another interagency flood coordination meeting. In attendance were mayors, city engineers, and emergency managers from towns up and down the Red River valley, FEMA representatives, Corps engineers and reconnaissance teams, local National Weather Service office employees, Small Business Administration and National Flood Insurance Plan representatives, North Dakota's congressional delegation (senators Kent Conrad and Byron Dorgan, and representative Earl Pomeroy), and dozens of others.

"You'd look over the people out there and it was a Who's Who of the flood fight in the Red River valley," NCRFC hydrologist Mike Anderson said. Anderson led the agency's team of four hydrologists and hydrometeorologists assigned to the Red River. For Anderson and his NCRFC colleague Steve Buan, the Red River valley was home; they'd both grown up there and still had family scattered from Wahpeton to Grand Forks. They knew the Red River. They even loved it.

"I can tell you right now," Anderson told the assembled group in Fargo, "that forecast tomorrow is going to say flood of record *or greater.*" He made sure to punch the last two words, and then paused. "Does everyone understand that? We're going to hit the flood of record at every location in the valley"—he paused again—"or *greater.*" To the city of Fargo, that meant 38 feet or more. To the city of Wahpeton, it meant 17.9 feet. To Grand Forks, it meant 49 feet.

On the 1997 Spring Flood Potential Map, which the National Weather Service issued the next day, the Red River valley was represented as a misshapen splotch of crimson. On this map, red indicated areas where flooding would be "severe." While other parts of the Upper Midwest showed moderately high flood potential, the Red River valley was the only area highlighted in red.

That same day, the number forty-nine was heard in Grand Forks for the first time. In this, its first numerical flood outlook for the season—its first solid number—the National Weather Service had calculated a crest of 49 feet for the Red River at Grand Forks. This was two-tenths of a foot higher than the city's official highest flood crest, 48.88 feet in 1979. The river, though, had been higher than that; 1897's unofficial crest of 50.2 feet was considered Grand Forks' highest. But the United States Geological Survey (USGS), the federal agency charged with constructing historical hydrographs for America's rivers, chose not to use hundred-year-old data on a river as dynamic and as ever-changing as the Red. So the 1979 crest of 48.88 feet was considered, for all intents and purposes, Grand Forks' flood of record.

The Red River's depth at Grand Forks varies, though not by much, during the year. Its normal depth is anywhere between eight and twelve feet. In Grand Forks, the river's flood stage is 28 feet. By all accounts, 49 feet would be a massive, dangerous flood, one that would test the limits of Grand Forks' levees and dikes, which could be fortified and topped to 52 feet.

The National Weather Service crest outlook was considered a "potential" crest, calculated with present snow cover plus anticipated normal precipitation for that area, for that time of year. Mike Anderson and the NCRFC hydrologists had chosen to issue this forecast two weeks earlier than they ever had before. They knew it was going to be bad and wanted people to know.

A week after the National Weather Service released its 49-foot outlook, the agency's director, Elbert "Joe" Friday, appeared on CNN to warn that spring flooding in the Red River valley would be "higher than ever before" and that people in the valley should expect "record flooding" in their towns. These kinds of statements constitute some of the strongest language in the agency's terse vernacular, but Friday went one step further to make sure the people in the Red River valley knew what he meant: "They're going to see more water than they've ever seen before in their lives." In Minnesota, NWS weather forecasters (responsible for precipitation forecasts, not river forecasts) were staging a major media campaign to emphasize the severity of the upcoming flood season. On March 1 Craig Edwards, an NWS forecaster for twenty-five years, told the *Minneapolis Star Tribune*, "This situation is the most serious I've seen since I've been here." Another article quoted hydrologist Gary McDevitt: "If we should get into a rain situation, it could be disastrous."

This kind of language kicked other federal agencies into higher gear. "We hope that residents will seriously consider taking preparedness steps now so that they are protected in the coming months should these forecasts hold true," said Roger Free, a FEMA coordinating officer.

Still, in Grand Forks, the National Flood Insurance Program enrollment logs were almost blank. The flood seemed so far away, and a crest of 49 feet seemed manageable. Many people living down near the dikes, in neighborhoods like Lincoln Drive, Riverside Park, and Central Park, kept reminding themselves that they had never even had seepage in their basements before, despite repeated flooding—the dikes had done their job. Even some insurance agents were dissuading people from buying flood policies. They considered it a waste of money.

On the far end of the University of North Dakota campus on the west edge of town, meteorology professor Leon Osborne was working in what could be described as a weather lab. The Regional Weather Information Center (RWIC) houses a prototype weather information management center, outfitted with Doppler radar, access to a network of automated observing stations similar to those used by the National Weather Service, a soundproof radio room, a television studio, an editing bay, and a graphics and animation station. The 2,000-foot laboratory is a weather analysis and forecasting crucible; it is, one could argue, a kind of condensed version of the North Central River Forecast Center in Chanhassen—but with academic wiggle room, constructed in the hope that the scientist-philosophers who work there will wed science with function.

Leon Osborne grew up in a north Texas farming community and came to UND after receiving a degree in physics from Utah State University and a masters in meteorology from the University of Oklahoma. Osborne, who looks like an ex–football player who might have let too many years pass between visits to the weight room, is the equivalent of the dean's list mainstay. He is a member of Sigma Pi Sigma physics honor society, Chi Epsilon Pi national meteorology honor society, a professional member of the American Meteorological Society, and a Sigma Xi member. He was, at UND, the big man on campus.

The RWIC would be the greatest accomplishment of Osborne's career, and the winter and spring of 1996–1997 would be its first test. Osborne and his staff were under enormous pressure. That fall the center had gone live. It had finally received state and federal funding to implement a highway weather forecasting system. The staff had divided nearly every road and interstate in North and South Dakota into sixty-mile segments. Now, every three hours, a forecast was generated for each stretch. Any driver in the Dakotas could now dial a cell phone and hear a precise, very local forecast. Osborne and his staff of eight employees—four on each shift—were prepared to produce fifteen thousand forecasts a day, twenty-four hours a day. Both states had planted hundreds of blue signs on the shoulders of major highways promoting the service, which Osborne had christened Advanced Transportation Information Systems.

However, Osborne had been told in no uncertain terms that if his system went offline for any reason—be it blizzard or flood—the funding would disappear, because he needed to prove the system's "survivability" was as close to one hundred percent as possible. Newly appointed federal secretary of transportation Rodney E. Slater had visited the RWIC that winter, arriving just ahead of a blizzard.

"Slater looks over his shoulder," Osborne remembered, "and says 'Leon, tell me: How bad is this blizzard going to be?'" Osborne stepped over to a computer and began to formulate a forecast. Slater stopped him and pointed to an unsuspecting young staffer, an underling, sitting alone at another computer.

"No," Slater said, "I want him to tell me."

"If the system went down, there went our funding," Osborne said later. "There went our program." The RWIC was the most important project Osborne had ever produced in his life, and he was determined to make it a success. But the very conditions he was forecasting could also be his undoing. To ascertain the survivability of his weather system, he needed to know how high the Red would crest. How would the Center itself be affected by a flood? Although the RWIC offices were on the far west end of Grand Forks, a relatively safe distance from the river, its hub for telephone communications—its lifeline, really—was in the U.S. West telephone building a block from the Red River. Only the slightest amount of flooding, just one levee breach, could put Osborne's program offline and bury it for good.

"I'd seen enough snow that you had to be blind not to see that there was going to be a major flood," he said. More specifically, "Given ideal snowmelt conditions, and based upon the amount of snow that we had and we were expecting to see—based upon the global weather patterns—we were expecting to see a flood that would be a record flood. If there were a record flood, and the city was not able to prepare for it, we would lose our program. The conclusion from our analysis was that we were shit out of luck." That was not precise enough; Osborne needed a reliable number, and he was unconvinced by the National Weather Service's 49-foot outlook. With sodden soil, ten feet of snow on the ground and more on its way, that outlook seemed absurd to him. Osborne set out to produce his own flood crest forecast.

On March 5, after Blizzard Gust had blown snow dust through the town on violent winds, a nominal spring arrived, mild and gray. The air grew warm, and the snowdrifts in town, still so high they formed nine-foot walls on both sides of city streets, started melting. The soil was saturated—an archive of the fall's rains and the winter's snows—and the snowmelt simply collected in giant puddles atop the earth. Interstate 29, the main corridor connecting Grand Forks to the rest of the world, had been closed for a total of eighteen days because of the blizzards. The town's civil resources—plows, National Guardsmen, the power company—had been overworked from battling blizzard after blizzard and the townspeople, too, were exhausted. The fight had been a good one, and they had triumphed, but they were tired. Everyone was looking forward to a warm spring.

After the ruinous Mississippi valley flood of 1965, the Corps of Engineers and the National Weather Service had made a deal: you show me your data, and I'll show you mine. That flood was considered, at the time, the Mississippi's worst ever for the seven-hundred-mile stretch between Royalton, Minnesota (about one hundred miles north of Minneapolis) and Hannibal, Missouri. Much of the anatomy of that flood was eerily similar to what had been happening in the Red River valley, and what would happen in the next weeks: an exceptionally cold and wet autumn that saturated the soil, a midwinter thaw, an above-average March snowfall, and an unexpected spring freeze that halted snowpack runoff. The 1965 Mississippi flood had caused $225 million in damage.

Until that point, there had been little communication between the two federal agencies. The Corps studied the mechanics of the river. The National Weather Service—then called the U.S. Weather Bureau—predicted its behavior. It often takes a disaster to force the federal government to reexamine the way it conducts business, and the 1965 Mississippi flood, simply because of its severity, brought to light the fact that greater understanding of American river systems might be gained if the two agencies shared information.

So it was in that spirit that two Corps hydraulic engineers from the St. Paul district office, Richard Pomerleau and Terry Zien, began their reconnaissance work for the National Weather Service. Pomerleau, in particular, seemed to be everywhere and able to do anything. A graduate of the University of Minnesota's Institute of Technology and a senior hydraulic engineer for the Corps, Pomerleau is also a nationally known expert in ice engineering. He has developed a highly respected emergency management spill model for the Upper Mississippi River. He is a skilled reconnaissance pilot, adept at gathering data under dire conditions.

"If we needed something," NCRFC hydrologist Steve Buan said, "he'd be able to figure out a way to figure out how to measure something. If he didn't have the equipment to measure it, he'd go back to physics principles and come up with a number." Richard Pomerleau is, in Buan's words, "MacGyver." Like MacGyver, Pomerleau and other Corps engineers have sophisticated tools in their toolkits. Likewise at the National Weather Service.

"In years past, you went out there with a coffee can, stuck it in the snow, melted it down and made your best guess, by hook or crook, how much water you could expect," said Paul Jacobs, northwest Minnesota's emergency coordinator for the Department of Public Safety. But the coffee can had now been replaced by remote sensing flyovers, satellites, automatic river gauges, and three-dimensional cameras attached to the bellies of survey planes.

The National Operational Hydrologic Remote Sensing Center, operating under the NWS's umbrella, is located next door to the NCRFC in Chanhassen. Its small staff is concerned with only one thing: snow. Its pilots collect snow data and analyze it. The mere amount of snow that has fallen in a certain location is empty data to a flood forecaster; he or she must know how much water that snow contains, and that will vary depending on the snow's character. Light, fluffy snow contains far less moisture than heavy, wet snow; it is entirely possible that a ten-inch snowfall in Grand Forks could yield twice as much moisture as a ten-inch snowfall in Bismarck. The moisture content—called snow melt equivalent—is an essential piece of data needed by flood forecasters because it determines the amount of runoff that will flow into a river during the spring thaw. Without this data, an accurate flood crest forecast is impossible.

The NCRFC, and numerous other National Weather Service river forecasting centers, utilize the Remote Sensing Center's small staff during flood season, requesting the services of two twin-engine planes, which make regular data-collecting flights. These planes, flying at five hundred feet, measure the gamma radiation emanating from the ground. The lower the radiation, so the theory goes, the more moisture on the ground, be it in the form of standing water or snow.

On other survey flights, three-dimensional cameras capture images of the floodplain, measuring elevation virtually house by house. Automatic river gauges—Grand Forks' was housed in a shed just off the Sorlie Bridge downtown—kept track of river depth, and transmitted the numbers to hydrologists in a continual stream of data. In the short history of advanced hydrologic data collection, this information had been routed directly only to hydrologists and others who were responsible for prediction. In 1997, though, a few Grand Forks city officials were wearing pagers clipped to their belts that displayed an hourly river level reading. The computer system at the city's emergency operations center could dial the modem on the Grand Forks river gauge and retrieve real-time river conditions. It was proving to be a year in which to show off how exact flood prediction could be. Any erratic river behavior would be telegraphed, literally and figuratively. Nature, it seemed, wouldn't be delivering any blows this year that the National Weather Service couldn't anticipate.

Anticipation was one thing; communication was another. The burden of communicating the severe flood threat to the city of Grand Forks rested on the shoulders of the National Weather Service and its hydrologists. If the citizens didn't know what was coming, none of this data meant anything.

"Technology has become a major player in getting us the information," Paul Jacobs said, "but we still depend on the people who use the technology and who are trained to interpret it." However, the further the coffee-can technique receded into the past, the less the men and women at the National Weather Service trusted human judgment—even their own.

The reconnaissance missions that Corps engineers Richard Pomerleau and Terry Zien were running consisted of regular low-altitude flights over various waterways in the Red River basin. Their main purpose was to gather hydraulic and hydrologic data in areas that contain Corps reservoirs. As a general rule, the Corps does not gather hydrologic data; what Pomerleau and Zien were doing for the National Weather Service was really a kind of favor. The Corps is concerned with hydraulics—the study of the mechanics of fluids, a somewhat fixed science. Hydrology, on the other hand, is concerned with the mutable behavior of rivers, the properties of flow, and the effect of water on the earth. Yet certain hydrologic "laws" could be considered fairly firm, and therefore provide the foundation for a predictive model—laws such as: in flood, the river will fall in the same way it rose. This particular "law" was so reliable, it might as well have been a divine commandment.

When the Red River entered flood stage in the beginning of April, the Corps' recon team began to gather data specifically for the National Weather Service. Pomerleau and Zien faxed their handwritten daily reports on the basin to NCRFC hydrologist Mike Anderson—meticulous reports whose details ranged from snow appearance ("The snow cover in the Wahpeton-Breckenridge area has taken on a grayish cast as the snow pack solidifies and compacts. The discoloration is probably due to increased water content on the surface") to the memories of local residents ("Farm lady said that the 1969 peak was higher but of short duration.") Anecdotal details like these were useful, even to the scientists at the National Weather Service. Despite the agency's high-functioning models and its contracted gamma flights, it still utilizes more than eleven thousand "cooperative observers"—many of them retired farmers or elderly farm widows. In many ways, these observers still provide the "coffee can" measurements that Paul Jacobs said had long since been replaced by high-tech tools.

The National Weather Service provides observers equipment—like rain gauges and yardsticks—and training materials; these may include warnings such as "Freezing rain (glaze ice) should never be reported as snowfall," or Byzantine instructions for extracting crucial data like snow moisture content. Although National Weather Service observers were "trained," many of them were elderly and living alone in remote locations, and, despite having lived through the worst weather North Dakota could offer, were perhaps more vulnerable during severe blizzards.

During Blizzard Elmo in January, two meteorologists from the Bismarck office received a phone call from a co-op observer named Florence Newsom. Her home in Hurdsfield, a tiny town halfway between Bismarck and Devil's Lake, was surrounded by ten-foot drifts, and she was unable to get to the Fischer & Porter rain gauge to change the monthly tape. The county road leading to her home had been closed for two weeks. The two NWS meteorologists—Vern Roller and Dan Markee—decided to visit Florence, who was eighty-two years old and living alone, and change the tape for her. They arrived at the blocked county road two miles from her house, minutes ahead of the Wells County snowplow. The plow became stuck when it tried to move one of the snowdrifts. After giving the plow driver a ride into town, Roller and Markee decided to walk the two miles to Florence's farmhouse. As they climbed over snowdrifts hardened by the frigid winds and nearly sixteen feet high, a "hungry-looking" coyote followed them. When the meteorologists finally reached the farmhouse, they found it was, indeed, surrounded by a levee of snow.

"After changing the Fischer & Porter tape," the meteorologists' report reads, "a cup of hot chocolate and a cookie were greatly appreciated."

People in the Red River valley liked the regional NWS employees; they were neighbors. Most of them had grown up near the river. They raised their families in the valley. The NWS was the farmer's friend, the city emergency manager's ally, a trusted comrade.

But after the flood of 1997, many people in Grand Forks found it hard to look any NWS employee in the face without feeling anger rising from their chest, into their throat, the words catching there. The National Weather Service, in the minds of many citizens, had ruined their lives.

On March 14, 1997, the National Weather Service issued a revised flood outlook for towns along the Red River of the North, raising the crest numbers for nearly every forecast point along its course—from its headwaters at Wahpeton down through Fargo, Halstad, Drayton, and Oslo. The only city on the Red that did not see an increase in its flood crest outlook number was Grand Forks. It remained at 49 feet. Ten days later, the Corps of Engineers told Grand Forks' city engineers to build the dikes to 52 feet, giving the city three feet of "freeboard"—breathing room.

At the RWIC, Leon Osborne and his staff had come up with a flood crest number. It was different from the number pegged by the National Weather Service. Far different. Osborne's analysis of the flooding situation in Grand Forks was not, in the purest sense of the word, hydrologic. Osborne had performed a kind of climatological and meteorological medley: he produced an aggregate number based on all the radar the RWIC had generated in the last few months; he created a high-resolution grid of precipitation that had occurred over the course of the winter; he sent staff out to perform snow moisture spot checks; he kept tabs on the distribution of snowfall; he utilized many of the same co-op reports the NWS was utilizing, then adjusted his own data to reflect what the observers were reporting. With this information, Osborne then compared the collected data with previous snowmelts, specifically the 1996 thaw.

"On the left-hand side of the equation, I have 1995–1996 snowfall and the 1996–1997 snowfall; on the right-hand side of the equation, I have crest level of 1995–1996, divided by the crest level of 1996–1997. It's a simple ratio." By applying the dynamics of the 1996 snowmelt to the nascent 1997 snowmelt—the snow moisture numbers, the precipitation numbers, and so on—Osborne could extrapolate, could project how the coming thaw would unfold. His analysis suggested one thing: "an incredible amount of water."

His forecast: 52 feet. Although only three feet higher than the NWS outlook, it might as well have been thirty. Even if the river stayed at exactly 52 feet, perfectly level with the tops of the dikes, it would take only the slightest change—an escaped canoe, a block of ice fallen from the undercarriage of the Sorlie Bridge, an unexpected rainfall—for the river to start pouring over the dikes.

But Osborne did not come up with his number by using a hydrologic model, something widely considered absolutely necessary to accurately predict a flooding river's crest number. He didn't take a thorough measurement of the water content of the snow on the ground. "I don't have to," Osborne said. "I have a pretty good idea at what temperature the snow was formed. There are standard relationships; given the nucleation temperature of the snow and the environment in which it resides after it falls, I can tell what the sublimation rate is going to be."

These are the words of a scientist confident in his own expertise, one who is even a little cocky. Osborne liked to use his tools to enhance his performance, not to dictate it, and for that reason felt comfortable filling in gaps in the data with his own educated guesses—something that was simply not done at the National Weather Service.

"Yeah, there was some subjectivity to it," Osborne said. "Human judgment came into it when we aggregated the precipitation because there were data voids. The radar wasn't hitting everywhere." Osborne could do this—could rely on his own judgment when certain data was absent—because the numbers he was generating were being used only to evaluate the flood risk to the Regional Weather Information Center itself, not to the city of Grand Forks. In fact, he made it a point not to step on any toes. "We were trying to be very respectful of the National Weather Service; I mean, that's their job, not ours. The last thing I ever wanted to do was to get crosswise with the National Weather Service."

On March 18, the hall at the National Press Club in Washington, D.C., was filled with news cameras, microphones, and network and newspaper reporters. Two National Weather Service officials stood at the podium: director Dr. Elbert "Joe" Friday, Jr. and Hydrologic Information Center chief Frank Richards. They were preparing to announce the potential for one of the worst flood years the United States had ever seen. The agency had invited FEMA director James Lee Witt and American Red Cross director Elizabeth Dole to join them at the news conference, hopeful that the presence of the U.S. government's disaster relief agency and one of the largest private relief organizations in the world would convey the urgency of its message. Both had declined to appear, and the National Weather Service "elected to go it alone." Friday and Richards very much hoped that the wire reporters would write stories that emphasized the certainty of severe flooding, and stressed the importance of proactive flood protection strategy, especially in the Red River valley.

"These could be the highest floods in those areas in the one hundred and fifty years we have been keeping records," Dr. Friday said when he stepped to the microphone at the Press Club. "You're going to see hundreds of square miles underwater. We want to make sure this doesn't come as a surprise to anyone."

Upper Midwestern states "have been depositing snow all winter like a savings bank," Richards added. "We'll be drawing it out of that account this spring."

The headlines and lead paragraphs that appeared in more than two hundred newspapers across the country the next day likely made Friday and Richards happy. *USA Today:* "The highest floods in 150 years in the northern Midwest could occur this spring as a result of a deep blanket of snow." Associated Press: "Friday predicted record-breaking floods on the Red River of the North in North Dakota and northwestern Minnesota." Reuters: "Spring flooding could be more widespread this year than in any year in the past decade, with the upper Midwest's snowbound winter leaving that region especially vulnerable." And in the small papers across North Dakota, the warning was duly noted. *Bismarck Tribune:* "Flood alert puts focus on N.D." *Wahpeton Daily News:* "NWS says major flood is probable." Ten days later, on March 28, the National Weather Service issued another revised flood outlook for the Red River valley. But the crest number for Grand Forks again remained the same: 49 feet.

The National Guard began "dusting" the Red River on March 31. A river that flows north tends to dam itself with chunks of ice during the spring thaw; a dammed river will flood. Dusting a river with sand softens the ice—the sand attracts the sun's thermal energy—and speeds up thawing, reducing ice jams. The 1997 dusting operation was the most extensive in state history. Helicopters made flyovers, and National Guardsmen hung out of the chopper doors and dumped dark sand onto the frozen river. On March 30, the National Weather Service issued an official flood warning—akin to a thunderstorm warning—for the Red River of the North, which meant the flood threat was immediate.

In Grand Forks the air was growing warmer and signs of spring emerged. Grass began to appear from beneath the melting snow, and the snowdrifts that had lined the streets all winter were shrinking. The balmy weather gave many people hope that the flood wouldn't be so bad. National Weather Service hydrologist Wendy Pearson remembered being challenged by a reporter who questioned whether the 49-foot crest number might be a bit of an exaggeration.

"He said, 'Out on the street people are saying we're not going to have such a bad flood,'" Pearson said. "They changed their minds and felt things wouldn't be so bad."

But in Utah a little blizzard was building, gathering strength as it pushed its way across the plains. It moved toward Grand Forks like a frozen tumbleweed, growing larger as it approached.

2 *River Town*

Towns will perish in major floods—many already have. The Mississippi has swept away whole communities while carving itself a new path. Mark Twain noted a number of Delta towns that became river debris, as well as a few that were simply exiled behind a newly formed sandbar, ending their run as river towns. The grandest American river city of them all, New Orleans, is probably doomed to the waters of the Mississippi and the Gulf of Mexico as the foundations of bayou shacks sink into the mud and city engineers worry about the skyscrapers and the French Quarter. There they have confined the Mississippi through various flood protection systems, as if it were an animal that could be caged. As Twain noted—as he celebrated—the river will flow where it wants, even if a city has built cement banks to contain it. This is what rivers do; the relationships between rivers and river towns are temporary affairs.

But the Red River of the North had managed a long-lasting, if sometimes volatile, relationship with its towns. There was no Mississippi-like history, with entire towns turned into islands overnight by cutoffs—the river shortening itself by rerouting its flow from a loop to a straightaway (the river, in Twain's words, "cleaves the banks away like a knife.") The Red was a relatively well-behaved river.

It stretches 533 miles from its source at the confluence of the Bois de Sioux and Otter Tail Rivers—near the twin towns of Wahpeton, North Dakota and Breckenridge, Minnesota—to Lake Winnipeg in Manitoba. It forms a riparian border between North Dakota and Minnesota, snaking its way across the floor of a massive, extinct glacial lake named Agassiz. The inscrutable whims of the Red River of the North are inspired, in large part, by this fossil inland sea.

Named for Harvard geology professor Louis Agassiz, Lake Agassiz was the largest Pleistocene lake on the continent. It was nearly as large as all of the Great Lakes combined, and its ancient crater is still visible today from the air. The loamy soil of the valley—sometimes called raisin cake— is what's left over from the giant lakebed. The secret of the Red's River valley's exceptional flatness and its nearly imperceptible northward tilt (the reason the river flows north) is found in the weight of the massive glacier that Agassiz believed once stretched from coast to coast (the professor liked to call glaciers "God's great plough"). When the wall of ice finally began melting, it receded from south to north, inclining the land ever so slightly toward the North Pole, and flattening everything in its path. North Dakota's wrinkles were ironed into a taut drift prairie.

The Red is a young, crooked river that hasn't had enough time to cut much of a path across the lakebed. Its channel is so poorly defined that it seems to be a writhing animal in a state of extreme discomfort: hairpin turns, oxbow lakes, stretches where the water seems unable to get up a head of steam. In places, its current is so sluggish that the river seems not to be flowing at all, to be a river of dark glass.

Geologists with the North Dakota Geological Survey have likened the muddy Red River to a convoy of ten-ton capacity trucks. On a typical summer day, the Red carries more than sixteen hundred tons of "suspended sediment" past Grand Forks. This is the equivalent, state geologists say, of 162 dump trucks, each carrying ten tons of mud, traveling northward through Grand Forks each day. Here the Red is a thin, shallow river (two hundred feet wide and eight to ten feet deep), but it is remarkably turbid. The river generally flows about one foot per second, or two-thirds of a mile per hour. Wherever the Red is going, you would probably get there faster on foot.

In 1848, long before whites had permanently settled at Grand Forks, Indiana geologist David Dale Owens, a thin man with large, lucid blue eyes, paddled up the Red River in early summer and noted the debarked trees and snapped trunks near the banks there. With his sharp geologist's eye, he saw the arboreal graveyard as evidence of "the power of ice in this river"— blocks of ice riding the Red's flood current that spring had cut through the riverbank forests like a giant axe. Three years later, the Red River flood of 1851 forced Norman Kittson of the American Fur Company to move his headquarters from riverside Pembina to St. Joseph (now Walhalla), about thirty miles to the west. The 1897 deluge, whose record was shattered a century later, inundated Grand Forks in similar fashion—damaging all twenty-five blocks of downtown, weakening bridges, and leaving a lake that was thirty miles wide and a hundred and fifty miles long. People and their livestock took refuge atop haystacks and roofs. Historic flood marginalia includes a steamboat finding itself docked on Third Street during the 1882 flood; in 1897, engineers rolled four locomotives onto to the Great Northern Railway Bridge to anchor it, preventing the floodwaters from washing it away. Old photographs of various Grand Forks floods look so similar, sometimes only the fashions of the day set them apart from one another. Streets filled with water, houses nearly submerged. People smile into the lens, wearing vests, suspenders, porkpie hats, dresses with frilly lace collars. There seems to be no sorrow in their faces.

You note the absence of emotion in those old photos because the pictures of people from the 1997 flood do show sorrow; it is deeply etched in many faces. In some faces, it will always remain. Maybe the North Dakota brave face was braver a hundred years ago than it is now. Perhaps the people back then hadn't come to trust the experts and the science. Perhaps they couldn't be as disappointed when they had no expectation that they, or anyone else, could divine what the river would do. No one led them to believe anything but the worst; in river towns, this constitutes logic. But with predictive science came comfort and complacency and the illogical belief that man can beat the river, even when the river is at its worst—so long as he knows what he's up against.

Before the plains states became a cliché for obsolescence, and the economy left Grand Forks and other Dakota towns in the dust of their own collapse, industry and agriculture and the Great Northern Railway advertised this region as the Promised Land.

In 1738 Pierre Gaultier de Varennes, sieur de la Vérendrye, put his hands atop the heads of Mandan chiefs and made them "his children." When Lewis and Clark arrived at Indian villages on their way to the "Great Western Sea" in 1805, they told the residents they had a new "father" in Washington: Thomas Jefferson. The Hudson's Bay Company, the North West Company, and John Jacob Astor's American Fur Company battled each other for Indian loyalty and animal fur. Forts appeared on the Upper

Missouri River, and the Red River valley became a point of transport for goods.

River forks make for good camps, and many towns in the new America of the Louisiana Purchase were built near confluences. In the late eighteenth century, the convergence of the thin Red River and the thinner Red Lake River had been a campsite for French fur traders. They called the small confluence *les Grandes Fourches*. The French had a penchant for overstatement.

There were only a few scattered wintering houses for traders when the Columbia Fur Company built a post on that site in 1826. It was a stop for métis families—people of mixed Indian and white blood—who hauled tons of supplies and buffalo robes between St. Paul and Winnipeg on the famed Red River oxcarts, wooden carts with screeching axles that could be heard for miles. The Red became a steamboat river in 1859, when St. Paul merchants, hoping to increase the trade, offered a reward to the first steamboat on the Red. The steamboats that plied the Red—the *Anson Northrup*, the *International*, the *Dakota*, the *Alpha*, the *Cheyenne*, the *Manitoba*, and the *Minnesota*—were sternwheelers that burned wood for power, and they populated the Red River as if it were a floating dockyard. But almost as soon as the steamboats were launched on the Red, it was over. By 1880, the railroads had arrived in Grand Forks.

Towns were built on rivers (like Grand Forks and Fargo and Williston and Wahpeton), on lakes (like Devils Lake and Fort Totten), on old military posts and Indian villages (like Fort Rice and Fort Yates, where Hunkpapa chief Sitting Bull was originally buried after Red Tomahawk led U.S. marshals to his cabin—the day when, as some Dakota Sioux put it, there was blood on the moon), and on railroads (Almont and Minot and all the rest, it seemed. Towns were built for railway stations, not the other way around, and for so long, a railroad line was a lifeline.) The discovery of gold in the Black Hills of South Dakota in the 1870s meant railroad tycoons would set down tracks to get people out there, to start empire-building. Steel ties were laid across Dakota Sioux treaty lands, industry taking precedence over promises made, as it has always seemed to do. The frontier was opening and people were coming, and they needed building materials for homesteads, crop seeds, and livestock; they needed pianos for the saloons.

When James J. Hill decided to build his transcontinental railroad in

1879, Grand Forks became the largest rail terminal between St. Paul and Seattle, as well as the headquarters of the Dakota Division of the Great Northern Railway—overseeing what was at the time, in sheer mileage, the world's largest main-line rail network. Now Grand Forks had it all. It had a river—one that was a clear path to Winnipeg for steamboats and scows. It had railroad companies in town—the Great Northern, the Soo Line, the Northern Pacific, the Manitoba. It had agriculture—sugar beets and pinto beans and flaxseed and canola and potatoes and barley and spring wheat and durum wheat and sunflowers. Homes were built with beams and planks floated upriver from Winnipeg. By the end of the nineteenth century, other industries had set up shop, including bottling works, breweries, and foundries. Grand Forks even had a semiprofessional baseball team, the Pickets.

Norwegian immigrants began moving into Grand Forks around this time, seduced by the railroads' foreign agents who haunted Oslo and Kristiansand and Trondheim with promises. The new North Dakotans built sod houses, cultivated the fertile valley soil, and found work on steamboats or at the local mill. In 1872, the five Norwegian families in town couldn't agree on a location for a schoolhouse; each family built its own school and hired draymen from local steamboats as teachers.

Scandinavian, German, and German-Russian immigrants made up only part of the influx, but they were often the only ones who stayed. Immigrants often came with their whole families—sometimes their whole village. The eastern plains became a checkerboard of ethnic enclaves. Whole towns spoke only German, or Swedish, or Danish, or Russian. Railroad men visiting these villages often had to bring translators with them. As a result, even today, when you ask a North Dakotan about his background, he's apt to answer with his ethnic heritage.

"You are now our children," James J. Hill told North Dakota farmers in 1915, "but we are in the same boat with you, and have got to prosper with you or we have got to be poor with you." It was not true. When the North Dakota farmer suffered, it was often at the hands of the outsider. Investors and bankers on the East Coast had supplied North Dakota with capital for the railroads that brought people and investment to the plains. Minneapolis grain brokers controlled commodity prices for the wheat that North Dakota farmers were trying to sell at the Minneapolis Grain Exchange, and St. Paul railroad and financial interests meddled in North

Dakota politics. As years passed, farmers found themselves under the thumb of large purchasers. They were lowballed and defrauded by grain elevator operators from out of state who graded flawless spring wheat crops far lower than what was fair. Grain prices rose and fell, commodity prices inflated or dipped, farms were subsidized or foreclosed—like ocean tides, capital crept into the state and receded. Worse yet were the severe droughts. In the years between 1935 and 1940 there was virtually no rain. Farmers shipped out their cattle because they had nothing to feed them, had no water for them to drink. Dust storms darkened the sky and blew topsoil off fallow wheat fields. In those five years, eighty-six thousand people fled from the dry, cracked soil of a rainless nightmare.

Yet Grand Forks was a kind of haven from the uncertainties of wheat farming and the anguish of failure. It was a city, a rare thing in North Dakota then, and still rare. It welcomed factories and processing plants and mills, and soon became a moderately important shipping and processing center for grains, sugar beets, potatoes and field seeds. It was still affected by the ups and downs of the Dakota economy, but perhaps not as severely as were the tiny towns scattered across the plains. With some industry anchoring its economy, Grand Forks was better off than most towns. For a time, Cream of Wheat was made in a Malt-O-Meal factory in town, infusing the air with the smell of buttered toast; the plant later relocated to Minneapolis.

The downtown corner of North Third and First Avenue—once the liveliest, most cosmopolitan corner in the state, with three opulent hotels, the Dacotah, the Fredericks, and the Ryan—made Grand Forks a kind of destination in a state with very few destinations. For many communities on the prairies, coteaus, and valleys of North Dakota, Grand Forks was the big city. In old photographs, the sidewalks of downtown Grand Forks look as crowded as any in Manhattan. The streets are packed with old Studebaker Roadsters and Chrysler Imperials, proof of prosperity. Downtown was a kind of palimpsest of small businesses. The 115 Club and Lounge. Dacotah Café. Paramount Theater. Metropolitan Opera House and its smoking porch. Humpty Dumpty Grocery Store. Elgin Dairy Lunch. Shave's Restaurant with its "20 cent meals." Anna Held Cigars ("Results of Cuban Treaty") and Geist's Palace of Sweets.

In the mid-1960s, the presence of the United States military, in the form of the Grand Forks Air Force Base—the nation's first Minuteman II

intercontinental ballistic missile site and control center—was a stabiliz-
ing force, providing jobs and housing. (Measured strictly by population,
the base would be the sixth largest city in North Dakota.) Intercontinental ballistic missiles stood at the ready in silos, needing only ten minutes'
lead time from the president for a full launch. Hidden beneath the land
like massive caskets, the silos seemed an appropriate commodity for North
Dakota, one it hoped never to export.

The 1970s struck North Dakota hard. Prices for grain skyrocketed when
the Soviet Union bought huge supplies of American grain. The boom
tempted many farmers to enlarge their farms and increase their capital,
while many non-farmers now tried their hand at agriculture. But debts
piled up, land prices climbed, the cost of farm machinery exploded—and
then grain prices fell. It was too late for most to get out of the game. By the
end of the decade, huge numbers of farms had been seized by creditors
and the state was desperately poor. North Dakota still hasn't fully recovered. Then, in 1995, thirty years after the first Minuteman was brought to
eastern North Dakota, the federal government ordered the exhumation
of the hundreds of missiles that were buried beneath the Dakota soil; the
missiles, and hundreds of jobs, were relocated to Montana.

A complex kind of pain seems to be concomitant to life in North
Dakota—the pain of seeing farms fail, the pain of seeing small towns collapse and die, the pain of seeing even the military lose faith in the land. At
some point, it seemed that the only things coming into North Dakota were
farm subsidy checks; everything else was leaving.

The Red meanders between the cities of Grand Forks and East Grand
Forks like a length of slack rope, curved here, curled there; at the south
end of Lincoln Drive neighborhood, the river loops back upon itself before continuing towards Central Park, downtown, Riverside Park, and
northward, towards Canada. Three bridges connect the cities, as well as
an old railroad bridge, which, at the time of the flood, was a pedestrian
walkway.

In the years before the flood, downtown Grand Forks was a modest collection of two-, three- and four-story stone buildings, a few with shops and
restaurants on the lower floors, and apartments and offices above. Its historic buildings—the pinkish, Romanesque-style Security Building, the
Herald newspaper building, the Grand Forks Woolen Mills, the Stratford

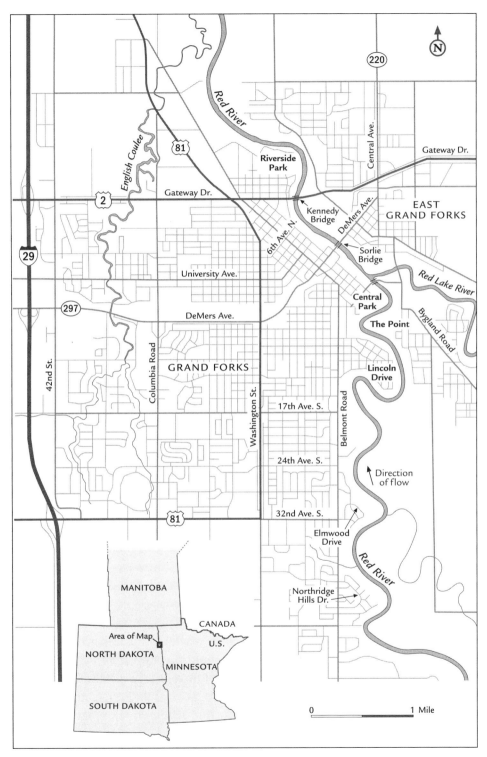

Grand Forks, North Dakota, and East Grand Forks, Minnesota

Building, the First National Bank, and the Empire Theater—were not particularly distinguished architecturally, but they were prized, and cherished as the city's heart. And in certain neighborhoods—Grand Forks was, before the flood, a city of neighborhoods—the architectural relics of the lucrative alliances of industry and agriculture languished beneath giant oaks and cottonwoods. The houses on Reeves Drive, just south of downtown, were large and splendid, with porticos, ionic columns, and verandas. Riverside Park, too, was a pretty neighborhood of distinctive, well-tended homes, parks, and gardens.

And then there was the Lincoln Drive neighborhood, built on a hook of land in a bend in the Red. It was a classic American neighborhood—small houses, each one unique, on straight, tree-lined streets, home to mainly working-class families. There wasn't much that was historic about Lincoln Drive—no notable former homeowners; no first-home-built-in-Grand Forks landmarks, as Riverside Park had. Though Lincoln Drive was built on a rounded spit, it had no river view. Those whose homes were closest to the river had instead a view of the massive, thirty-nine-year-old dike that formed a kind of earthen saucer in which their homes, and the rest of Lincoln Drive, existed. It was a hearty, happy Dakota neighborhood.

But during the early and mid-1990s, downtown Grand Forks was largely shuttered, vacant, and dying. For two decades, businesses had been sneaking out of downtown and into the growing business district in western Grand Forks, close to Interstate 29. The city's two hospitals moved there too, along with a number of restaurants and department stores. The town was almost unrecognizable from what it had been mid-century, the last time it could be considered a thriving city. Before the 1997 flood hit, one of the most important questions facing the city was how to save downtown. And unspoken was the question of whether it was worth saving at all. These riddles fell to the new mayor of Grand Forks—a former waitress and long-time mayor's secretary named Pat Owens.

Patricia Owens was a pretty, petite fifty-six-year-old with deep brown eyes, a pixie haircut, and a strong prairie accent that clipped her words and tightened her vowels. She had spent most of her life in the Grand Forks area. She grew up on her family's farm in East Grand Forks, spending most of her childhood working with her father and brothers in the potato fields or helping her mother prepare meals for the farm workers—the Native Americans and Mexicans who came to the valley during harvest season. During harvest, the Owens home resembled a boarding house; the family housed the workers in their spare bedrooms and served meals at the kitchen table. Many of the workers came back year after year; they were, Owens would later say, part of the family.

"We all have warm blood running through our veins," Owens remembers her parents telling her. "We're not all given the same opportunities, but we're basically one human race. We're all humans."

Owens' mother and father were quiet people, devout Catholics who read the Bible every day. They sent their only daughter to Sacred Heart Catholic High School, where she graduated in 1958 at seventeen. She married her husband, Bobby, just after commencement and moved with him to Greenville, South Carolina in 1959. She spent her first weeks in Greenville trying to find a job, but each time she began to introduce herself, her interviewer cut her off, telling her they didn't hire "Yankees." She finally found a job working for a blind attorney who, although white himself, dealt only with African-American clients.

After a year, the couple, and their new baby girl, Robin, moved back to Grand Forks, and Owens settled into married life. Her married life, however, was far different from that of most wives in Grand Forks at that time: she worked. She waited tables for a while, then took a job as a stenographer in the city auditor's office. In 1964, Owens moved into the mayor's office as a secretary. She became pregnant a month later and worked until the day she delivered.

The mayors Owens worked under considered her indispensable. She was sometimes called the mayor's ombudsman. She knew the workings of the city in a way that most city employees did not. She was a repository of answers, tips, and goodwill. When Owens was on vacation, days were slower in the office; if constituents knew she wasn't going to be there, they didn't bother calling or dropping by. Owens had a way with people. They liked her. And Owens was most comfortable dealing with people one on one.

But in 1996 the mechanic wanted to drive the Mercedes, one might say—and so Pat Owens made plans to run for the office of mayor of Grand Forks. Her opponent was a retired Grand Forks school administrator named Moine Gates. Gates was a fifty-five-year-old ex-airman from Plaza, North Dakota, a small town sixty miles southwest of the Minot Air Force Base, where he had been stationed as a young man. Gates had taught business classes at Grand Forks Central High School for twenty-two years and also served seven terms as a Republican lawmaker in the state house of representatives. He had recently worked as the Grand Forks school district technology director and was preparing to retire that June, planning on exploring blue highways with his wife in their RV. But then the mayor's job opened up and he decided to set his wanderlust aside.

Moine Gates was a savvy man. He knew how to win this election. He joined the Grand Forks Chamber of Commerce—a kind of requisite secret society for ambitious local politicos—only a year before he announced his candidacy. The business community, a powerful and intimidating coalition of business owners, bankers, and other influential players, wanted its own candidate, and Gates was groomed for the job.

Although Pat Owens had been heavily involved with the Chamber for years and had worked her way onto its committees, Gates was given a chairmanship on the governmental affairs committee almost upon his arrival on the board. As the election neared, the Chamber announced that it was backing Gates for mayor. In this city, where the Chamber of Commerce has substantial power and sway, the endorsement gave Gates an enormous advantage. In Grand Forks, it was a scandalous and, some council members thought, scurrilous political move. Bob Brooks, a city councilman and then the chairman of the Chamber's leadership committee, had supported Gates up until the Chamber's bewildering endorsement. He had assumed the Chamber would endorse Owens, who had been part of the Chamber for years.

"I thought it was a virtual slap in the face," Brooks said. Brooks switched camps and supported Owens. Robert and Mary Kweit, both professors in the political science and public administration department at UND, had watched the 1996 mayoral election with great interest. Robert, an ex-New Yorker used to such political maneuvers, did not find the Chamber's endorsement of Gates so baffling.

"The tension between Pat and the Chamber? She was a girl."

Owens tried to fortify her campaign with other sources of support. As a former city employee with more than thirty years of service, Owens was a familiar face in town and a favorite co-worker of city employees. By all accounts she knew how the city worked and she knew how to get things done. She also corralled the votes of Grand Forks school district employees who disliked their former boss, Gates. Owens picked up a strong labor vote on the north side of town with the endorsement of the Democratic Nonpartisan League. She was also the choice of another powerful coalition: city employees. In interviews with the *Grand Forks Herald* prior to the election, Owens sold her skills to the city's voters.

"I believe I am a very good consensus builder . . . I will be a very visible mayor . . . If you can build consensus, you have the citizens involved, then they feel like you're being up front with them. There's no hidden agenda." *Consensus.* She said the word so often that it became part of her platform. At the time, Grand Forks voters responded favorably to Owens' approach to governing. However, one segment of the population already had trouble with the idea of Pat Owens as mayor—people who had trouble with the idea of a female mayor. When the *Herald* asked Owens how she thought citizens would react to a female mayor, she said, "Over the years I haven't had a lot of problems with gender."

But she had. And she would have more. On May 15, 1996, the *Herald* ran a story headlined "Gates: Owens feeling stressed."

"You've got to be able to operate under stress," Gates was quoted as saying. "If this is causing stress to one or more individuals, then what are they going to be like as mayor?" When a reporter asked Owens if she detected any sexism in Gates' campaign, she risked saying yes. Gates laughed when told of Owens' statements; during a local television interview he said, "Pat is a nice lady in the job that she is in right now . . . however she does not have the leadership skills nor the decision-making abilities."

As the election neared, Owens' campaign funds dwindled. She mentioned this to a *Grand Forks Herald* reporter, who quoted her on it. The next day Owens found a fifteen-hundred-dollar check in her mailbox. The attached note read: "You gotta run. I hate this guy."

Gates' tactics forced people to examine the definition of fair play in a local political contest. What was a reasonable assessment of a candidate's weaknesses and what was sexism? Could a man get away with criticizing a female opponent for poor decision-making skills and emotional tendencies, as Gates had charged, especially if he offered no proof? Was it fair comment or political sexism? Gates never provided any real evidence of Owens' alleged weaknesses. But this would not be the only election in which Pat Owens would be called "emotional" and "indecisive."

Despite the overwhelming support of the business community, Pat Owens beat Moine Gates. It was a landslide, with Owens carrying 76 percent of the vote. She became Grand Forks' first female mayor.

But then, only nine months into her term, Mayor Pat Owens faced a disaster of almost biblical proportions.

3 *Watersick*

Mike Anderson's business card does not have the National Oceanic and Atmospheric Administration seal printed on it, as his colleague Steve Buan's does. Instead, below his name, position, and office address at the North Central River Forecast Center is a drawing of a tiny, drenched dog sitting in a pool of water and looking forlorn. The hydrologist doesn't say the dog is his alter ego, but if you know Anderson's story, you don't have to ask.

Mike Anderson grew up in Wahpeton, North Dakota—the headwaters of the Red River of the North. He spends so much time on the North Dakota side of the Red River, despite living in a Minneapolis suburb, that his boss, Daniel Luna, says he chooses not to ask Mike in which state he files his tax return. Anderson, a handsome man with white hair and a moustache, is unreservedly kind, and well-liked among the hydrologists at the NCRFC. In 1997, Anderson was the primary National Weather Service forecaster for the Red River of the North. Each of the NCRFC's sixteen river forecasters is responsible for one primary river basin. In addition, each serves as backup forecaster for a secondary basin, and must be equally well versed in that area. Anderson's second basin, for example, was the nearby Souris River, and he knew it as well he knew the Red. Moreover, it would not be unusual for Mike Anderson to swap rivers with colleagues Steve Buan and Mike DeWeese; the hydrologists are expected to be able to handle any river in the entire North Central forecast area, which stretches from Michigan to Missouri, from North Dakota to Indiana. In 1997, however, the NCRFC assigned five hydrometeorologists and hydrologic forecasters to the Red River full time: Mike Anderson, Steve Buan, John Halquist, Mike DeWeese, and Pat Neuman.

"The Red is a different animal," Mike Anderson said years later. It was his way of explaining why one-quarter of the NCRFC's staff was assigned to a single river in a forecast area of 850 rivers and tributaries during flood season. On a typical day, Anderson might attend meetings, work on peripheral projects, and then hunker down to study, analyze, and forecast for his basin. During flood season, when he arrived for his shift in the morning, he analyzed data that had arrived overnight—river data, precipitation data, snowmelt data, and so on—then ran it through the runoff model. And then he started asking himself questions. Lots of them.

"'Is that data correct? Does it follow in line? If you had a ten-foot jump in the river and there hasn't been any rain there or snowmelt for the last month, you know that possibly, probably, the gauge that's sending us that piece of river data is incorrect. We need to check this because that doesn't look right—can you get us supplemental data? We normally don't get river data from this location, because it's not a forecast point—it's not even a data point—but we'd really like to know what's going on there.' Then, if all the data is right, you get into the guts of the model. Is it routing the water from Wahpeton to Fargo at the correct rate, is this looking good?"

As spring runoff approached, these were the kind of questions Mike Anderson was asking himself about the information he was receiving about the "animal" for which he was responsible. In short, he was doing what he had done for more than twenty years, and he was good at it.

The North Central River Forecast Center is housed in a long, low brick building in Chanhassen, a western suburb of Minneapolis, 322 miles from Grand Forks. Inside, hydrologists and hydrometeorologists formulate and issue river, reservoir, and flood forecasts using computer models. These predictions (called "forecast guidance") are transmitted to other National Weather Service forecast offices. These smaller offices are responsible for issuing predictions and outlooks to the media, water resource managers, and the public.

The NCRFC is one of thirteen National Weather Service river forecast centers in the country and is responsible for thirty-two major river systems and drainage areas—specifically, the St. Lawrence River drainage, the Upper Mississippi drainage and the Hudson Bay drainage, of which the Red is a part. It must track the behavior of more than 850 smaller rivers and tributaries in the Dakotas, Minnesota, Iowa, Wisconsin, Michigan, Illinois, and Indiana, as well as parts of lower Canada. It monitors 450 official forecast points.

The Red wasn't the only river in the three drainage areas that was flooding during the spring of 1997. In fact, that year, the Minnesota, Wild Rice, Sheyenne, St. Croix, Maple, Buffalo, Red Lake, Snake, Marsh, Pembina, Two Rivers, Little Minnesota, Redwood, and a large portion of the Mississippi were flooding, as was Devils Lake in North Dakota. Between March 14 and May 2, the NCRFC issued 10,186 forecasts for rivers in the basins of the Red, the Minnesota, and the mainstem Mississippi; 492 of the forecasts—over one-fifth—were for floods of record. In other words, these were the worst floods those rivers—and the towns on them—had ever experienced.

The Red River of the North is not a particularly high-profile river for the National Weather Service. It doesn't demand the kind of attention from forecasters and engineers that the Mississippi River does—or at least it hasn't until recently. As North Dakota's Geological Survey had been noting with increasing alarm since the early 1990s, the flooding pattern in the Red River valley had been steadily worsening. Mike Anderson, using the particularly obtuse language of hydrologists and meteorologists, calls it a "current rotation of high water"—a wet cycle.

Flood outlooks for the Red River valley are usually issued one to two months before the expected peak flooding. Compared to other river systems and other forecast centers, this long lead time—advance warning, really—is unusual; it is possible only because floods in the Red River valley are usually due to snowmelt, not rain or snowfall. Because of the terrain—the NCRFC's hydrologist-in-charge in 1997, Dean Braatz, calls the valley as flat as a "fry-pan"—melting snow often has nowhere to go but into the river, especially if the soil is already saturated, as it was in the spring of 1997.

Hydrometeorological technician Lynn Kennedy worked at the year-old Grand Forks National Weather Service office that issued the NCRFC forecasts. By February of '97, he was taking phone calls from Grand Forks city employees who were concerned about what they were hearing around town. They weren't just curious; they had work to do. Each city along the course of the Red was already designing its flood protection system.

"They had to decide what action they were going to take, and they cannot decide what action to take if we tell them they are going to have 'severe flooding,'" Kennedy said. "'How high is "severe" on my dike? Forty-nine feet is a level on my dike I can work with, but "severe" I can't work with.' So we wanted to get these numbers out. But the sooner you get the number, the wider the range of probability." Forty-nine feet was an outlook. It was not yet a forecast. Few outside the National Weather Service understood the difference.

Forecasts are short-term estimations, the kind of weather information that is a staple of local news programs and on which picnic plans and baseball games are based. At the National Weather Service, river forecasts were formulated through a computer model with a five-day lead time. Outlooks are a different story. Because they are longer term—often with months of lead time—they are far less accurate and are produced and presented only as general guidelines, rough estimates. Terms like "average," "below average," "above average" and "severe" are used in outlooks instead of specific numbers. If an outlook does include a number, it is hedged with qualifications and caveats regarding its reliability and precision. The message the NWS hopes to convey with these caveats is: don't take this number to the bank.

The National Weather Service had been producing its spring flood outlooks in the same way for the Red River valley for decades, taking into account climatological data, long-term temperature forecasts, and anticipated precipitation—which, in the NCRFC's hydrological model in 1997, was always, as default, "average." Hydrologists had no way to propose to the computer model a situation in which snowfall was heavier than average, as it was in the winter of 1996 in Grand Forks. Outlooks were based on static "scenarios," not pliable hypotheses. For those decades, the NCRFC used only two precipitation scenarios: "normal precipitation" and "zero future precipitation." That is, the model could assume *either* an average amount of snow or rain during the spring snowmelt (based on the previous thirty years) *or* no snow or rain at all. Of course, the outlook that assumes no precipitation will almost always be wrong, and the predicted river crest will always be exceeded. The outlook that assumes "normal future precipitation" has a 50 percent chance of being equaled or exceeded. Both scenarios were unlikely to occur, but they gave hydrologists a baseline from which to work, and it gave everyone else a rough idea of what to expect. That is the way it had been done for decades, and judging by the National Weather Service's track record, it had worked exceptionally well.

What was less dependable was the public's ability to distinguish an NWS outlook from an NWS forecast. People tended to interpret them as equal, often considering them to be the same product, with the same degree of reliability. This was a grave mistake.

So much seemed like simple mathematics and plain common sense to everyone outside of the National Weather Service offices. Lots of snow, lots of snowmelt. River prone to floods, flooding river. Flood-prone river plus lots of snow—big flood. But it would prove far more complicated than that.

Later, in the National Weather Service's published assessment of its performance during the 1997 flood, it noted what was perhaps the major problem with the outlook model the hydrologists were using at the time: "Since the outlook process does not produce an explicit probability of exceedance and the historical sample of outlooks is fairly small . . . exceedance probabilities involves a degree of judgment." The question of judgment would soon come into play. Would the scientist act independently of his computer if he had to?

In mid-March, Leon Osborne had called a small staff meeting at the Regional Weather Information Center (RWIC) on the UND campus to discuss the 52-foot crest number that he had calculated independently of the National Weather Service. The number was meant to be a secret, but someone at the meeting leaked it to family or friends, and within a few days, the RWIC was being inundated with calls from Grand Forks residents who had heard something about 52 feet. Should we buy flood insurance? most of them asked.

"We were saying yes," Osborne said. "I guess myself and other people wouldn't deny it, wouldn't deny what our thinking was." He himself had been stunned when his insurance agent had tried to talk him out of purchasing a flood policy. "'You don't need flood insurance,'" Osborne remembers the agent telling him confidently. "'You're out of the floodplain; the National Weather Service says it's not going to get that high. Don't waste your money.'" Osborne wasn't the only person in Grand Forks given that advice.

The first two days of April 1997 were warm in Grand Forks, and the spring runoff commenced; Red River tributaries began to rise rapidly. The Sheyenne River, feeding the Red near Fargo, was rising nearly five feet a day in spots and was nearly eight feet above flood stage in others; the Wild

Rice River's ice cover had cracked, sending floes down the river like floating islands, and the river had risen four feet in one twenty-four-hour span; the Maple River had reached flood stage. Water overrunning the banks of these rivers could spread across the floodplains unchecked, like milk spilled on a kitchen table. There was simply no room in the watersick soil for any additional moisture.

To make matters worse, the Red's headwater in the northeast corner of South Dakota was also overfed by nearly thirty inches of melting snow, and the Red's main channel was still blocked by winter ice. The unbroken ice would almost certainly create a huge amount of backwater, with ice jams acting as massive dams. The Red was still flowing under a thick cover of ice, and it was rising as more and more water surged into its channel from bulging tributaries and a bloated headwater.

On April 3, sandbagging and dike building began in Grand Forks as the Red entered flood stage at 28 feet. The city brought out its sandbagging machine—a contraption that looks like an octopus, with a central funnel and eight chutes. Volunteers held open burlap sacks under the mouths of the chutes, tied the sacks shut with heavy twine, and tossed them down a human chain to the dike. Corps engineers, who had been studying the Red at Grand Forks for years, trying to design a reliable flood protection system, began filling and stacking sandbags. The Corps had deployed construction crews to Grand Forks in early March, and nearly $2.8 million had been already been spent on temporary flood protection. Huge military trucks roared through town, some loaded with clay, others with sandbags. Along the human chains near the dikes, people talked about the river. More and more, the conversations were about a 49-foot crest. Some people, however, mentioned a 52-foot crest. Few on the chains believed them.

Corps engineers knew that when it comes to crest predictions, even the smallest unit of measure is significant. As the world's largest public engineering management agency, the Corps had been constructing flood protection systems on American rivers and waterways for over a century. Though it was founded in the late 1700s, its first disaster relief operation occurred in 1865 when Corps engineers helped freed blacks survive flooding along the Mississippi. For the next fifty years, the Corps would attempt to reshape, restructure, and reroute rivers. The Mississippi and Ohio got the most attention because they were commercial highways. The Corps removed sandbars, ripped snags from the riverbed, built wing dams and locks. When steamboat traffic was highest on the rivers, the Corps piloted dredge and snag boats up and down the rivers, tearing roots and fallen tree limbs out of the water. They called their boats "Uncle Sam's tooth pullers." The Corps' experience in flood protection and river engineering was unparalleled.

When the 1997 flood occurred, the Corps was working with the city of Grand Forks to engineer and design a floodwall to protect the neighborhoods at the foot of the dikes from a catastrophic flood. They had been haggling with the city councils of both Grand Forks and East Grand Forks since 1985. Feasibility studies for various flood protection systems filled file drawers at the Corps regional office in St. Paul. One study in particular would, in the months after the flood, come to be very important to the people of Grand Forks. But for now, it was filed away, forgotten.

On April 4, as Grand Forks was shoring up the dikes, the little blizzard from Utah rolled into town under the name Hannah. South of Grand Forks, in Wahpeton, an icy rain had been falling for hours. As it moved towards Grand Forks, temperatures fell. Sharp, icy raindrops began falling in the city late that night, glazing streets and coating the spindly black branches of elms and maples. Then the winds picked up, carrying the frozen rain slantwise. The rain turned to snow a few hours later, the gusts now at sixty miles an hour. With the winds at hurricane strength and the snowfall intensifying, the National Weather Service designated Hannah a top-category blizzard.

Hundreds of power line poles and towers throughout the valley buckled under the weight of the snow and ice. In Grand Forks, the power supply had been cut to a quarter of normal, and bursts of blue light illuminated the night sky as power lines broke and crashed to the ground. Nearly three hundred thousand people from the Canadian border down the Red River valley to the middle of South Dakota lost electrical power. Some were without power for a week. All interstates and local roads to Grand Forks were closed, preventing emergency vehicles from reaching those in need of medical attention. In Fargo, officials pulled the city's snowplows off the road for hours, fearing the big plows themselves would get stuck in the snow. High winds made emergency airlifts of medical supplies impossible; they also toppled a number of television and radio towers. Many households lucky enough to still have electricity now lost their only contact to the outside world—and the broadcasts that warned them to stay off the roads and to keep their livestock in barns.

A Lankin, North Dakota man named Troy Swartz froze to death after his car lodged in a snowdrift on an empty country road. A farmer named Kenny Visser found twenty of his cattle and forty hogs drowned in the Wild Rice River floodwaters, the corpses frozen solid in the ice. In Bismarck, Tim and Peg Rogers and their thirteen-year-old son, Josh, were finally on their way home to Grand Forks from a hockey tournament after parts of Interstate 94 had been closed for days. The four other Rogers children were back in Grand Forks with relatives. The night before the family left Bismarck, their hotel had lost electricity when local power lines snapped under the weight of the snowfall. As they drove east toward Grand Forks they saw the land scattered with splintered power poles, trees shorn in half and cars buried under snow. Peg thought it looked like a war zone. The highway was covered with ice. Tim and Peg watched in horror as a SUV spun out and rolled across the road in front of them, the passengers' belongings flying through the broken windows. When they stopped to help, they found the family inside alive but shaken. Tim and Peg waited with the family until help arrived, sharing the blankets they kept in the back of their car. An hour later, they loaded up for the slow crawl back to Grand Forks. Peg started to worry about her parents, whose home at 301 Polk Street was built on that little spit on the Red River called the Lincoln Drive neighborhood.

At the National Weather Service office in Grand Forks, Blizzard Hannah made things a lot more complicated. That, as Mike Anderson later put it, "was when everything kind of went into the kettle for us." Power outages had affected communications systems both there and at the Fargo office, and all surveillance and reconnaissance flights were canceled. The NCRFC's Doppler radar was of little use. Interference garbled incoming data so that the computers could not detect the amount of water in the snow Hannah had dropped on Grand Forks. Yet Anderson still desperately needed that information to feed into his computer model; otherwise the model—and the crest prediction—were going to stagnate. The NCRFC hoped that some of the co-op observers would manage to collect their data and relay it to the office. But Friday, April 4, passed with no co-op reports; Saturday, no reports; Sunday, no reports. They were snowed in or unable to find their equipment beneath the huge snowdrifts that had accumulated around their homes. Hannah had left many of them with no heat and no phone line, and they were huddled in living rooms with blankets pulled around their shoulders, waiting for the storm to let up. The last thing on their minds was checking gauges that were buried under snowdrifts. No information was coming into the National Weather Service. As a result, time, in essence, stood still, and the computer model was falling behind.

Hannah brought flood protection operations to a standstill for three days. The city was paralyzed and the river was swollen, and despite the National Guard's dusting efforts, ice jams were damming the river upstream. The Red's feeder rivers were pouring into the main channel, and the ice chunks were piling up in the ever-quickening, ever-growing river, creating a kind of dam. Although Hannah had delivered only six inches of snow, it had been a strange, damaging blizzard whose effects would be far-reaching.

On April 5, the NCRFC began staffing its Red River desk twenty-four hours a day. The next day, the Red crested at its headwaters in Wahpeton at 19.44 feet. Once the flood crest passes Wahpeton, it normally takes ten to twelve days to reach Grand Forks, a distance of about 133 miles as the crow flies. But this time the Red would crest twice at Wahpeton, nine days apart, sending two flood swells down the river.

Meanwhile, across the river in Minnesota, the town of Ada had been evacuated. One farmer told a National Weather Service employee that he had found his cattle frozen to death in an ice-covered pasture. On April 7, with the eighth blizzard of the season still in progress, President Clinton declared North Dakota a disaster area for the second time that year.

Spring was seventeen days old on Monday, April 7, but by any standard, it was a cold, biting winter day. The NCRFC received a couple of co-op reports from observers who had managed to take a "snow cookie" and call the number in; Tuesday, a few more reports; Wednesday, when phone lines were largely restored to the Red River valley, the NCRFC finally began receiving reports at a near-normal rate. Mike Anderson debated with himself, and with his model, over changing the outlook crest for Grand Forks.

"The blizzard came, we stayed with forty-nine," he said. "Sunday, we stayed with forty-nine feet. Monday, forty-nine feet. We stayed with forty-nine feet." The computer model, however, wanted Anderson to do something that would have seemed slightly mad: *lower* the crest outlook. "Due to the cold that infiltrated the runoff, our model just looked at it as not being warm enough to melt the snow. You haven't got the water running into the river channels. Our forecast model said, 'Whoa, here it's shutting off the runoff, water isn't getting to the stream, I think we're showing a crest of forty-seven feet.' And we knew that wasn't right; we knew the snow was out there. There's no way we're going to cut back on it." Not lowering the crest outlook was, to the National Weather Service, almost a brave thing to do. Yet Anderson couldn't increase it either. He simply didn't have the data.

"We didn't have a real solid handle on how much water had really run off right up until when Hannah hit. How much water was in the system, still here? How much did Hannah really drop? And then you have the blowing snow, and you hear about twenty- and forty-foot drifts. Well, that's fine, but on the lay of the land, what kind of water do we have there in that frozen snowpack? There were a lot of variables; and that's why we held on to that forty-nine feet."

On Tuesday, April 8, Lou Bennett, the warning coordination officer for the NWS office in Fargo, made some phone calls and arranged for a North Dakota Civil Air Patrol mission to temporarily take over recon duties for the remote sensing planes that had been grounded in Chanhassen during the blizzard. The patrol's flight lines were videotaped and the tapes sent overnight to the NCRFC for analysis. Four more flight runs took place in the next week, and each time, the video was sent to the NCRFC. For all the trouble, though, little usable data came out of the flights, and the hydrologists were not in a position to postulate. There was nothing to do but wait.

As soon as the blizzard had ended, flood protection operations in Grand Forks had resumed. Though the sandbagging line was a flood-season ritual, this year it felt different. When Peg Rogers and her family arrived back in Grand Forks, and after checking on her other four children, she and her son Josh headed immediately for Lincoln Drive to help sandbag the dike there. Peg felt the uneasiness.

"There seemed to be an unspoken fear," she said later. "It was like if we said it out loud, it would be real."

The dikes, levees, and floodwalls surrounding Grand Forks were city engineer Ken Vein's dominion. Vein is a soft-spoken, outwardly serene man with sandy-brown hair with a touch of gray near his ears and in his moustache. Upon a first meeting, he strikes one as reticent to the point of timidity. This is a first impression. Ken Vein is not timid.

Vein knew early in life what he wanted to do, even if he didn't yet know there was a name for it. His elementary school teachers noted Vein's skillful drawings; he was, they told his parents, a quick study. Vein's twin brother, Charlie, was similarly inclined and equally talented. The boys' keenness for engineering appeared in the months after their father died, when they were ten years old, and from then on they were preoccupied with details, as most engineers are. Life became a kind of index of specificity, of beauty found in unlikely objects: the intricate mathematics of flow through a sluice gate, the delicacy of a displacement current. Engineering also allowed one to disappear into equations and mechanics and carefully sidestep human emotion. "Emotion will kill you every time," Vein has said.

During the next ten years, Ken and Charlie took drafting classes, interned at the Grand Forks Air Base engineering department, and surveyed for the NoDak Rural Electrical Cooperative. After graduating from UND in 1976 with degrees in civil engineering, they founded their own engineering firm, Advanced Engineering. Vein joined the Grand Forks engineering and public works department in 1984 and was named city engineer in 1992. In 1995, he was named the director of public works, while retaining his job as the city's chief engineer. He was now overseeing the work of nearly two hundred employees. One year later he found himself struggling to keep a massive flood in check, which he had done. But the 1996 flood was nothing compared to what he was facing now.

Vein knew he had to create a line of defense of the sort that was without precedent in the city's history. The thirty-nine-year-old dikes around the city—the "public dikes"—had been topped off and fortified with sandbags and clay during other severe flood seasons. When Vein received the initial NWS outlook in late February, he had designed a flood protection system that could defend the city from a cresting river of 52 feet. But private dikes surrounding neighborhoods farther down the Red, were not part of the city's levee system—and this posed a problem.

The public dike system consists of a series of levees built on public property and on private property with a public easement. But at many spots in the city individual citizens had chosen to build sandbag dikes around their homes or neighborhoods for added protection. While emergency dikes could be raised and sluice gates in the sewer system could be lowered, the people living behind the private dikes might or might not raise their dikes to the same level. If they didn't, and the river overtopped these private dikes, the whole city would flood. To avoid this, Vein and his staff designed a mini–flood protection system for every property along the river. He ordered a virtual sandbag factory set up to fill bags and get them to the homes along the waterways.

Vein received NWS updates and forecasts by fax. He had been given two numbers by the agency—the 47.5-foot outlook (no future precipitation) and the 49-foot outlook (with "normal precipitation"). His 52-foot wall of dike and sandbags left Vein feeling the city was well prepared. "I had faith in the National Weather Service and we designed our system based on their projections," he said later.

But at the National Weather Service, a period of silence had begun. Nearly ten days would pass between Hannah's appearance and the NWS's first operational forecast, issued on April 14—one, maybe two lifetimes in the agency's measurement of time. The recent blizzard had stopped data collection in its tracks, including the gamma flights, the radar sweeps, and the co-op reports. Even many river gauges were inoperable, encrusted with ice. The problems the agency was facing were not relayed to the city of Grand Forks or any of its other customers. For nearly a week after the blizzard ended, the people of Grand Forks heard not a word about the Red River from the agency. To some it may have seemed as if Blizzard Hannah had lulled National Weather Service into a kind of trance. NCRFC hydrologists would have considered that a bad analogy, though; instead, they might say the blizzard forced them into straitjackets, placed burlap sacks over their heads, strung them upside down, then walked away, saying, as she left, "Let's see you get out of this, Houdini."

The "normal precipitation" numbers that the National Weather Service relied on had just been doubled in one unexpected weather event. In fact, the total snowfall on the ground was now double the amount that had been on the ground in the weeks before the horrific 1897 Grand Forks flood, the one that produced a flood of 50.2 feet.

One full week passed before the National Weather Service was able to add Hannah's 2.66 inches of snow moisture to its computer model. And while it seemed a given that the snowfall from Hannah would drastically affect the runoff and, therefore, the Red's flood level, it was not that simple. In Upper Michigan that spring, for example, snow with record-high moisture content was *not* resulting in high river levels; in fact, only moderate runoff occurred there that spring. This inconsistency is one of the hallmarks of river behavior; rivers are variable, and so are their floods. The Red is an unusually capricious river, even when it is at normal levels, and so its floods are even more dynamic.

Back in Grand Forks, dike patrol began in earnest. Residents walked the tops of the dikes in two-hour shifts, wearing vinyl vests and carrying radios. They stared at the river and looked for bad spots in the dikes—cracks. The Red no longer looked red; it was now an amalgam of its usually mild, tea-colored feeders, tributaries that had suddenly morphed into dark, ice-filled torrents. Huge amounts of mud and sediment were flowing through the Red's channel now. Grand Forks police officers reminded townspeople that it was illegal to gawk at the flood-fighting efforts—City Ordinance No. 9–0105, Section 2, which also outlawed gaping at fires, traffic accidents, riots and "other disasters." They also reminded residents that boating on the flooded river was illegal; two men canoeing the Red were ordered to shore.

The days following Hannah were bitterly cold. In the second week of April, temperatures had dropped, as much as twenty degrees below normal. At night, the mercury hovered near or below zero. The sudden chill refroze any water that had melted during the brief spell of mild weather, including the ice on smaller rivers in the valley. Livestock were caught in rivers and creeks that had iced over in minutes. In fact, all over the Red River valley, more than 10,000 head of cattle were killed in the blizzard (a statistic that included the unborn calves pregnant cows were carrying), along with 1,255 hogs, 3,422 sheep and a thousand chickens and turkeys.

The spring runoff, had, essentially, frozen in place, and the river was behaving exactly as the National Weather Service's model said it would. It wasn't rising.

To understand what happened in Grand Forks, one must understand the mentality of a community living on a river that floods regularly—nearly every other year and with increasing severity since 1950. Despite efforts by federal agencies such as FEMA, flood-prone communities continue to build on the floodplains, refuse to purchase flood insurance and are, for the most part, complacent. People who build homes in floodplains believe that earth and clay can keep a river out of their backyards. It had worked before. But at some point, perhaps when they are standing in their living rooms, knee-deep in river sludge, knee-deep in their sodden possessions, they come to understand they were wrong. But the federal government pours millions of dollars into flood-control programs along rivers like the Mississippi and the Red each year, and much more when those programs fail. Floods kill about one hundred Americans each year, and cause nearly four billion dollars in damage annually. In some years, just one flood can do that much damage. Rebuild the cities, rebuild the dikes—and the floods still come.

In Grand Forks in 1997, the complacency was widespread because the town had pushed back a brutal flood just the year before, and had done it well. The 1996 flood was classified as one of Grand Forks' five worst; it was also what is known as a hundred-year flood. Such phrases express the severity of a flood in terms of its probability, its statistical frequency. The more remote a flood's chance of existing, the more dangerous the flood. A hundred-year flood is one that would be expected to occur only once in a century; it has a one percent chance, however, of occurring in any year. Imagine the odds that one town, situated on a river that stretches more than five hundred miles, would suffer a hundred-year flood one year, then find itself destroyed by one the next year.

In March, FEMA had implemented its public service campaign, encouraging—almost begging—Grand Forks residents to purchase flood insurance. The warnings were largely ignored; only about a thousand people in a town of fifty-two thousand insured themselves against flood damage. Most citizens felt confident that the river would crest far below the top of the dikes. There was no reason to purchase supplementary insurance if the river wouldn't reach them. And that, citizens say, is what the National Weather Service told them in its outlooks and predictions.

The word "severe" had not been ignored in Winnipeg, Manitoba, 144 miles downriver from Grand Forks. There, city officials were watching Grand Forks very closely. Forty-seven years earlier, Winnipeg had been dealt a flood that destroyed more than ten thousand homes and caused close to $650 million in damage. Since then, the Red had flooded in Winnipeg, but it has never since escaped the banks. That's because Winnipeg and the Canadian government built a twenty-nine-mile ditch with a series of dikes to divert floodwaters around the city. Winnipeg dug the Red a new channel, forcing a fork at the entrance of the city, like a riparian beltway. Two steel gates, planted so deep in the riverbed that boats pass over them unimpeded, can be raised to a height of fifteen feet, diverting floodwater into the ditch, called a floodway.

The diversion took six years to build, was completed in 1968, and was—in terms of cubic yards of earth moved (100 million)—a bigger construction job than the Panama Canal. The floodway was so extensive that Apollo astronauts claimed to see it from space. The ambitious project, which cost $63 million (the equivalent of about $500 million today) was initially nicknamed Duff's Folly, for then Premier Duff Roblin who had insisted upon the diversion after the devastating 1950 floods, despite overwhelming public resistance and ridicule. Since 1968, however, the diversion has protected Winnipeg from eighteen severe floods, saving the Canadian government billions of dollars. And in the spring of 1997, when the city of Winnipeg raised the diversion gates at the entrance of its floodway, it asked Duff Roblin to do the honors at the hydraulic servomotor console.

Anyone standing on one of the softly rounded earth dikes at Grand Forks in the first days of April 1997 could see that the Red River was engorged and that its ruddy water was rising so high, so quickly, that the banks were disappearing under it. On April 2, the city's only newspaper, the *Grand Forks Herald*, had proclaimed that the city and surrounding river communities "are better prepared than ever before" to handle a flood. Forty-nine feet was no problem. Terry Bjerke, a mailman who lived well away from the river, was not worried. "We've been here before," he remembered thinking. "Fighting floods is how winter ends. Big deal. Do some extra stuff.

City says we're protected. We're good for three feet over the flood crest."
Grand Forks was a city behind walls, behind those formidable dikes, which
curled around the city like a comma, an engineered promise to protect.

On April 10, temperatures climbed into the forties and stayed there for
three days. People wandered around the city in windbreakers, happy in
the fresh, warm breezes. The frozen flood began to thaw. Spring runoff
commenced afresh.

The North Dakota National Guard had spent its winter digging towns out
from under blizzards and carving passable streets out of the gigantic snowdrifts. But after Hannah hit and the Red entered flood stage, the Guard
brought out its showpieces. It assembled its battalion of dump trucks, tractor-trailers, power generators, forklifts, D-7 dozers, loaders, and helicopters to fortify dikes up and down the banks of the Red River, from the
top of North Dakota in Grafton to the bottom of the state in Wahpeton.
And from Bismarck, a virtual army of state and federal agencies crowded
towards the riverbanks to fight the coming deluge—North Dakota's Division of Emergency Management, Water Commission, Highway Patrol, and
Civil Air Patrol; the Army and Air National Guard, the U.S. Coast Guard
and Department of Transportation, FEMA, and "Emergency Preparedness
Liaison Officers" from the U.S. Army, Navy, and Air Force. Other agencies
occupied the small niches of need that went unfilled by the larger agencies—State Radio Communications, the North Dakota Departments of
Human Services, Health, and Agriculture; the U.S. Forest Service, and the
U.S. Geological Survey. In the days leading up to the flood, the towns on
the Red River became alphabet cities, and Acronym became a kind of second language.

It was bad from top to bottom. Upstream (south of Grand Forks) the
river was flooding small towns on either side of the Minnesota-North
Dakota border in succession. The blizzards—which had turned nearly
every county in eastern North Dakota into a federal disaster area—and
now the flooding had turned the winter and its thaw into a classic Dakota
brawl with nature. Despite the difficulties the season had delivered, many
North Dakotans were charged by the thrill of fighting the river.

The North Dakota Civil Air Patrol was flying daily surveillances for
state and federal officials who were already trying to assess flood and blizzard damage in terms of dollars. On Friday, April 11, one crew flew NWS

representatives over the Bois de Sioux and the Red Rivers to examine ice congestion in the respective channels. The Corps of Engineers' flood reconnaissance team faxed Mike Anderson and Mike DeWeese at the NCRFC with a report of "rotting" ice in the Red at Grand Forks, with the river gauge reading just a hair over 42 feet. The recon team, Terry Zien and Richard Pomerleau, scrawled a note on the bottom of the report: "Grand Forks called—media is requesting a crest value and time. I told them to stick with your 'near' crest until tomorrow but you may want to update early in the AM." But the National Weather Service did not issue an update the next morning.

On Saturday, April 12, the U.S. Coast Guard conducted a "white sheet survey" over small towns on the Minnesota side of the Red; if residents were stranded by floodwaters and needed evacuation, they were asked to hang white bedsheets outside their houses. A farmer found 150 of his cattle drowned in the flooding Beaver Creek—a tributary of the Goose River which is, in turn, a tributary of the Red. In fact, farmers all over the counties closest to the Red River and its tributaries were still losing livestock. The severe blizzards had caught some farmers off guard. Frozen cattle carcasses were scattered across farmland in clumps. The North Dakota Department of Agriculture began receiving reports that the power outages caused by Hannah had left farmers helpless; without power, the electrical pumps that supplied water for their livestock were useless. Pregnant cows, dehydrated and sickly, began aborting.

Meanwhile, the Corps of Engineers had been steadily draining water from the Lake Traverse reservoir, located on the North Dakota–Minnesota border, into the Bois de Sioux River, a main artery of the Red. The reservoir had filled to capacity and was in danger itself of flooding the surrounding small communities. The Corps increased the releases into the Red River watershed to 7,000 cubic feet per second (cfs), adding a significant amount of water to an already flooding river system. And on the day of the "white sheet survey," the releases of water from Lake Traverse began flowing into the Wild Rice River, another Red River tributary. There was simply too much water in the system. Many of the people observing the rivers in the Hudson drainage—Corps employees, NWS hydrologists, state environmental officers, U.S. Geological Survey employees—were astounded. People who had spent their lives recording the erratic behavior of rivers began to tell each other they had never seen this much water, that, as NWS hydrologist Wendy Pearson would later put it, they had "never seen water do this."

On the outskirts of Grand Forks, farmers watched the snow slowly melt, the water lying atop their fields like giant panes of glass. In places where the snowmelt could find an exit, it rushed through tiny culverts and escaped across dirt roads. It was flowing in places the farmers had never seen it flow before. Later, some people thought that habitual drainage of valley wetlands for crops—something farmers had been doing for more than one hundred years—contributed to the severity of the 1997 flood. But even the valley's original wetlands could not have contained a flood of this size.

By April 13, the flood had reached a height that shattered town crest records in Halstad, Minnesota and in Fargo. The pilots and observers who were running recon flights and contracted gamma flights over the basin for the National Weather Service relayed what they saw on the ground below: it looked, they said, like an ocean of water was trying to push its way through the slender, crooked course of the Red River.

Late that afternoon, in discussions about the National Weather Service's crest prediction for Wahpeton, the Corps discovered that the NWS was using an outdated rating curve for that forecast point. A rating curve is a simple X/Y graph that displays a river's height on the vertical axis and its flow, in cubic feet per second, on the horizontal. The Corps' St. Paul district office supplied the NCRFC hydrologists with the current rating curve. Glitches like this sometimes happened during a flood season, and they were usually caught.

In Grand Forks city officials and National Weather Service hydrologists were watching the Red's behavior upstream carefully; the flood was moving north like a slow-moving tidal surge.

4 *Red River Rising*

Two days earlier, on Thursday, April 10, the National Weather Service had issued its first flood crest outlook in a week. It was the same number— 49 feet—that it had been predicting since late February. The prediction was perplexing to many people who had just spent a week shivering in homes that had lost power and heat due to the blizzard. Hannah had dropped about six inches of snow on the city of Grand Forks, and there was no telling how it would affect the Red River's rise. The agency, however, seemed to be saying that the additional moisture would not affect the flooding river in any way.

Peg Rogers, who had been sandbagging the Lincoln Drive dike near her parents' home since returning from Bismarck, had spent days looking at a river almost dead even with the top of the levee. "Have any of these people looked outside at the level of the water?" she remembers thinking. The number forty-nine had been on everyone's lips, on every newscast, in every weather report for nearly two months. It was something that was easy to hold on to. Sociologists studying the Grand Forks flood would later call it an "anchor point." And yet, even with a 49-foot crest burned into the collective mind of the city, people still looked at the river and felt uneasy. Many began to believe that the people in charge were terribly mistaken.

And in the back of Mike Anderson's mind was the dread that he might, in fact, be mistaken. To a hydrologist, numbers are constantly in motion. They adhere to certain laws and they make sense, but they are always animate. For a week, however, Anderson had been working with dead numbers. They had not changed because no data had arrived from the outside to warrant a change. The numbers he had to work with were the same numbers he'd had before Hannah hit. With his lifeless numerical data in front of him, Anderson turned to the North Central River Forecast Center's second set of eyes—the Corps of Engineers' Flood Reconnaissance Team.

Richard Pomerleau and Terry Zien could see just from looking at the Red River at Grand Forks that it was rising more quickly than the National Weather Service computers at the NCRFC said it was. It was as if those computers were modeling a completely different river. But Mike Anderson was hesitant to stray into a land of hypothesis, where decisions drift from objective science to subjective human observation. He was especially hesitant because the National Weather Service computers and their models knew the lay of the land and the flow of the river in more precise detail than the people feeding them data did. The agency's River Forecasting System could, in a single mechanized glance, assess the Red River from its source in Wahpeton to its drainage into Hudson Bay, and spit out, among other things, discharge values, river flow in cubic feet per second, the effect of snow runoff from the basin into the stream channel, and predicted river crests for any of the seven forecast points on the U.S. side of the border.

Anderson hesitated to alter the crest number because there was no new information upon which to base an updated prediction. Blizzard Hannah had hit before the NCRFC had gone into operational forecast mode—meaning it had still been operating in the less precise world of outlook. A guess would have been unscientific. Mike Anderson was groping down a darkened hallway.

Dean Braatz, the NCRFC's hydrologist-in-charge, would later call Monday, April 14 "a pivotal day." Temperatures were rising rapidly and the snow pack had started to ripen, a hydrologic term for thaw. After ten days without a change the National Weather Service now bumped up the crest prediction one foot, declaring the Red River at Grand Forks would crest at 50 feet sometime between April 19 and 22. The river was currently at 43.70 feet and rising.

This prediction was different: it was the first operational crest forecast of the season. An operational crest forecast has a lead-time of only five days, but it is far more reliable than an outlook. April 14 was the earliest possible date for such forecast—the crest was now as little as five days away. To get this number, Mike Anderson had noted that the computer model

projected a crest flow of 110,000 cfs for April 19, which was then translated by the rating curve to a stage of 50 feet. It was, in Anderson's words,
"a simple conversion."

A rating curve, a basic X/Y graph, reflects the relationship between a
river's height, or stage, and its rate of flow, called discharge. It is a tool that
hydrologists use to predict how high a river will be at any specific discharge
number; that is, by plotting a certain amount of water rushing through a
river channel, it is possible to predict just how high the river is going to be,
based on the river's past behavior. A rating curve is "built" from regularly
gathered data, data that is merged with previous data on stage and discharge during other floods in that river's history. Each point on the curve
represents a measurement made by the U.S Geological Survey at any time
during the period of record. There could conceivably be thousands of these
points, of these measurements, on a single rating curve. And the curve is
drawn across them like any mathematical curve would be—as a best fit.
The rating curve is used to predict at what height the river will crest at a
given flow rate. It is a vital, but perhaps the least complex, component in
the National Weather Service's River Forecasting System hydrological
model. The rating curves the NWS uses are supplied and updated peri-
odically by the U.S. Geological Survey, the federal agency responsible for
measuring river flow throughout the country. Most updates to rating
curves take place after a flood, when new measurements have been made.

To produce a rating curve for the Red River of the North at Grand
Forks, USGS staff routinely take discharge measurements off the downtown Sorlie Bridge at various times during the year, when the river is at
different levels. At a certain stage—say, 27 feet—the volume of water passing through the channel will be 15,000 cfs. Another ten feet—up to 37
now—and the measured discharge is around 32,000 cfs. These numbers,
theoretically, should not change much; that is, the Red at 27 feet at Grand
Forks should always be flowing at a rate of 15,000 cfs.

The USGS takes discharge measurements at every conceivable river
stage, plots these numbers on a graph and draws what NCRFC hydrometeorologist Steve Buan calls a "best-fit curve," or a single-value rating
curve (Fig. 1). Essentially, it tells the NCRFC hydrologists how high the river
will be at a certain measured discharge, based on observed fact. Since the
National Weather Service deals, in its internal calculations and models,
in discharge only, and not stage, it relies on this rating curve to convert

discharge into stage—to a number that the general public will understand. While a NCRFC hydrologist will immediately recognize 110,000 cfs going down the Red River as a major flood, a layperson may not. But if you tell her the river will crest at 51 feet, she knows what to expect.

When rivers rise past their highest historically observed crests, the USGS makes additional measurements and supplies this information to the National Weather Service which, in turn, uses it to update and supplement the rating curves. But the USGS does not extend these curves beyond observed flows; it simply can't. Once a river has risen beyond its highest observed crest, the USGS continues to take flow measurements and relay them to the National Weather Service, but by then the rating curve is officially out of date.

The rating curves the USGS had supplied the NCRFC had worked almost flawlessly for every forecast point along the Red River. But at Grand Forks, the National Weather Service was struggling to make sense of a river that, to their human eyes, looked like it was rising rapidly and would crest higher than 49 feet. Yet the computer model didn't seem to indicate a higher crest.

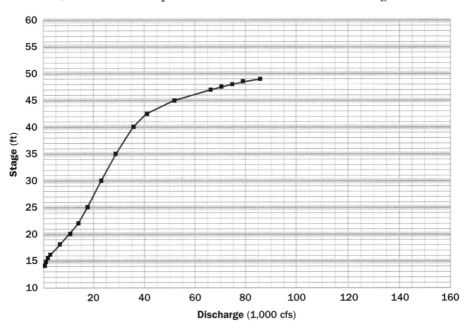

Fig. 1.
East Grand Forks Rating Curve (USGS Rating No. 18)
used by the National Weather Service, April 1997

The model's outer limit—the highest crest it could accurately predict—was Grand Forks' then-highest modern flood crest: 48.88 feet in 1979. The curve did not extend past that number because a number higher than that had not been observed before. It would have to extrapolate—the machine would have to guess.

In 1927, after the great Mississippi flood, Isaac Cline said that Weather Bureau policy dictated that flood crests be formulated using only "all water in sight," or verifiable data. Seventy years later, the National Weather Service still had neither the time nor the funding to create flooding scenarios that extended into the realm of imagination.

For nearly everyone in Grand Forks, the National Weather Service's one-foot increase was mildly troubling. For city engineer Ken Vein, however, it was a grueling directive. With any small hike in the crest prediction, Vein would have to add huge amounts of clay and sandbags to the top of the dikes. And every time he directed city employees, Corps workers and volunteers to add a foot of elevation to the dikes, it was no longer simply raising a few dikes—it meant adding thousands of sandbags along miles of levees.

With the river in flood, Ken Vein had grabbed the city's attention, not because he was quotable, like Pat Owens, or gregarious, like East Grand Forks mayor Lynn Stauss, but because he was imperturbable and hard to read.

"I keep my emotions within," Vein told a *Herald* reporter days after the Red River crested. "You could put it that way." Often seen in black cowboy boots and western-style shirts with a bolo tie, the forty-two-year-old's tranquil exterior hid a fierce intensity and an unyielding belief that he knew what was best when it came to the city's infrastructure.

Vein kept a paging device on his belt that gave him the river level readings every hour as well as the rate of rise. It was telling him the river was rising faster than it should have been. "We were approaching the forecasted crest elevations," he said. "And I'm thinking, something is terribly wrong here; this thing isn't slowing down." With temperatures now in the fifties and sixties, the remaining snowpack—including the snow dropped by Hannah ten days before—was flowing into the Red by gully, coulee, and overland. By Tuesday, April 15, more than a million sandbags had been filled and stacked by more than twelve thousand volunteers in Grand

Forks. On the sandbag lines, rumors of a 52-foot flood crest persisted, the result of the leak from Leon Osborne's staff meeting at the RWIC. Now, eye to eye with a fast-rising river, it didn't take long for the sandbag telegraph to turn the rumor into a disputed fact, reported this way by the *Grand Forks Herald:* "The numbers sometimes change, but the message essentially is the same: The Red River will crest at 53 or 54 feet this spring, some 4 to 5 feet above the record crest, and that officials are covering up the prediction to prevent panic from spreading across the valley. Well, the rumors are false, according to the National Weather Service in Grand Forks."

The employees at the Grand Forks National Weather Service office were aware of these rumors, but they mentioned them to Mike Anderson only in passing.

"I vaguely remember one of the techs talking to me [about Leon Osborne]," Mike Anderson said. "This was the first time I'd ever heard this guy's name, this professor who was saying something higher. It was right in the heat of the thing, so we had to filter out a ton of things. We had some of these other forecasters filtering phone calls for us, because we didn't have time to talk just to John Q. Tech someplace. Take the message. Unless it was Rich Pomerleau or Terry Zien or one of the four or five key people, we didn't talk to anybody else outside of the conference calls."

During a flood event, local NWS offices, as well as its river forecast centers, are inundated with phone calls from amateur forecasters, politicians, city leaders, and private citizens. "You only had a quart of time and you had two gallons of information coming at you," Anderson said. There was no time at the NCRFC for rumors.

But the people in Osborne's briefing at the RWIC knew the 52-foot crest number was no rumor. It was unconfirmed, unendorsed, and unofficial information—only National Weather Service numbers could be called "official"—but it was not, at least at the RWIC, considered "rumor." Stung by the *Herald's* article, and the curt dismissal the *Herald* attributed to the Grand Forks National Weather Service office, Leon Osborne called his staff together and told them, "Don't answer any more phone calls on this subject." He instructed his staff to tell anyone who called with a question about the flood crest that "We'd prefer you listen to the National Weather Service." However, if the caller asked whether or not he or she should buy flood insurance—as he or she always did—Osborne told his staff to say, unequivocally, yes.

At the time, Osborne felt he was doing the right thing. The National Weather Service was under federal mandate to provide forecasts for floods and other weather events. The Corps of Engineers approved—and financed—only the building of dikes to a height sufficient to hold back the forecasted crest; anything extra would have to be financed by the city.

"Obviously they felt I was doing things I should have stayed out of," Osborne said later. "But that's like a physician that sees that another physician doesn't have the right diagnosis. We don't have a Hippocratic oath in meteorology, but maybe we should."

But Osborne backed off and let the National Weather Service do its job.

The United States Geological Survey staff had been taking regular flow measurements from various bridges up and down the Red River valley. As the floodwaters multiplied, they, too, began to see water flowing in areas in which it had never been observed to flow before. Now, instead of only gauging river discharge, USGS teams were dispatched to observe and estimate the volume of water flow across highways, and measure the discharge from ditches and small culverts now pouring into the Red.

At 10:10 AM on Tuesday, April 15, USGS employees measured the Red at Grand Forks at 47,400 cubic feet per second at a height of 45.72 feet. The USGS relayed this information back to the team of NCRFC hydrologists on the Red River project in Chanhassen. It was compared to the model simulation flow and crest numbers, and it now matched within four-tenths of a foot. Everything seemed to be working with near pinpoint accuracy.

That same day, the Corps was finding that the ice jams on the Red River were causing so much backwater that they needed outside advice. Richard Pomerleau and Terry Zien contacted Kathleen White from the Cold Regions Research and Engineering Laboratory in Hanover, New Hampshire. The lab is part of the Corps' Engineer Research and Development Center, and houses the world's best and most complete collection of scientific and technical literature on the cold regions of the earth. White, who specializes in ice jam data collection, mitigation, and control, had spoken a number of times during this flood season with both American and Canadian officials. Near Winnipeg, the Red was flowing under a nearly unbroken sheet of ice, and the potential for jams was high. After speaking with White, Winnipeg city officials had decided to drill holes in a seven-mile stretch of the river to weaken the ice. They called out nine arctic vehicles called Bombardiers, which look like car-sized snowmobiles. Lined up, the Bombardiers drilled a hole every minute. The cost to the city of Winnipeg was estimated at $40,000. This kind of operation was too expensive for most of the small cities along the Red's course.

After consulting with Kathleen White, Pomerleau and Zien visited NWS hydrologist Wendy Pearson at the Grand Forks office and told her what the experts had recommended to U.S. cities along the Red: apply rhodamine dye to the ice to dissolve it. The cities decided to stick with sand.

Early on Wednesday, April 16, the National Weather Service re-issued the same forecasted crest number: the Red at Grand Forks would crest at 50 feet, but now it placed the crest on April 22 or 23—the next Tuesday or Wednesday—even though the river had just risen more than three feet in a little more than twenty-four hours.

At 9:20 that night, the 1997 flood officially became the worst on record at Grand Forks when the river rose above the 48.88-foot crest mark set in 1979. The river was only inches away from the National Weather Service's original predicted crest of 49 feet, and was flowing at more than 82,000 cfs. Now the National Weather Service found its calculations going off the top of the rating curve. Imagine computing a statistical problem on a graph and finding yourself drawing your line off the top of your paper. When the river rose past the 1979 crest, this was, literally, the end of the line for the National Weather Service's rating curve.

Mike Anderson and the team of NCRFC hydrologists assigned to the Red River knew this would happen. They knew back in February that because they were predicting a flood of record, that they would have to extrapolate the existing rating curve. They had done it countless times before. That wasn't the problem.

"Obviously we know that we can get at any location higher than the previous flood of record," Anderson said. "I mean, we do it five times a year or ten times a year. Our model has a way of extending that rating curve."

The computer model is pre-programmed to automatically extend a dead-end rating curve by choosing one of three extrapolation methods: linear, logarithmic, or hydraulic extension. The National Weather Service's model chose its method automatically as well—an action built into its operating system that selects the best method for the data at hand—and this time the model chose the logarithmic extension. The model produces a simple extension, based on how the river has behaved prior to that last point on the rating curve.

"It's like ballistics on a Howitzer shot," Steve Buan said four years later in the conference room at the NCRFC. "It's a trajectory."

"It works," Anderson said. He's earnest, a scientist sure of the integrity of the tools he uses. But he paused and added, with emphasis, "If you have a *normal* rating curve." For Mike Anderson, the difference between success and failure would be no larger than a half-inch loop on a simple graph.

The Red's mean discharge during the year is around 2,630 cubic feet per second. During flood season it flows at a rate three and a half times that. At its worst, in 1897, it was flowing at 85,000 cfs. On Wednesday, April 16, the river was two days away from an extraordinary 136,900 cfs.

One cubic foot equals about seven and a half gallons; the Red River at Grand Forks, squeezed into a narrow channel made even narrower by dikes on both banks, was trying to push the equivalent of more than a million gallons of water per second through a strait that normally accommodated 19,275 gallons per second. In other words, it was as if fifty-two Red Rivers were trying to flow through one Red River's channel.

The Red had crested at Wahpeton (for the second time) the day before at 19.44 feet: about a foot and a half higher than Wahpeton's former flood of record. In three days it would crest at Fargo at 39.72 feet, two and a half feet above record. A day later, at Halstad, Minnesota—halfway between Fargo and Grand Forks—it would crest at a little more than a foot and a half above record. Up and down the Red, the river was surpassing towns' floods of record by one to two and a half feet at most. A pattern was beginning to emerge, and Mike Anderson and Steve Buan noted it.

On the far south end of Grand Forks, on Elmwood Drive, Mary Lien picked up her camcorder and, from her porch, began a slow pan of her back lawn, which was still covered in crisp snow. Slowly she zoomed in toward a convoy of dark green trucks with piles of sandbags in their beds, driving over the newly erected clay and earth dike that East Elmwood residents had been told to build just weeks before. A yellow earthmover appeared from the other side of the dike. She focused the camera on the machine for long minutes as it dug up the hard winter soil surrounding the dike. The roar of diesel engines. The hollow metal clanking of the earthmover. The complete absence of the sounds of nature.

Jim and Mary Lien and their six children, all but one in their late teens or older, had been sandbagging and patrolling the dike since early April. They had watched as their neighbors hired moving vans and loaded their belongings into them. As Mary panned away from the dike with her camcorder, she zoomed out for a survey of her back lawn. Somewhere past the stand of cottonwoods on the edge of her property the ice-covered Red River was growing ever larger.

Downtown, sandbagging also continued. Peg Rogers, her son Josh, and many of the people of Lincoln Drive sandbagged until two or three in the morning, working by floodlight and listening to the Red lap against the sandbags piled atop the dike. People were silent. No one was making jokes anymore. They seemed to be listening intently to the sound of the ice-clogged river. The energy that had electrified the city—the kind of exhilaration that stirs a man just before he enters battle—had become fear. Peg Rogers thought about her parents. Their little home on Polk Street stood in the shadow of the dike. If the dike broke, the house was gone.

Earlier that day, the University of North Dakota had canceled classes for the remaining four weeks of the semester to add students to the volunteer ranks, as sandbagging had been upgraded to a twenty-four-hour operation. Students were given the option of accepting the grades they had maintained to date or requesting an incomplete. Down near the university, students pitched sand and clay along English Coulee, a normally picturesque campus stream now kept in check by stacks of sandbags. People living nearby worried about the coulee because it, like the Red, was looking less and less familiar as the flood season progressed. Ken Vein, whose home overlooked the coulee, had earlier told the *Grand Forks Herald* that he believed the houses along the coulee were safe, "providing there are no surprises." The coulee, slight as it is, is part of an extensive flood control system completed in the early 1990s. It is a miniature version of Winnipeg's massive floodway.

Along the coulee's channel, a levee collects runoff from the upper half of its drainage basin and sends it into a structure that slows the flow to no more than 450 cubic feet per second. It is a kind of hydraulic colander that empties the excess flow into a diversion channel. Three miles down that channel, another structure reroutes most of the diverted water into a ditch that carries it around the city before dumping it back into the Red River north of Grand Forks. This system allows no more than 20 cfs to pass through the coulee's main channel, which gives it the appearance of a mild, meandering brook. The diversion project was designed to keep western Grand Forks and areas around the university from flooding.

The Red River's main channel at Grand Forks was not diverted in this way. On both the Minnesota and North Dakota banks, the river was held in check by dikes, the oldest form of flood protection. But if a system like the English Coulee diversion had existed on a larger scale for the Red River at Grand Forks in 1997, towns downstream—Pembina, for example—would have flooded worse than they did, even if Grand Forks had been spared. In the world of hydraulic engineering, collateral damage in battle is inevitable; and sometimes certain wars are simply unwinnable.

The evening of that same day, April 16, the city of Grand Forks held a public meeting at the Civic Auditorium with mayor Pat Owens, city engineer Ken Vein, and Jim Campbell, the emergency operations manager. Owens had been feeling anxious about the National Weather Service's crest prediction. Each time she thought about what could happen if the dikes failed she got goosebumps.

"Intuition told me what was happening," she said. Five minutes before taking the stage at the auditorium, Owens pulled Campbell aside and said, "Jim, I think I need to tell them to voluntarily evacuate. We need to tell them we just don't know." Campbell agreed. Owens, Campbell, and Vein took their seats on stage and faced a crowd of residents who lived in the riverbank neighborhoods—Lincoln Drive, Riverside Park, and Central Park. Owens looked into the audience and told them to pack up their things and move out of their houses, out of the neighborhood. Some people in the crowd laughed.

"I hope most of you will, on your own, decide to move somewhere else until this is over," she told them. "It is unknown to all of us what will happen at fifty feet."

Meanwhile, USGS team members were valiantly continuing to measure discharge under terrifying conditions. Some of them literally dangled off bridges; others didn't have to, since the water was within arm's length of the girders. These discharge numbers were relayed to Mike Anderson at the NCRFC and compared to the discharge numbers predicted by the model, which was now operating with the extended rating curve. Everything still matched up, but the next twenty-four hours would change everything.

As the sun crept above the straight-line horizon of the Red River valley on Thursday, April 17, the river was at nearly 50 feet, and the first cracks began to show in the dikes at Grand Forks. However, an editorial in the *Herald* newspaper that landed on doorsteps that morning admonished residents to stop believing rumors, specifically the one about a 52- or 53-foot crest. "Do not make up rumors," editor-in-chief Mike Jacobs wrote, "Do not spread rumors. Do not believe rumors." The same issue featured a front-page info box answering "5 vital flood questions." Question Four read: "Will the river crest at 53 feet?" The *Herald* responded: "That's a rumor." Ken Vein had also expressed his faith in the National Weather Service again, hoping that a vote of confidence from the city engineer would help put an end to the "rumors." "My level of confidence is high. They've got sophisticated computer models, and we're farther downstream than Wahpeton and Fargo, so they've got more data for Grand Forks."

At 8:50 that morning, the hydrologists at the NCRFC received the latest discharge measurement from Grand Forks. The flow was 82,700 cfs, with a corresponding river stage of 49.94 feet. For the first time, the National Weather Service model's simulated flows were diverging from the flows actually being observed for that height. About three hours later, Mike Anderson revised the crest prediction to 50.5 feet. The USGS noted that, as feared, ice jams upstream appeared to be causing fluctuations in the rate of rise. Moreover, in Minnesota's Red Lake River, which flowed into the Red at Grand Forks, a large jam had formed at the town of Crookston and was causing rapid changes in river stage there. Acting as a dam, it was holding back huge amounts of water. When it broke, it would likely send a flood swell towards Grand Forks.

The Grand Forks Fire Department switched from a three-shift to a two-shift workday. The Grand Forks Air Force Base assigned five hundred airmen and women to monitor dikes and staff the temporary shelter that would open that evening at the Grand Forks Civic Auditorium. The state highway patrol closed the northbound lanes of I-29 north of town because nearly nine inches of water was flowing across the four-lane highway.

At the Emergency Operations Center that had been opened in the basement of the police station, Jim Campbell and Pat Owens returned again and again to a closed-circuit television to keep tabs on the dikes. Two master sergeants from the air force base had designed a system by which city officials could have a live view of the levees. A cameraman wearing a twenty-five pound metal frame backpack outfitted with a small transmitter walked the dikes, keeping his lens trained on trouble spots. The transmitter relayed the signal to a more powerful transmitter mounted atop a county-owned van and, from there, the signal was sent to the emergency operations center, where Campbell and Owens watched the transmitted images.

KCNN, a news and talk radio giant in eastern North Dakota had become a twenty-four-hour flood information station. Dispatches were issued: sewers are full; water plant close to going under; don't take showers; don't flush the toilet. KCNN also became a kind of on-air rumor mill, with many callers sharing second-hand information. More than once, city leaders phoned to clarify or refute claims made by panicked citizens. When someone called in a rumor that the Kennedy Bridge was closed, people grew frantic. To many, that prospect must have seemed like a white flag, a precursor to full surrender to the flood. The rumor caused such alarm that Pat Owens went on the air to assure everyone that the bridge was still open. She begged citizens to stay calm. "I am asking people not to panic. We will fight it to the very end." It would be little more than twenty-four hours before the Kennedy Bridge was closed.

In the basement of the police station, the emergency operations center was a crowded cotillion of city and state agencies, each with its own table: the Corps of Engineers, the city engineer, the sheriff's department, the health department, the police, the National Guard, the Air Force, and so on. City attorney Howard Swanson, who had just returned from business in Milwaukee, arrived there to find the mayor had been asking for him, wishing to discuss the legalities of evacuation orders. As Swanson and Owens conferred in a hallway, Ken Vein walked by and interrupted their conversation. He wanted Swanson to get on the phone and persuade the state and local contractors to send more bulldozers, dump trucks, Payloaders, and tractors.

"Do I get the title of Heavy Equipment Coordinator?" Swanson joked. Within hours, Swanson had lined up over ninety North Dakota Department of Transportation dump trucks from across the state. After his brief announcement on city radio asking area residents to lend their bulldozers and dump trucks to the flood fight, dozens of farmers phoned to say they were willing to drive their tractors into town.

After sandbagging all night, Peg Rogers went to her job at the United Day Nursery on Chestnut Street. Through bleary eyes, she watched toddlers building miniature dikes in the nursery's sand table. Around one o'clock a visibly terrified woman rushed into the nursery, swept her child off the floor, and headed for the door.

"The dike's broke in Lincoln Drive," she said. "It's filling up with water." Peg immediately thought of her parents in their home there, and of her seventeen-year-old daughter who was helping them move furniture and other belongings to the second floor.

In Lincoln Drive, civil defense sirens were blaring, a shrill suggestion that they pack up their things and move out of the neighborhood. Panicked homeowners dropped whatever they were doing and spilled out of doors, running full speed out of Lincoln Drive. "The dike's failed," people shouted to one another. Someone said he had seen a wall of water on its way up Polk Street. Humvees and ambulances drove up and down the streets, with police officers barking evacuation orders through public address systems mounted on the roofs of their vehicles: "All residents please evacuate the area and go to the Civic Auditorium if you need shelter."

Peg Rogers arrived at Euclid Avenue, a street on the knoll overlooking the saucer that was the Lincoln Drive neighborhood. National Guardsmen and women were trying to keep frantic relatives from rushing down into the neighborhood. Peg tried to move past one Guardsman, but he stopped her.

"You can't go in there," he said.

"My parents and daughter were in there just a half hour ago," she told him.

"I can't let you in," he said. "But don't worry; we won't leave anyone behind." In a panic, Peg wandered around the periphery of the neighborhood, trying to find a way in. It would be one long hour before she found her elderly parents and her daughter safe at Peg's sister's home. They had joined the exodus before Peg arrived.

Then, as unexpectedly as the civil defense sirens had started, they stopped. People were now trickling out of Lincoln Drive, rather than running. National Guardsmen were turning a blind eye to people who wanted to slip past the checkpoints. The dike hadn't broken. It had, instead, developed six massive cracks running lengthwise through the dike, and they were beginning to seep water. The pressure against the sediment and clay dikes was enormous. The river was trying to become a lake. The Lincoln Drive dike had been a reliable shield against a number of severe floods. Pat Owens, who was seventeen years old when it was built in 1958, was not particularly surprised that they were leaking.

"I just had a feeling that one would go," she said. It hadn't "gone" quite yet. Corps engineers and Emergency Operations Center (EOC) officials tried to improvise. At the cracks, they began to lay down more sandbags, a kind of mini-dike to hold in the leaking water. The city had run out of clay. Ken Vein began sending bulldozers to dig up the Lincoln Drive golf course and the soccer fields at Bringewatt Park.

After tearing up the golf course, city soccer fields, and even private land in search of clay for the dikes, Vein and his crew ran out again. They had to have more. With no other options, Vein directed the Corps and National Guardsmen to begin digging up more of the city parks and extracting as much as clay as possible. Even sand was running low now; city and Corps engineers raided the golf course's sand traps. Throughout that afternoon and evening, the National Guard stacked the dikes with more sandbags and clay mined from the city's recreation grounds. Volunteers attached plastic sheets to the sandbags, tucking them into crevices, and threw the sheets over the dike into the Red River. The idea was that the water pressure would force the plastic against the cracks and seal them tight. In the late evening, hundreds of volunteers were still laying sandbags and patrolling the river. Officials from the EOC and other city leaders had been congregating along the dikes to help Corps workers inject a mortar mixture into the cracks. Neil Schwanz, a Corps spokesman, told the *Herald* that the dikes were secure, even as the Red River was breaking in waves on the sandbags above the top of the earth dike.

In a corner of the EOC, Ken Vein and his staff were bent over maps, trying to determine the strength of the dikes, plot fortification strategies, and pinpoint vulnerabilities in the city's infrastructure. Corps engineers, too, had every intention of keeping the Red River out of the streets. A sharp-witted, highly decorated young engineer named Lisa Hedin was in charge of the Corps' efforts in Grand Forks.

Hedin, an athletic woman with light brown hair and limpid blue eyes, was, in 1997, one of only a handful of female engineers in the St. Paul district office, and she was one of the Corps' best and one of their brightest. Just as a good pool player can see every shot after the break, so the Corps comes to every project ready to run the table. And if a typical Corps project is pocket billiards, Lisa Hedin is Minnesota Fats. Hedin was intrigued early by the unique problems presented by bodies of water. While other kids her age were playing with Barbie or G.I. Joe, Hedin was skillfully engineering road systems in her sandbox and building snow dams in the gutter during the spring thaw. From the time she was in junior high school, there was never any question that she would be an engineer.

She came to the Corps as a hydrologic engineer, and worked on river problems while going to graduate school at night. Eventually she would earn her masters in civil engineering. It was obvious that her bosses at the Corps recognized they had a rising star on their hands, and they honored her twice with the Army's Superior Civilian Service Award. What was happening in Grand Forks now, however, would test her skill and her fortitude in a way no other project had, or likely ever would.

She and the rest of the city and Corps engineers were facing an extraordinarily difficult problem, one that even the concentration of brainpower camped in the EOC was having trouble solving. Unlike the rest of the Center, which was abuzz with the incessant ringing of telephones and increasingly desperate shouting from station to station, the engineering room was silent. The engineers were at work—coolly assessing weaknesses and methodically searching for advantages. Yet Lisa Hedin could feel panic approaching. So could Ken Vein. Still, the aura of the engineering room remained churchlike, and as the engineers quietly studied the contour maps, they may have been praying.

All over Grand Forks, residents had already started praying. In churches, clergy lead their congregations in prayer. Reverend William Sherman of St. Michael's Catholic Church, a World War II veteran who had been part of the occupying forces in Japan in the days after it had been bombed, led special prayers during morning and afternoon Masses. On that Thursday afternoon, as volunteers scrambled to fortify the Lincoln Drive dike, Sherman walked the Riverside Park dike and said the rosary. The patron saint of floods is St. Gregory Thaumaturgus, whose best-known miracle was stopping the River Lycus from overflowing. Sherman, though, was thinking a lot about St. Columban, another flood patron saint—a man who had been stranded on a remote island in the Irish Sea.

In St. Paul, at the Corps of Engineers headquarters, engineer Patrick Foley was taking a look at an old rating curve from a Corps feasibility study. The Corps' St. Paul district headquarters is a square, modern armory set in the middle of downtown. With its perfect corners, its hulking, clean profile and its nearly windowless façade, it is undeniably an engineers' building. The narrow streets that form its boundaries—for it takes up one small city block—are a stone's throw from one of the Corps' main charges: the Mississippi River. Unlike the National Weather Service, whose offices are often tucked in remote, suburban locations, the Corps prefers to have its responsibilities literally in its sights.

Of the three major federal agencies handling rivers and their floods, the Corps is the only one that deals in anything outside of observable fact. When it comes to the science of rivers and river control, the Corps can often make engineering seem artful. While the National Weather Service and USGS rarely venture outside of the boundaries of observable fact, the Corps thinks about and plots the "what if's" of river behavior. What if the Red River channel were two hundred yards to the left? What if it were routed around Grand Forks rather than through it? What if its flows reached 136,900 cubic feet per second? The Corps is a confident agency, certain of its ability to control rivers, to adjust their roving courses, to "correct" their bad behavior.

Among other tasks—such as civil works projects, disaster response, and water resource management—the Corps studies rivers: topography, the vegetation growing on its banks, the effect man-made structures have on its flow and its grade. The National Weather Service, on the other hand, is concerned with what a river will do in conjunction with any number of meteorological factors. As a result, the Corps spends much of its time collecting data that the NWS would consider irrelevant. The NWS, on the other hand, spends its time collecting perishable data—such as soil moisture levels and snowmelt forecasts—that are of only passing interest to the Corps.

Patrick Foley began to trace the river's rate of rise against its flow on the rating curve from an old feasibility study for a proposed Grand Forks ring dike designed by the Corps some years back (Fig. 2). The curve was a non-predictive tool used by the Corps to determine how the Red River would behave at Grand Forks *if* the city were surrounded by a ring dike. Detritus from the earlier study, this particular rating curve was like a caricature of the current rating curve the NWS was using. Its flow-to-stage ratio produced a steeper curve. The reason: this rating curve assumed a tightened river channel, one corseted by an extensive dike system identical to one that the Corps had proposed to the city of Grand Forks in 1994. One effect of a tighter river channel would be a higher river level for any given discharge, something that was happening to the Red River at that moment for unknown reasons.

"I tracked it to check the curve we were using to design our levee, and also to see if there was anything unusual going on in the river. If we see unexpected deviations with the USGS measurements made in the early part

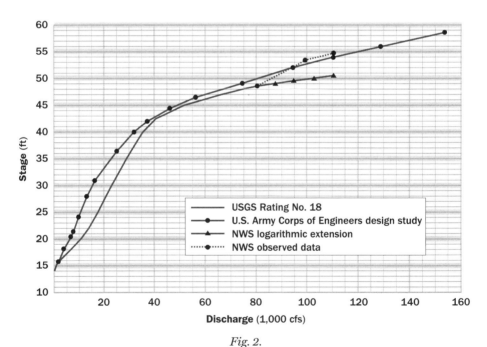

Fig. 2.
U. S. Army Corps of Engineers design study rating for East Grand Forks based on a proposed ring dike

of the flood, there might be something unusual going on," Foley said. When Foley compared the two curves, he noticed very little deviation.

In addition, Corps engineers had extended this rating curve to imaginary levels beyond the 1979 crest. The engineers could do this for one simple reason: it was not using the curve as a predictive tool. No one was counting on them to predict the flood crest. If they were charged with that task, they would not have used *this* rating curve in a hydrological model because it was unverifiable. Its extension past the 1979 crest was calibrated on educated conjecture, not hard data, and in federal forecasting, conjecture is not an option.

Further, the city of Grand Forks had turned down the Corps' ring dike proposal. This dike system was not in Grand Forks; the river channel had not been modified in this way; water did not flow through the channel in the way this rating curve suggested it would. The rating curve was not operational.

So while Foley found it interesting that the Red River's current stage-to-flow ratio was adhering to this rating curve, he did not feel compelled to notify the NWS about it. It was, in his mind, a simple coincidence. He did, however, share this information with his boss, Ed Eaton, the Corps' chief of water control. After looking at the curve, Eaton agreed that it "offered no clear insights into the flood's behavior."

Even if Foley and Eaton had felt it necessary to alert the NWS to how well this curve seemed to match the Red River's current behavior, they still may have hesitated; although the two agencies were working closely together during 1997 Red River flood season, there were still boundaries they dared not overstep. Officially, "The St. Paul District recognizes and respects Congressional mandated responsibility given to National Weather Service for issuance of public forecasts, watches, and warnings . . . the St. Paul District neither presumes to take over the mandate given to the National Weather Service by Congress for forecasting of river stages nor does the Corps perform oversight and quality control over the National Weather Service. . . . Unless the St. Paul District staff have good reason to question National Weather Service forecasts, the forecasts of these professionals are not questioned on a routine basis as this would be a wasteful duplication of effort on the part of two federal agencies."

After dismissing the rating curve Pat Foley had shown him, Ed Eaton pulled out another Corps document for Grand Forks, a historical hydrograph for Red River floods at that forecast point; he noticed something "odd" about it. Historically, the anatomy of a Grand Forks snowmelt flood included a steady rise, then a slight deceleration during which the river's stage might hover. Then the river would begin rising again about another two feet before reaching crest levels. Eaton was concerned because it was already late in the game and the Red was showing no signs of slowing. The Red wasn't following the pattern. Eaton decided then that he had "good reason to question," and got on the phone to the NCRFC.

Late that afternoon Lisa Hedin, Ken Vein, and Al Grasser cleared off a table in their office at the Emergency Operations Center and spread a few maps across a table. For the first time, there seemed to be a palpable fear in the room. Hedin began to swear—and between her angry, frustrated curses, she was saying what all the other engineers were now saying: there's no high ground to fight from.

Ken Vein's assistant, engineer Al Grasser, had been working as hard as his boss to keep the city safe, but, as he later told a *Minneapolis Star Tribune* reporter, he "could kind of see the writing on the wall." Grasser would later call that Thursday night the worst of his life.

Veteran helicopter pilot Dale Dobesh had spent the past week flying over the flooding Red River valley for Minneapolis CBS-affiliate WCCO-TV. The station's hangar in St. Paul was itself flooded by overflow from the Mississippi, and Dobesh had moved his base of operations out to a tiny suburban airport called Flying Cloud. From there he made daily flights up and down the course of the Red with WCCO photojournalists. On Wednesday, Dobesh had flown over Fargo with two of them and saw the same writing on the wall that assistant city engineer Al Grasser had seen. The next day, Dobesh walked into the WCCO news director's office and told him that he needed to send the "A-team" to Grand Forks.

The news director agreed and immediately dispatched the station's first-string reporting team, including photojournalist Bill Schwabe and Don Shelby, a veteran anchor and former investigative journalist who was eager to get out from behind the desk and back into the field.

Dobesh and the A-team left for Grand Forks within hours. After refueling in Moorhead, across the river from Fargo, Dobesh continued towards Grand Forks, flying at about five hundred feet. On the ground beneath, Dobesh saw cattle, horses, and even wild deer stranded on islands of dry land. He steered the chopper away from them so as not to frighten them into the water.

"There were spots where the river covered from horizon to horizon with only some roads and trees sticking out," Dobesh said. "The riverbed was visible because the ice had not broken up, and it formed this ribbon of ice across this expanse of water. I'll never forget that sight."

After locating her parents, Peg Rogers and her son Josh decided to cross the Murray Bridge and volunteer to sandbag in an East Grand Forks neighborhood called The Point. As the sun disappeared behind the thin prairie horizon, huge floodlamps buzzed on, casting pale beams of light on the exhausted faces of the sandbaggers. During a coffee break, the civil defense sirens blared again and the volunteers saw a military truck barreling towards them with a National Guardsman leaning out the window, yelling something to them. As the truck got closer, Peg could hear him shouting that The Point's dike had failed somewhere upstream. He was telling her to leave immediately. Peg and Josh ran across the Murray Bridge, the river licking at the undercarriage of the deck.

After locating her other four children and dropping them off at the flood headquarters and temporary shelter in the Civic Auditorium, Peg drove towards downtown where her husband, Tim, who worked for the U.S. West telephone company, was trying to save a phone cable under the Sorlie Bridge. Downtown was deserted, but not under an official evacuation order yet. Night had fallen and the sound of the angry river seemed louder than it had during the day. As Peg handed her husband some food she had bought from one of the few stores still open, huge chunks of ice fell from the bridge into the river with a deafening clap.

The civil defense sirens sounded again, and Peg saw another National Guard truck racing toward them. Another dike had failed, the driver told them, and they had to leave this place immediately. Tim sent his wife off ahead of him; he had to retrieve a load of equipment from a manhole. He promised he would do it quickly. Peg left reluctantly, crying.

"I felt so helpless," she said later. "It was like we were in a slow-motion movie and were just waiting to see what was next." Peg went home. As she tucked her two youngest children, ten-year-old Shaun and one-year-old Mitchell, into bed, she told them everything would be fine in the morning and they would have a good laugh about the hysteria of the day before. They believed her, and she had almost convinced herself.

The Red River was already a foot past the National Weather Service's initial crest prediction and nearly two feet higher than its highest historical crest. The Corps water control chief, Ed Eaton, had called the NCRFC just as Mike Anderson and the other Red River hydrologists were reviewing the same hydrograph that had so alarmed him. They agreed with Eaton that the forecast needed to be raised, but chose to raise it to 50.5 feet rather than 51.5 feet as Eaton had urged.

"We felt that the current forecast of fifty to fifty-point-five feet was justifiable and correct for the information we had available," Mike Anderson said, "which included Corps of Engineers recon information." A few hours later, however, the National Weather Service revised its crest prediction to 51.5 to 52 feet any time on Friday or Saturday. The stubborn ice jam that had been damming the Red Lake River at Crookston finally broke, and sent a surge of floodwaters into the Red's channel at the forks. The river was rising so fast and so high that the NCRFC hydrologists were having difficulty keeping up with it.

Around nine o'clock that Thursday night Pat Owens, who, along with her staff, had been spending twenty-hour days at the Emergency Operations Center, decided to head home to change clothes, do a load of laundry, and catch a few hours of sleep. She planned to be back downtown around four in the morning. Ken Vein, who had been working virtually around the clock since flood operations began weeks before, had also gone home to get some sleep, leaving Al Grasser and the volunteer sandbagging crews to continue trying to maintain about three feet of freeboard above the river with sandbags and clay. But the river was rising too quickly and the dikes were leaking. Grasser called his boss a few hours later and asked him to come back. When he arrived, they headed down to Lincoln Drive.

At the Lincoln Drive dikes, Vein and engineers from the Corps began assessing the dikes' strength. If the water running through the cracks in the dikes was clean, they tried to patch. If the water was murky, running dark with clay, they abandoned the dike because it was on the verge of collapse.

"We realized there was no way to stop this," Vein said. "We cannot stop it."

Like Al Grasser, NCRFC hydrologic forecaster Mike Anderson considers that Thursday night one of the worst of his life. "Things really went to hell in a handbasket within twenty-four hours."

"I think that up until that day, everybody that we'd talked to"—including Richard Pomerleau and Terry Zien, who had looked at this river from every conceivable angle—"thought everything was going fine. We didn't get any indication from the field that things were going awry. It just went awry in twenty-four hours, literally," Steve Buan remembered.

That night, the entire Red River crew had come into the NCRFC (they were normally split into two shifts, and had been working around the clock since March). Mike Anderson and Steve Buan were sitting in front of their computers in disbelief. Something was terribly wrong. "Things had gone to pot," Anderson remembers. Though they wracked their brains for an answer, no one at the NCRFC could figure out why things were not matching up. The model and the river it was modeling had gone their separate ways, it seemed.

"We had history at Wahpeton, Fargo, Halstad, Hickson, then the other tributaries," Buan said. "How far above their floods of records had they crested at? You'll have a hard time finding any of those points were much in excess of two feet over their flood of records. All of sudden now we're like a screaming eagle about forty-nine feet, and it's going up. Why? Then it flies by fifty-one. We're two feet above flood of record, and it's still going up. What's going on? It was starting to fall outside the norm. I mean, we look for patterns. It's like any scientific discipline, you're looking for reasons and explanations. Why was this one starting to act so different from the other ones?" Buan paused, still incredulous four years later. "Try to explain that."

Mike Anderson could explain it: "We knew that we were in never-never land."

Earlier that day, the NCRFC Red River crew had noted a discrepancy between the simulated discharge in the model and the observed discharge figures from the USGS. It was unclear what this meant, and it was unclear where the problem lay—in the data, or in the model. Like most scientists, Mike Anderson and Steve Buan immediately suspected bad raw data. Moreover—and ultimately more significantly—the rating curve's conversion from discharge to stage was lagging behind observed river levels. That is, as the discharge increased, the river rose much more rapidly than the model was saying it should at that discharge. Something strange was happening on that rating curve. The Red had presented Mike Anderson with a grim riddle, and he had to solve it before "half a town" disappeared.

This was the riddle: although the National Weather Service's discharge numbers were spot-on—what it had forecast was almost exactly what was being observed—those numbers were not correlating with the river stage numbers. The Red seemed to be adhering to its own rating curve, one in which 110,000 cfs in the river channel did not, in fact, translate to 50.5 feet, as the USGS rating curve said it should. The river was shooting past that number, and the National Weather Service couldn't keep up. The single-value rating curve—that gently rounded mathematical curve—had grown a mysterious offshoot; the observed river stage was now so different from what the rating curve said it should be at the observed discharge that the rating curve now looked, if drawn on a sheet of graph paper, like a divining rod (Fig. 3). It seemed to adhere to no pattern, and that, more than anything, frightened the Red River hydrologists.

"It just started to come and come," Anderson said. "We started looking at that and saying 'Wait a minute, how can we go any higher? Okay, we'll raise it from forty-nine to fifty-point-five.' Well, you come an hour later, and thanks to people like Pomerleau and Ken Vein, we're told 'This baby is not slowing down.' And we've got recon out here on these little coulees and water is just a-whistlin' through these things. We're far from leveling off."

Why was this happening? Why would this rating curve, which had worked immaculately for not only the entire 1997 flood season at Grand Forks up until this point, but also for a number of years prior, suddenly fall apart? Why were things so different in Grand Forks? It was as if the Red at Grand Forks—or maybe the fossil inland sea Agassiz—had spontaneously begun to obey the gravitational pull of the moon, rising to meet it. What was happening at Grand Forks was that inexplicable, and as unlikely.

As Mike Anderson and Steve Buan were struggling to re-map the flooding river, and unbeknownst to anyone at the time, the embankment at Hartsville Coulee, ten miles to the south of Grand Forks, breached. The coulee, which runs parallel to the Red on its east side and which serves as an outlet for excess floodwaters, had sent yet another flood surge barreling downstream towards Grand Forks. Almost at that very moment, a USGS crew was taking one more measurement off the Sorlie Bridge, which was quaking as the torrent rushed passed. The crew was astonished when their gauges read an impossibly high flow—145,000 cubic feet per second. It was a leap upwards, more than twice the peak flow of the Red River during the 1979 record flood. The USGS repeated its measurement, just to be sure: 145,000 cfs. When this information was relayed to Mike Anderson, his first inclination was to be suspicious.

A few hours later, the USGS crew, suspicious of the data themselves, begged a National Guardsman to drive them back onto the Sorlie Bridge. The bridge was now partly submerged and the guardsman hesitated. He asked a National Guard major for permission and received it, with this directive: the major would ride along and if he gave the signal, the guardsman was to put the Humvee in reverse and get off the bridge, whether or not the crew, or the major himself, was on board. The Humvee crept onto the bridge. The USGS crew walked over to the edge, icy river water flowing over their shoes, and lowered their meter into the river.

145,000 cfs.

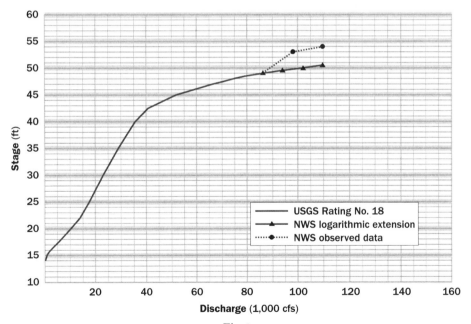

Fig. 3.
East Grand Forks Rating Curve showing the divergence
between the NWS's logarithmic extension and the actual river discharge and stage

The Hartsville breach had greatly changed the dynamic of the river, if only for a few hours. But no one on that bridge knew of the breach, so a terrifying mystery began to unfold. When the USGS measured again the next day, the river's velocity had slowed, even though the river itself was still rising. But it would be two weeks before anyone learned of the breach, so the strange discharge numbers were mystifying and deeply alarming to the USGS crew. When these numbers were relayed to Mike Anderson once again, he was still reluctant to believe them. If the USGS crew hadn't seen it with their own eyes, they wouldn't have believed it either.

In downtown Grand Forks, Richard Pomerleau and Terry Zien were among the last people to cross the Red River before the bridges were closed, all the while relaying information to the NCRFC via cell phone. This thing isn't slowing down, they told Steve Buan.

Buan put down the phone, turned to Anderson and said, "It's all over, Mike."

For the people in Grand Forks, it was just beginning.

5   *Flood and Fire*

Pat Owens had just put a load of laundry in the machine at her home on South Seventeenth Avenue, the west side of town. It was one o'clock on Friday morning, April 18. She hoped to grab at least an hour of sleep before returning to the operations center downtown. The mayor had just fallen asleep when her phone rang. It was Charles Grotte, the assistant public works director. "Mayor," he said, his voice strained. "You gotta come back." As Owens drove to the police station, she saw water shooting out of the catch basins and manholes in the streets. Sump pumps buzzed. The sound of water—in all its permutations—was everywhere.

When Pat Owens walked into the police station, which had become the city's nerve center, she saw Lisa Hedin and other Corps engineers sitting with Al Grasser and Ken Vein. To Owens, the looks on the engineers' faces told her Grand Forks was losing the battle. They cleared a space at the table and spread out maps of the city for her. They pointed to the Lincoln Drive neighborhood, tucked inside a hook in the river. The dikes there were not in good shape, they told her. They were riddled with boils—signs of seepage and often the last indication that the dike is about to fail. The clay supply was gone; the overland floodwaters had filled the extraction sites. They told Owens that people were still out on the dikes, sandbagging and surveying the river. "We've lost it," they told her. "We're losing it. And you're the only one who can order an evacuation."

"Pull 'em off the dikes," Owens said. When her advisors pressed her on the evacuation order, Owens paused and thought, "God, if I evacuate the city, they're going to impeach me." An evacuation of an experienced flood town would be a controversial order. If the mayor evacuated without due reason, sending thousands of people to the outskirts of the city to watch the land stay dry, the move would be deemed hysterical, and it would cost the city thousands of dollars. On the other hand, if she didn't evacuate now and the water continued to leak into the city at the current rate, there might be no safe way to evacuate later. It was no sure bet that the city would have enough equipment and staff to do a full-blown evacuation under duress. Owens wanted to wait a few hours until daylight; she hated the idea of evacuating neighborhoods in the dead of night. People would be frightened.

Each chunk of earth that crumbled off the dikes downtown was not just deterioration; it was, to the city's engineers, a deeply personal failure. They had not built the dikes that had protected the city for forty years, but they had drawn the battle plans for this flood season, and they were getting beat.

A young engineer called Owens aside. Tears had gathered in the corners of his eyes. "The dikes are failing," he told her. "And it's my fault." Owens realized that the engineers were now forced to watch the dikes— their dikes—disintegrate, to see the weeks and weeks of laying sandbags and digging up the city parks for clay add up to nothing. Owens told the young engineer that the failing dikes were not his fault, that everyone had done the best they could.

Ken Vein, who had been injecting mortar into the lateral cracks in the Lincoln Drive dike, realized that further fortifying the levee was useless. "It was impossible," he said. "Everybody had been pretty much physically and mentally exhausted by that time anyway. We realized we were not going to be able to raise the high ground."

Vein and his engineers were now scrambling to contain the flood rather than prevent it. "We were trying to keep ahead of it as much as we could through the rest of the city and, in the area that we lost, to contain it," Vein said. "We knew that water flows downhill so once this area filled, it was going to fill areas farther to the north. Lincoln Park to Central Park through downtown to Riverside."

The mayor issued the first evacuation order for the Lincoln Drive neighborhood at about four o'clock that morning, and evacuation operations began immediately, with the civil defense sirens blaring. Guardsman John Burke got a call at the National Guard base fifteen minutes later. The city needed trucks to evacuate people from the river's edge neighborhoods. John had already closed up his mobile home and sent his wife and kids out of town. Now he had to get the people of Grand Forks to do the same thing. John and his fellow Guardsmen started going from house to house in Lincoln Drive, knocking on doors and telling residents to leave immediately.

"I don't know how you describe it," John said. "A real state of disbelief." As the sun lightened the sky, DeMers Avenue, one of the city's main drags, became jammed with traffic heading west out of town.

Down on the dikes near Lincoln Drive, Mike Rudrow heard the sirens. He had been on dike patrol, looking for cracks and watching the rising river. His house was one of the closest to the river, built against the base of the dike. He would have to abandon it. For the few minutes before the sirens sounded, though, Rudrow had a chance to contemplate the eerily calm, inscrutable sounds of the river just before it broke the dike; the almost imperceptible sound of the water seeping through the dike walls. It was quiet in Lincoln Drive. The silence didn't last long.

People rushed to their cars, groggy and bewildered. Anyone who thought this evacuation was another false alarm, only had to watch the water—the river—finding new channels on Maple Street, on Chestnut Street, pooling around car tires and people's shoes. One woman, as she evacuated, meditated on the idea of everyone praying to God at the same time "to stop these waters, 'cause we can't; we tried."

Residents of the Central Park and Riverside Park neighborhoods who weren't awakened by the civil defense sirens, were roused at six o'clock by National Guardsmen and women pounding on their doors, announcing evacuation orders. In Lincoln Drive, the dike continued to leak, the cracks spitting out the mortar that the Corps and the city engineers had pumped into them just hours before. Across the river, East Grand Forks was similarly overcome.

Two hours later someone saw water rushing out of the north end of the Lincoln Drive golf course like a small tsunami. The Lincoln Drive dike had finally been overtopped.

At ten-thirty that morning two Corps of Engineers officials—Colonel John Wonsik, chief engineer of the St. Paul district, and flood executive officer Robert F. Post—participated in a conference call to the Corps' headquarters in Washington, D.C. Corps brass had been hearing rumors—mainly from North Dakota's congressional delegation—that the National Weather

Service's forecast was low, and that the Red might go as high as 55 feet. It was now at more than 52 feet. Four hours later, Wonsik and Post contacted the NCRFC and urged the NWS hydrologists to increase the forecast "to convey urgency." The NWS did not alter the crest prediction.

"I remember this call very vividly," Mike Anderson said. "The current stage was three feet above the previous flood of record. The Lincoln Drive dikes had overtopped six hours before. The two cities were being evacuated. If the National Weather Service forecast would have read, for example, fifty-three to fifty-six feet, what would have been done differently by those directing the flood fight, and the cities of Grand Forks and East Grand Forks?" It was too late.

A few miles upstream, and south of downtown, Mary Lien turned her camcorder on once again and focused it on a human chain tossing sandbags down toward the dike. The sound of low-flying planes and military helicopters caused few to look into the sky; in just a few hours, it had become mere background noise. From the back window of her home, Mary saw jagged ice floes and half-submerged trees reaching spindly fingers towards the sky.

"The corner of the dike needs height," Mary said, narrating. "They're putting sandbags on top of the dike they just built last week." A helicopter descended slowly from the sky to inspect the river. Mary turned the camera back to her neighborhood. Here on the far south side, the East Elmwood neighborhood was abuzz with trucks, sandbaggers dragging sacks to the dike, National Guard Humvees, and emergency vehicles. "Might be the last chance to take a look at this area," Mary said. A couple of hours later, her daughter Kristen took the camcorder and walked through their home, taking what seemed to be that last look at photographs, books, the living-room sofa, a beautiful china hutch, and the family's piano. The radio crackled from the living room. "Empty bags are available," the announcer said. "But there is no sand available for private dikes. There are no private contractors to provide sand." Kristen moved the camera from item to item, methodically, almost meditatively.

Around noon that day, a dike holding back the flooding Red Lake River— which joins the Red at Grand Forks—was overtopped. East Grand Forks neighborhoods Sherlock Park and Griggs Park were evacuated and quickly submerged. At two-thirty a hole appeared in the dike protecting Grand

Forks' Central Park neighborhood, closer to downtown than Lincoln Drive, and water began pouring into the streets there. Two hours later, across the river, the entire city of East Grand Forks had evacuated.

John Burke and the National Guard drove around the streets of Grand Forks in five-ton Humvees and army trucks, looking for people who had defied the evacuation orders to monitor their sump pumps. People flipped their porch lights if they wanted a ride and the Guardsmen took them to the Red Cross center set up at Red River High School, or the armory.

"You'd go pick up people and then you come back twenty minutes later and the water's moved up three more blocks," John said. "Pretty soon it just ran like a river." By now the streets were empty and the Humvees' headlights were underwater. Some streetlights worked. Some didn't. Most windows were dark. If the Guardsmen saw a light, they worried there was someone they had missed and stopped to check. As they plowed through water four feet deep in residential streets near the river, John saw furniture floating in people's homes.

Though the water had completely engulfed Lincoln Drive and was rushing through downtown, some people still refused to leave. John saw a boat tied to a tree in someone's front yard down on Cherry Street; later that night the boat was tied to the deck. At Eighth Avenue and Oak Street, John and some of his colleagues spotted a marooned car. Inside, an elderly woman refused to leave her vehicle and demanded that the Guardsmen pull her car out of the water.

"She was stubborn as hell," John said. When he looked over the woman's shoulder he saw a little white dog paddling around in the backseat, surrounded by floating bananas and grapes. The Guardsmen finally convinced the woman to climb into their truck. She set her shivering wet dog on John's pile of fresh clothes and commanded the Guardsmen to gather up the packs of cigarettes that were still floating near the dashboard of her car. By the time they reached the hospital, John was hypothermic, and he wondered how the elderly woman, who had been sitting in the icy river water for more than fifteen minutes, stayed so animated. As if in answer, she pulled John aside, produced a paper bag from her coat and opened it. "This is why I had to hold on to my bag," she whispered. Inside was a quart of vodka.

As a boy in northwest Texas, Leon Osborne had been often been awakened in the middle of the night by tornado sirens. It had been thirty years since he had felt that nerve-tingling electricity. But when he heard the civil defense siren coming from downtown, he was, for just a moment, a small boy in a Texas farmhouse terrified by another tornado.

On Thursday Osborne and his family had spent the entire day sandbagging along Northridge Hills Drive, out by the Sunbeam neighborhood where they lived. Located on the far south side of Grand Forks, the neighborhood was built, like Lincoln Drive, on a bend in the Red River. Osborne's home stood within throwing distance of Optimist Park.

"We had already moved everything out of the basement," Osborne said, "at least everything that we could." He and a son had spent hours moving family belongings and twenty years' worth of scientific journals from the first floor to the second. In between trips, Osborne slipped old journals beneath his sofa and other furniture to get a little more elevation. As he climbed up and down the stairs, Osborne thought about the RWIC. He knew he had to get back there as soon as possible.

In Grand Forks, the air had grown almost balmy—sixty-one degrees. Snow was now thawing so fast that its melt flowed through culverts and ditches like little wild rivers. The amount of runoff these tangential streams were adding to the Red's main channel was difficult, if not impossible, for USGS teams to calculate. By mid-afternoon, the Red was rising at a rate of more than six inches an hour. Hydraulic engineers from the Corps' St. Paul district office advised Mike Anderson that it was likely the river would exceed the National Weather Service's new forecast by one to two feet. The river was already at 52.2 feet.

In neighborhoods a little farther from the river than those that had been evacuated, people constructed mini-dikes around their homes, stacking sandbags and installing water pumps. Neighbors helped each other fortify. Downtown, the four bridges spanning the river between Grand Forks and East Grand Forks were engaged in their own battle with the Red. Earlier in the afternoon, the Murray Bridge in East Grand Forks shuddered when nine feet of water rushed through a collapsed dike to the south. Now the river had reached the steel underbellies of all the bridges crossing the Red at Grand Forks; soon it would be flowing two to three feet deep over bridge roadways. With four bridges, one after the other, obstructing the river's flow, it was as if the Red had been partially dammed four times in succession.

The National Weather Service revised its crest prediction to 53 feet. It was guesswork. Some in Grand Forks would later say it was common sense. Either way, it came too late. Three hours after the newly issued prediction, the last East Grand Forks riverside neighborhood went under. In The Point, a river's edge neighborhood across the bridges from Lincoln Drive, only chimneys and second stories of houses could be seen. When Pat Owens was told The Point was gone, she began crying; it was the neighborhood in which she had spent much of her time as a child.

Around this time another conference call took place, involving Corps Flood Executive Officer Robert Post, emergency management officials from Minnesota and North Dakota, representatives from both governors' offices, and NCRFC forecasters. Robert Post urged Mike Anderson to increase the forecast to 55 feet, and to issue it as a forecast range instead of a single-number prediction in order to "communicate a certain degree of uncertainty in the forecast instead of the accuracy implied by the single value forecast." At five that afternoon, the NCRFC received a phone call from North Dakota Senator Kent Conrad about "a fifty-five-foot crest value, origin unknown." The call was transferred to Mike Anderson's desk, and he picked up the phone.

"How are things going?" Conrad asked Anderson. *How are things going,* Anderson remembers thinking. *What the hell do you tell a U.S. Senator?*

"Well," Anderson said, "Not well."

"Listen, if it's going to go any higher, I'd appreciate it if you call me back," Conrad said. Anderson said he would, but Conrad's phone call added even more pressure to an almost unbearable situation.

"Now the congressman is calling directly to your office. That's all you need to think about."

By early evening that day—Friday, April 18—the Red River had reached the roofs of the houses in Lincoln Drive, including Mike Rudrow's. Peg Rogers' parents' home was also completely submerged and everything in it was lost. But they were safe. A few hours later, at 8:21 PM, the NCRFC issued a revised crest forecast of 54 feet, choosing not to go with a forecast range "as urged," the Corps flood chronology later noted, "by all the conference call participants." Mike Anderson phoned Senator Conrad to let him know about the revised forecast.

"Thanks," Conrad said.

"We're just playing catch-up now," Mike Anderson said later. "That's all we're doing is playing catch up. It was nothing but frustration."

"We went with fifty-four feet because the water was already at fifty-two-point-five," Buan said.

"And there was nothing to back it up," Anderson said. "We just said well, it can't go more than a foot or a foot and a half higher. Well, we'd said that for three days already; it can't go any higher. Because of things like the previous history on the river, it just can't go any higher." He paused. "Never again will I say it's impossible to go higher."

Some people had ignored the sirens, believing the evacuation orders to be an act of civic hyperbole. And, technically, it would be about five hours before the entire city—not only the riverside neighborhoods—would be under a mandatory evacuation order. After receiving phone calls from citizens telling her of the many people in the bars drinking who should be evacuating, Pat Owens issued a ban on the sale of alcohol in the city.

Rex Sorgatz, then a twenty-four-year-old University of North Dakota senior, was one of the few people left in the downtown district. His second-floor apartment was fifty feet from the Security Building, and though everyone else in his building had left for higher ground, Rex had decided to wait the flood out and take advantage of the quiet time to work on his novel. That night Rex, a low-key, red-headed, modish English major six weeks away from graduating, looked out his window at a deserted downtown. He called his friend Simon, a graduate student who lived in an apartment building across Third Street, around nine that evening. They decided to take a look at the state of things downtown. Down by Urban Stampede, a coffeehouse by the railroad tracks that split the downtown cluster north and south, Rex and Simon saw that water was flowing over the tracks and that the nearby police station was now a kind of island. They watched as corrections officers led a chain of prisoners out of the station, across a plank and into a waiting van.

Rex and Simon then made a half-hearted attempt to cross the old Burlington Northern Railway bridge—then a pedestrian bridge—into East Grand Forks for their nightly drink at Whitey's Bar. A National Guardsman stopped them, telling them that the water was too close to the underside of the bridge for them to cross safely. On the way back to their block, Simon told Rex he was going to leave. Rex decided to stay and, after moving his car to a nearby parking ramp, returned to his apartment and fell asleep.

Just as Rex had been phoning Simon that evening, water had appeared in the street in front of the police station. The Emergency Operations Center would have to move quickly. City engineers grabbed all the utility plans, maps, and hydraulic data tables they could carry and fled. EOC staff unplugged computer hard drives and monitors and carried them out to waiting vans. It was an escape. And as more and more reports came in from the dikes, the more the panic seemed to build. Yet the people at the EOC had to set the example—their job was *not* to panic. As the waters closed in, the convoy of vehicles headed to the new hub of operations was out at the Rural Technology Center at the University of North Dakota.

Just as floodwaters began creeping towards the police station downtown, the phone rang at St. Michael's Catholic Church. Father William Sherman picked it up. It was the county jailer. "Hey, Father, I've got seventy prisoners and ten guards and I've got twenty minutes to get them out of here." The Grand Forks County Jail was in the basement of the police station, where Pat Owens and the city staff had been strategizing. He asked Sherman if the prisoners could bunk in the parish's youth center. Sherman told him there was plenty of space, and he looked forward to it. The prisoners arrived soon after in their orange jumpsuits with bedrolls tucked under their arms.

Pat Owens and her advisors evacuated the police building. The basement was full of water within thirty minutes of their departure.

At eleven that night, Sherman got a phone call from KCNN radio announcer Scott Henning. "Father," Henning said, "You better say something encouraging to the people." Sherman had seen the church workers furiously plugging drains all over his church, he knew that the city workers had abandoned the dikes, and Grand Forks was in danger of being completely lost; he struggled to think of something of proper weight and religiosity. He heard himself saying something his mother had told him when he was a child: "If God takes care of the birds and bees, He'll take care of you, too."

At midnight, Tim Rogers called his wife, Peg, from downtown. He told her to wake the children, move as much out of the basement as she could, and pack a few things; they were losing the town. Peg woke her children and they began moving the "important things" to the upper stories of their home.

"I noticed that my oldest son had moved his hockey trophies and pictures to the top shelf in his closet; he didn't want to lose them," Peg said. "We worked as fast as we could but time went faster." Outside, Peg could hear the civil defense sirens blaring, police and fire sirens screaming, and National Guardsmen shouting instructions over loudspeakers mounted on the roof of their trucks: "Please leave your homes. Bring medications and personal items. Please leave immediately." Peg gathered her children and grabbed the suitcases.

By midnight, all engineers and volunteers had been pulled off the dikes. The city was now operating out at the University of North Dakota, and in one quiet office, Ken Vein and Lisa Hedin were again staring at the maps of the city's dikes. It was now clear that the Red River was going to completely overtop them—some already had been overtopped— and that the floodwater was going to spread deeper into the city than they could have anticipated. A hallway meeting between Vein, Hedin, city attorney Howard Swanson, and Colonel John Wonsik resulted in a decision to build a dike down Washington Street, the main east-west dividing line in Grand Forks. If anyone had suggested a few days earlier that homes west of Washington Street, which is about a mile from the banks of the Red, would get water, it would have seemed laughable. But now, with reports that water was rolling through each downtown street as if each were a tributary of the Red, a decision had to be made regarding those very homes. Swanson, however, was concerned that if the floodwater flowing towards Washington met a dike there, it would raise the water levels east of Washington—in Lincoln Drive, Central Park, Riverside Park, and downtown. Vein said he didn't believe that would happen, but was willing to take the risk.

"And I said, you know the criticism is going to come up at some time that by doing this we are saving some people's property to the consequence of somebody else's," Swanson remembers saying to Vein. "He said 'I know, but if I don't make some decisions here, we're going to lose the whole city.' "

At 1:15 in the morning on April 19, the Grand Forks water plant failed. There was now no source for drinkable water. Forty-five minutes later, *Herald* reporters saw raw sewage flowing down the alley next to their building and the downtown filling up. They fled their offices. Three hours later, water would be four feet deep in downtown. The Red had not just submerged the city, it was flowing through it at about 4,000 cfs—faster than its average rate in the channel of 2,899 cfs.

At 3:30 AM, KCNN reported a traffic jam on North Dakota Highway 18, the Interstate 29 detour towards Fargo. An hour later, Sherman conducted the last mass before evacuating the church (the prisoners would be farmed out to various county jails across the state). Three people attended the mass, all wearing hip boots. By the time the sun rose over the Red, the Belmont dike had been lost, the Corps of Engineers had abandoned all flood fighting operations, the water plant had failed, downtown was under four feet of water, and Mayor Pat Owens had ordered evacuation of all areas in Grand Forks east of Washington Street.

The river was still rising.

At 6:00 AM the Grand Forks river gauge was swallowed up by the river, and all communications with the gauge were lost. The gauge's last report read 52.89 feet.

When Rex Sorgatz awoke that morning, he looked out his window and saw that Third Street had become a river channel six feet deep.

"I knew I probably should have left last night," he said. But he had several gallons of bottled water and lots of canned goods and there was little chance that the water would reach his second-story apartment. He looked around his apartment, with its provisions, and thought to himself that he was beginning to resemble the holed-up Freeman in Montana he'd interviewed for the *High Plains Reader* the year before. "I'm not going for nothing," he thought.

In fact, the weather was so lovely—sunny and warm—that Rex decided to take the Toni Morrison novel he was reading, *Jazz*, and head up to the roof to read and sunbathe. He watched a National Guard boat cut a wake down one of the side streets and fetch a blind man who had been stranded in his apartment. The Guardsmen spotted Rex on the roof of his building and shouted up to him, asking if he needed a ride out. Rex waved them on.

"I actually had a great time watching all this water flow through my downtown." A few hours later, Rex returned to his apartment and lay down for a nap.

Meanwhile, out at the new EOC, Pat Owens had constructed a makeshift command pyramid. Her emergency manager, Jim Campbell, had suggested she establish a hierarchy of authority. Pat designated Ken Vein, Jim Campbell, and Howard Swanson as "managers"; all decisions were to go through one of them. Across the river in East Grand Forks, the USGS set up a temporary gauge to measure river flow, replacing the one they had lost under the floodwaters. They put it on the deck of a local restaurant.

Out in the Sunbeam neighborhood, Leon Osborne and his family packed their car with assorted belongings and some food from their freezer and headed towards Red River High School, the nearest shelter. When they arrived, Osborne told his wife and children to wait in the car while he registered. When he walked into the gymnasium, he saw people he recognized from around town, but they didn't seem to see him.

"The faces on the people were of total surrender," he said. "Many of them still had mud on their face. It was just this total surrender." Osborne wanted to get out of town, had planned to do just that, and his family was ready to go. But then he thought about the RWIC again. "It just dawned on me that I can't give up yet. I made the decision then that rather than leave we would come to the University, come to the RWIC, and we would keep this facility up and running as long as possible."

An hour later, after driving through water that had escaped the English Coulee across DeMers Avenue, Osborne and his family had moved into the RWIC's forecasting center. As university employees left town, many of them made a pit stop at the RWIC to drop off provisions. Someone brought sleeping bags. Former UND president Tom Clifford and his wife Gayle gave Osborne all the drinking water they had stockpiled. The RWIC had no running water, the restrooms were not working, the air filtration system had malfunctioned, and the cooling system had broken down. The building was beginning to smell of the raw sewage that had backed up in the plumbing system. Osborne's wife, an employee of a local bank, decided to take their two youngest children to Larimore when she heard that the bank was opening a temporary shelter there. Osborne's oldest son, John, a sophomore at the university, chose to stay with his father. He, along with

Osborne and a RWIC staffer named Bryan Hahn, would spend the next ten days doing the work normally done by twelve RWIC employees. Anything to keep the system online.

The flood was now a national news story. Don Shelby had brought a ten-foot inflatable Zodiac raft along because he had reported on floods before and knew there would be none to spare to the media. He also brought a small six-horsepower boat engine from his garage and attached it to the back of his raft. Downtown had been cordoned off; the water was six to eight feet deep in the downtown streets next to the river. Few had seen downtown as it was at that moment. Most of the reports were coming from National Guardsmen and the people evacuating the area. The water was too deep for the police to drive through, so they were living on rumors like everyone else. The reporter stopped a Grand Forks police officer he saw standing on a spot of dry land on Washington Street.

"We're going in," Shelby said. "Sooner or later you guys are going to have to leave and we're going in."

"We'd arrest you," the police officer said.

"Some things are worth it," Shelby replied. "Come with us. It'll be a reconnaissance for you guys. You don't have boats yet." It was true; the Grand Forks police didn't have boats and they didn't have men on the scene. The cop gave Shelby and photojournalist Bill Schwabe the okay and hopped in the Zodiac with them. They boated down to DeMers Avenue. Live power lines skittered in the water, and transformers sparked and bubbled. The water was dank and full of poisons from fuel cells, PCBs, and sewage. Schwabe shot the submerged city. The afternoon was still and quiet except for the low grumble of the motor and the rush of the river echoing off the buildings. As the trio approached the Security Building on Third Street—an old Grand Forks bank on the National Historic Register—they heard an alarm buzzing. It seemed to come from a pink brick building next to the old bank. Shelby, who was in the back driving, slowed the raft and tried to locate the source of the distress signal.

"We've had problems with these alarms going off down here because they short out and send out these burglary-in-progress signals to the police radios," the cop said. The alarm got louder as the men approached the building, and Schwabe grew annoyed because he realized the piercing alarm would mar the audio on his film. They continued on their tour, then headed back to their position on Washington Street, about a mile outside of downtown. As they unloaded the raft, they looked over their shoulders and saw a giant plume of black smoke rising over downtown.

Out at the Emergency Operations Center, Howard Swanson walked outside to use a Port-a-Potty. A chopper blasted past him, flying extremely low. Suddenly he heard the buzz of dozens of chopper propellers and saw a dark veil hanging over downtown.

"I could smell the smoke, I could see the smoke, I could hear the helicopters. In fact, the ground shook as I walked to this Port-a-Potty. And then the fear—not only now are we dealing with water, we're dealing with fire. At that point, I thought we were going to sustain loss of life."

Pat Owens' cell phone rang as she was running into the Emergency Operations Center. As she fumbled with the phone, she glanced at a television on one of the desks. The city was in flames. When Owens finally answered the phone, it was her emergency manager, Jim Campbell, calling to tell her the downtown was on fire.

"I felt like a fist hit me," she said. "You read in the Bible, the end of the world? That's how it felt."

Downtown, fire had engulfed the Security Building and was threatening to spread to the rest of the block. The first firefighters arrived by boat, having been downtown performing last-minute evacuations of apartment-dwellers who had either refused to leave their homes or attended "flood parties." No one had yet asked Rex Sorgatz to leave. In fact no one seemed to know he was there, only yards away from the burning Security Building.

The fire engines that responded to the call could not get close enough to the flames and still operate—the water was so deep in the streets that the engines died almost immediately. To make matters worse, firefighting couldn't begin until the stragglers—those who had stubbornly ignored the evacuation orders—had been removed. Meanwhile, the fire spread from building to building.

Around five that afternoon, firefighters entered Rex's apartment building, which was now ablaze. They ran down the hallways of each floor, pounding on doors with the butts of their axes, screaming "Fire! Get out now!" Rex was awakened by a deafening series of pounds on his door. Still sleepy, he stumbled to the door, opened it, and looked down the hallway; the firefighters, assuming the building was empty, had moved toward the exit. They turned around and saw him standing in his doorway. They told him his building was on fire and he had to leave immediately. Rex didn't believe them, but put on his coat and grabbed his backpack; he believed the noisy operation was a scare tactic to flush stragglers out of the evacuated areas. But he had lost his sense of smell the year before and couldn't detect the smoke that was apparent to everyone else near that burning block.

The firefighters led Rex down the fire escape on the back of the building.

"As soon as I walked outside, all of a sudden it was about a hundred fifty degrees and the flames were flying up in the building next door," he said. When he saw the fire was real, he tried to turn back to retrieve his computer, which contained his unfinished novel and every piece of writing he had ever composed. The firefighters stopped him. He couldn't go back.

"This whole block will be gone," one of them said to him as he guided Rex to a waiting Coast Guard boat docked near the bottom of the fire escape.

"Where do you want to go?" the Coast Guardsman at the engine asked Rex.

"Hawaii," he replied.

With the fire trucks dying in the middle of the streets, engines dead, the city of Grand Forks had no immediate means to fight the inferno. Firefighters aimed their hoses upward toward the flames and watched as only weak streams trickled out of the nozzles. There was no water pressure in the hydrants. Some firefighters tried to siphon water off the streets to fill the fire hoses. A few began using portable extinguishers and water buckets, while others searched for more people who had refused to evacuate their apartments.

Calls were made to various agencies: to the Grand Forks Airport to see if any crash trucks were available (they could operate in deeper water than the fire engines), to the Minnesota Department of Natural Resources (DNR) to request airtankers to drop retardant on the blaze, to the National Guard for lowboy trailers to hoist the fire engines out of the water and make them operational again. National Guardsman arrived quickly and lifted the fire trucks onto the beds of their tractor-trailers to keep them from flooding. Firefighters in hip waders struggled through icy water, trying to contain the blaze, but their water pumps continually failed. There was no water pressure. The fire spread to other historic buildings. The fire chief concluded the only feasible way to control the blaze was to take it from above.

Out at the airport, WCCO-TV helicopter pilot Captain Dale Dobesh had just touched down to refuel. During his flyovers with WCCO photojournalists, he had watched the flames leap from one building to the next.

"I couldn't help but feel completely helpless, as far as firefighting was concerned," Dobesh said, "knowing the tremendous loss that we were witnessing. And we were just 'taking pictures.'" The captain wondered if he might join the firefight. Years before joining WCCO, Dobesh had worked a number of forest fires under DNR contracts with Minnesota and Wisconsin, dropping water by helicopter. He remembered the buckets the air firefighters used, the kind with a trap door on the bottom, which, when lowered into a pond, lake, or river, would fill quickly. The copter pilot would then fly to the hotspot, douse the flames, then return to the water source and begin all over again. Dobesh was green, then, and took his critique from the fire boss over beers at the end of the day.

"Through these lessons about fuel types, wind conditions, number of firefighters and how they were deployed," Dobesh said, "one begins to absorb some very useful firefighting training." Now Captain Dobesh decided to temporarily relinquish his media duties and join the firefight.

It took hours to organize the aerial assault, and in that time the fire spread even further. DNR air tankers arrived from Bemidji, piloted by some of the same men Dobesh had worked with earlier. One air tanker made the first flyover, but then operations had to be suspended temporarily. Another media helicopter had taken over the airspace above downtown Grand Forks. The man flying the chopper was a daring, cocky pilot from another Minneapolis television station. The pilot, who had been flying for thirty-seven years, was known in media circles for the remarkable footage he had gathered of a Minnesota tornado in 1986: He had flown his helicopter right next to the twister. Now he and his chopper were hovering over downtown, preventing DNR airtankers from beginning their firefight. Pilots from other media outlets, who had steered away from the burning block, tried to radio the pilot and tell him to get out of the way. He didn't respond.

After ten tense minutes, and after shooting the footage he wanted, the rogue copter pilot finally steered out of the air tanker's path. Minutes later, all choppers in the area were summoned to the Grand Forks Airport, where they loaded gallons and gallons of water into their bellies. Civilian and military helicopters, television helicopters, a Canadian crane chopper with a 2,000-gallon bucket normally used to control hotspots in forest fires, and even firebombing planes all took to the skies above downtown Grand Forks and, like an aerial funeral procession, dropped water and fire retardant on the blaze one by one, then turned back to the airport for more ammunition. The DNR firebombing planes—used to fight forest fires— dropped retardant that fell like red sheets of rain. People who remained in Grand Forks watched the sky grow crowded with helicopters. Bob Brooks, a Vietnam veteran and future city councilman, turned to his wife at their home near the interstate and said, "God, it's like Vietnam." He was not the only veteran in town who, looking at the sky above Grand Forks that day, saw Saigon replayed.

Captain Dobesh met the city fire department's battalion chief Bruce Roed at the airport, and the two men took a quick survey flight over downtown as the firefight continued. As they hovered there, Chief Roed asked Dobesh if he would help the fire department locate hotspots, which were increasingly difficult to find because of the black smoke billowing from the blaze. Dobesh agreed, and they returned to the airport to coordinate with what Dobesh called "the *big* helicopter crew." A Skycrane helicopter was refueling. Its 2,000-gallon bucket sat on the tarmac next to it. Dobesh made a quick mental calculation. With water weighing eight pounds per gallon, one drop from the Skycrane would hit its target with the force of 16,000 pounds—or eight tons. Anyone left in those burning buildings would surely be killed. The earlier retardant drop was like a sprinkle; this would be like cement falling from the sky.

The fire department, however, was certain everyone had been evacuated, and decided to go ahead with the operation. By eight in the evening the fire had torn through three city blocks. Over at the university, Rex Sorgatz and other students sat on the roof of the Old Science Building and watched the planes drop the red dust on the fire. The Skycrane filled its gigantic bucket in the raging Red, then, in a magnificent cascade, released the river water on the fire it had started. By this time, Rex's apartment building was a smoldering shell. His friends patted his shoulder, but said nothing.

The river was still rising.

At the Grand Forks Air Force Base hangar, evacuees crowded around the television sets and watched the downtown burn. In small towns across the plains, other evacuees did the same thing. Peg Rogers, whose husband was still frantically working to save the telephone plant downtown, monitored the fire from Larimore, where she and her children were staying with friends. She had not heard from Tim, but hoped that "no news was good news."

Less than twelve hours after the fire started, eleven buildings had been lost or heavily damaged, but it had been doused. Along with Dobesh's chopper, the Skycrane helicopter made sixty water drops before all the hotspots were extinguished. While Dobesh was hovering above downtown, something caught his eye east of the Sorlie Bridge in East Grand Forks.

"We noticed a house burning—only the top half and the roof was sticking out of the waters," Dobesh said. "We told the Skycrane to drop on the house so the sparks wouldn't start up more homes." The huge chopper dipped its bucket into the Red, then proceeded to the house fire just off the river's banks. As it prepared for its flyover, Dobesh watched from his helicopter not far away. The Skycrane approached the tiny home and when it passed directly overhead, the pilot released all 2,000 gallons of river water in the bucket. When eight tons of water hit the roof, the house crumpled like origami and sank into the floodwaters surrounding it.

At ten the next morning—Sunday, April 20—the Grand Forks water supply ran out and Pat Owens declared a twenty-four-hour curfew. At United Hospital, John Burke was evacuating patients. Helicopters—National Guard, police, civilian, whatever could be found—were lined up at the hospital, flying patients to any nearby or faraway hospital that had room for them. Most had been moved to hospitals in Fargo and Moorhead but some patients found themselves as far away as Iowa, with little or no notice to relatives.

Willard Guerard, Pat Owens' ninety-two-year-old father, was evacuated from his farm five miles outside of East Grand Forks. He had been at home with his animals, watching his daughter's numerous television appearances and keeping tabs on the flood that was swallowing her city. But when overland flooding threatened his home, the Coast Guard sent a helicopter out to the farm to get him. He refused to leave without his pets—a dog and three cats. The Coast Guard allowed him to take them along on the helicopter ride back. It was the first time Willard had ever flown.

The river was still rising.

Makeshift shelters were quickly assembled all over the valley. The Red Cross established one at the Grand Forks National Guard Armory. The Grand Forks Air Force Base opened an F-16 hangar and ordered nearly three thousand cots for displaced homeowners who had no reason to believe that, although their homes might have suffered some water damage, they would not return to them when the flood subsided. Red River High School and Valley Middle School became home to hundreds; and thousands of Grand Forks citizens scattered across the Dakota prairies and the Minnesota valleys on either side of the Red River. To get to Minnesota, one had to drive seventy-five miles south to Fargo and cross the Red there; all other bridges were closed. Some were submerged. At the Grand Forks Civic Auditorium shelter, people were being asked to leave, as the shelter was in danger of flooding. Outside the front doors, Bob Brooks was shaken to see a tough local legislator crying into his hands.

Pat Owens and her husband were now living at the air force base, where airmen and women had set up cots in the jet hangar, along with banks of free phones for residents' use. From the hangar, which was a provisional shelter, people headed towards Minot, Rugby, Buxton, and Mayville.

The inundation of national media and federal agencies continued and Pat Owens was the woman with whom everyone wanted to speak. Daily televised press conferences began at the Emergency Operations Center, with briefings for evacuated residents, scattered around the region.

That Sunday, two days after the Lincoln Drive dike was overtopped, Pat Owens stepped in front of a microphone during a press conference. Dressed in a canary-yellow rain slicker and holding an engineering map of the city's dikes, she made another plea to the holdouts still ignoring the evacuation orders: "Walk away from those homes. Walk away from those buildings." And, moments later, "As I talk to you this morning, my own home is going under. Now I'm in the same bucket with the rest of you."

This statement would come back to haunt her. Her white split-level on South Seventeenth Street was located in the heart of the non-historic district; it was just a few hundred yards away from the consumer wonderland on Washington Street. Her home was nearly three miles from the Red, and that her home was even touched by river water was a testament to the size and power of the flood. But it was only touched. This flood inflicted many gradations of loss, of hurt, and people kept score. When Owens was flown over her street in a helicopter to survey the damage to her home, the water was breaking in waves upon her driveway; she believed it was doomed. Nearly a week later, after the Red had started to recede, the *Fargo Forum* would erroneously report that "Mayor Pat Owens lost her own home in the flooding." Later, when she allowed herself, and other Grand Forks residents, back into their homes, she found several large cracks in the cement walls in her basement, but no other real damage.

But at that April 20 press conference, as the Red River was invading Grand Forks, and as a fire burned the city's face beyond recognition, she said: "People need to stick with me, because I need them, too."

Over at the university, professors scrambled to save books and journals from the first floor of the Chester Fritz Library, which was flooded by runoff from the English Coulee. Some journals were left behind, considered esoteric and not worth saving; but others, including original maps of the Panama Canal, were virtually priceless. These were loaded on to library carts for reshelving on the upper stories of the library.

"You wouldn't want to be a freshman in library science next year," UND alum Marv Larson told a *Herald* reporter as he loaded journals and books into boxes.

Evacuees from Lincoln Drive, who were camped in various cities across the Dakotas and Minnesota, as well as at the air force base, heard about the fate of their neighborhood in snatches of information, gleaned from second- and third-hand reports and rumors. However, on April 20, those who had access to the *Grand Forks Herald* discovered the awful truth.

"I hate to even say this," said Craig Charbonneau, who had fallen asleep in his home on Oak Street, unaware of the evacuation order and who had had to canoe through Lincoln Drive to get to dry land, "but houses are literally floating on the Lincoln Drive area."

Leon Osborne's son John was trying very hard to help his father run the RWIC. During the day, he was answering telephones, but that just about was all he could bring himself to do.

"He would spend the rest of his time pretty much in a—I wouldn't want to call it a state of confusion," Osborne said, "but a state of despair." It was then up to Osborne and Bryan Hahn to run the whole program—twenty-four-hour-a-day weather forecasts, as well as a nonstop information board. The program's "supercomputer" was located in another building on campus, and Osborne and Hahn took turns checking the sump pump powered by a generator there. Osborne posted updates on the RWIC's web site in regular intervals, and evacuated Grand Forks residents returned again and again to the site to check on the situation. Soon, those people were calling Osborne at the RWIC at all hours of the day and night. Many were angry—at whom, they weren't sure, but it was Osborne who always picked up the phone.

"Whenever these people would call and wanted to express their utter frustration," Osborne said, "well, it was one of those things—you just had to sit there and take it. It seemed like the only time that people would really call would be late at night, and I don't know if it's because they couldn't sleep and they wanted to call and just go ballistic. I've been around some and I've heard an awful lot of colorful language, but I learned words that I had never heard before."

Osborne was living on peanut butter and jelly sandwiches, his eyes glued to a computer screen, his ear glued to a phone. He was taking "paper towel baths" with cold water in the rank bathroom. His son was breaking down under the stress, and Osborne was about to do the same. Bryan Hahn noticed his boss was acting strangely.

"I think he recognized I was pretty much at my limit," Osborne said. "I was trying to tough it out. They just came to the conclusion that I needed to get out. The threat of violence wasn't used as much as it was implied." The three-man crew spent a few hours at the Red Tag Diner, out by the interstate. It was one of the only places in town that had hot water. The first time Osborne walked into the diner and laid eyes on the woman literally ladling out servings of hot water, he asked her to take the bucket and pour it over his head.

Peg and Tim Rogers and their children had packed their van with a few bags of personal belongings and headed out of town during the first night of mandatory evacuations. After stopping at Peg's sister's home out on the air force base, the Rogerses moved on to Larimore where a family they had never met before offered them shelter for as long as they needed it. Tim, meanwhile, was shuttling back and forth between Larimore and Grand Forks. He was still working for U.S. West, which was trying to get the ruined communications systems back on line. U.S. West's offices stood less than a block from the burned-out downtown block, and seventeen workers were there operating sump pumps and building ring dikes around the building. They hooked up large air blowers to gas generators and blew air at the telephone cables to keep them dry. Many of the workers hadn't left the offices; they slept on cots and received food and supplies from military boats. Their efforts, city officials would say later, saved Grand Forks from further devastation, because the telephone lines were crucial to coordination efforts.

Late on Sunday, Tim Rogers told his wife he had to work in town around the clock and that she should take the children to stay with relatives in Preston, a small town in southeast Minnesota.

"As we started down I-29, all we could see was water. It was like an ocean," she said. "We stopped in Fargo to eat, and it was so odd watching the kids eat and looking all around us, knowing that no one there knew we had no home." When Peg and the kids reached Minneapolis, they stopped at the Mall of America. There, a man overheard young Nick asking his brother Josh about how on earth the family would get back on its feet. The man asked where the boys were from; when they said they had just come from Grand Forks, the man wrote out a check for a hundred dollars and handed it to Josh. During the last stretch to Preston, Peg and her children stopped at a McDonald's to use the restroom. Peg noticed a can on the counter that was being used to collect money for the flood victims of Grand Forks.

"It was then that I realized we were totally dependent on others," she said. "I started to cry because there was no lying to myself as to what was happening."

Late that evening, Pat Owens, on the advice of the Grand Forks fire chief, ordered the demolition of the half-gutted buildings that used to be the heart of downtown. Eleven buildings would be knocked down—among them the burned shell of the Security Building, the *Grand Forks Herald* newspaper headquarters, and the Empire Theater. Before the demolition, though, photographers framed shots of the still-smoking block. The black scars the fire left on the Security Building marked an unusual path. Fires seldom turn corners—this one did. It appeared the fire had tried to run from the river.

At eleven o'clock the next morning, Monday, April 21, the river crested at 54.11 feet; it would hold for nearly twenty-four hours before slowly receding. The '79 crest record had been shattered by nearly six feet; it exceeded the National Weather Service's first prediction by nearly five feet as well. It would be weeks before the river would fall to normal levels, and Pat Owens, the people of Grand Forks, and the rest of nation could only wait to see if anything would be left when the waters fell back between the banks.

6 *Devastation*

Grand Forks looked like an occupied city. The only vehicles operating in town were Humvees, tractor-trailers, helicopters, firebombing planes, and boats. Thousands of people were camped in the F-16 hangar at the air force base. Three blocks of downtown looked as if they had been bombed—the rubble still smoldered. Each structure that had been irretrievably damaged was historic; they were the face of the city. The Heritage Building. The Empire Theater. The First National Bank. The Security Building. And six more. The *Grand Forks Herald* newspaper building was destroyed—one hundred and seventeen years of regional history in its archives. North Dakota U.S. Congressman Earl Pomeroy rode with the Coast Guard, surveying the damage downtown. Wearing a Coast Guard lifejacket, dirty jeans, and heavy workboots, the congressman sat in the back of the fourteen-foot boat and took notes as a Guardsman navigated the murky floodwaters. "I never thought I'd be taking a boat ride down DeMers Avenue," he told a reporter. "Everywhere I look, I see destruction. I can't begin to comprehend the amount of money it's going to take to get Grand Forks back on its feet."

The city was haunted by the ghosts of those who left—all fifty thousand of them. Ninety percent of Grand Forks' population had been evacuated. Across the river, all nine thousand residents had left. North Dakota Senator Kent Conrad asked Mayor Pat Owens if she realized that she had just conducted the largest evacuation in United States history since the burning of Atlanta in the Civil War. She hadn't; perspective would come later. Eleven thousand homes and businesses were damaged or gone. Every downtown business suffered significant damage, though the definition of "damage" would prove to be slippery.

On the outskirts of town, cows were marooned on high ground and thousands of animal carcasses—mostly cattle and pigs—littered the land and clogged streams and tributaries. Decomposition, hastened by the warming temperatures, suffused the spring air with the unmistakable smell of rotting flesh. Teams of National Guardsmen and women began collecting and disposing of the carcasses throughout the valley, and within a month had buried more than 13,700 carcasses and removed 950 from waterways or, in the words of the state agriculture commissioner, picked up "eleven million pounds worth of dead animals."

The water supply was contaminated by broken fuel tanks and human waste that had escaped the sewage system, and Pat Owens was told that it would be at least three weeks before safe water would become available from the taps. There was no water for showering, cooking, or drinking. A few hours after the Red crested, the National Guard hauled "water buffaloes"—2,000-gallon tanks of fresh water—to a Ramada Inn on the west side of Grand Forks. People lined up with plastic jugs and waited their turn.

Rumors began to circulate that toxic gas had been discharged by a foundering chemical plant. City and emergency management leaders had warned of a possible loss of electrical power at CF Industries, which stored anhydrous ammonia. At a Monday-morning press conference, CF Industries superintendents scrambled to quash the rumors, admitting that they had asked Emergency Operations to build a clay dike around the plant to protect the tanks, but assuring citizens there was virtually no chance of toxic gases being released.

The *Grand Forks Herald* continued to publish despite having no home. Using the printing facilities of a fellow Knight-Ridder paper, the *St. Paul Pioneer Press,* the *Herald* staff worked from the computer classroom of an elementary school in Manvel, about fifteen miles north of Grand Forks. They were determined not to miss an issue. After receiving the *Herald*'s copy electronically each day, the *Pioneer Press* printed thousands of papers and flew them back to Grand Forks on an early-morning charter flight. Writers scrambled to get their stories on time; the paper's editorial deadline had been moved up five hours. The pressure to deliver was enormous. On top of that, many of the *Herald*'s writers and advertising staff had lost their homes or suffered major damage. Editor Mike Jacobs was one of them.

As he was lighting fires under his staff writers to meet the new, nearly impossible deadlines, Jacobs told a reporter from the Minneapolis PBS affiliate that he was thinking about the *Herald* building. He had watched the Red wash through it. Then he had watched a fire destroy it, along with so many important things he wished he had thought to take with him when he left. He thought about a book his sports editor had been working on; the young man had just given Jacobs the manuscript to proofread, and Jacobs had placed it in his briefcase. In the confusion of the evacuations, Jacobs had forgotten his briefcase. Now the manuscript, and the disk on which it was saved, were either soaked or burnt. Either way, the book was gone. Jacobs' home, too, was full of things he knew or believed were gone. His collection of rare North Dakota books—"one of the finest collections of North Dakota books in existence"—was the product of a careful and expensive forty-year search. He could only shake his head.

"We knew we were going to win because we've always won before," he said. "It just didn't occur to us that the river has that kind of power."

Grand Forks residents had scattered across the plains of North Dakota and northern Minnesota, bunking with relatives and friends. Those who could not find sanctuary at the crowded air force base were welcomed into homes in dozens of small North Dakota towns. At the base and over the radio, strangers declared their homes open for anyone who needed a bed and a good meal—for however long they were needed. A seemingly endless stream of announcements over the PA system at the base informed evacuees that, for instance, a farmer in Grandin had room for four people and a dog, or a family had six beds and a pullout couch for anyone who needed them. Just outside of Lakota, North Dakota, on a shoulder of the highway leading from Grand Forks to Devils Lake, someone had posted a sign on behalf of the city that read: "We have Rooms for Lots. You're Welcome."

The entire city of East Grand Forks had been forced to evacuate. At the Bemidji State University fieldhouse, East Grand Forks mayor Lynn Stauss vented his frustration to two hundred of his displaced constituents. He didn't identify the object of his anger by name, but everyone in the audience knew who he was talking about.

"They missed it," he said, "and they not only missed it, they blew it big." The crowd's applause echoed in the large gymnasium, making it seem as if all nine thousand East Grand Forks citizens were sitting in on the mini-rally. "If you'd known it was going to be fifty-four feet, every one of you would've had flood insurance; every one of you would've taken your valuables out of your home and protected them." Stauss, a boyishly handsome fifty-two-year-old schoolteacher, had been heating bottled water in an electric percolator in order to shave and sponge bathe. He was in better shape than many of his constituents who had not had a shower in days and wouldn't for a few more. After his speech in Bemidji, Stauss traveled to Crookston and Thief River Falls and repeated his angry criticism of the National Weather Service to applause from East Grand Forks' temporary refugees.

"This is not really predicting, changing it a foot in a day," he said. "Anybody could do that." Anybody—Mike Anderson, Steve Buan, Mike DeWeese, John Halquist, and Pat Neuman—heard clearly every word Stauss was saying. Stauss's criticism cut the quick, but the men continued working their twenty-four-hour schedules. They hoped to do for other cities downriver what they hadn't been able to do for Grand Forks. Corps flood control manager Tim Bertschi told a newspaper, "Boy, that's got to be an awful job to have."

"I don't care if they are upset by my comments," Stauss said. "Because when you depend upon somebody for a prediction, either make a good prediction or don't make any prediction. If they had just said, 'We don't know and we're scared this year,' that would have alerted people and alerted every government agency and we would have seen many more people take flood insurance. And now what do we have? Family pictures, heirlooms, and other valuable things that were important to people, all floating and gone. We can replace buildings but we can't replace those valuable things."

Rex Sorgatz had escaped with three hefty tomes—*Clarissa, Orlando, Tom Jones*—along with *Death in Venice* and two pairs of jeans. Everything else in his apartment was gone, including his own novel-in-progress. In the days following the downtown fire, Rex had stayed with his girlfriend's parents at their home in a small North Dakota town, then had moved to International Falls, Minnesota for a few weeks. In between he was interviewed by National Public Radio, CNN, the *Grand Forks Herald*, and *Time Magazine*. One reporter asked Rex if he thought the missing fifteen apartment dwellers on Third Street were dead or alive.

"I don't know Ed, I'm not exactly a firefighter," Rex said. Two weeks after his hasty and unexpected departure from his apartment, Rex returned to downtown Grand Forks, alone, on a cloudless, quiet night.

"Lights were out everywhere downtown, but there was enough moonlight to see I would probably never set foot in Whitey's again." The old East Grand Forks speakeasy had indeed been ruined, and only its famous horseshoe bar had been salvaged. Whitey's demise was particularly depressing for Rex, who had spent almost every night of his college career in one of the bar's wooden booths with friends, homework, or both. On May 12, the *Herald* reprinted an editorial Rex had written for the Fargo alternative weekly he used to edit with his friend Ian Swanson, who lived nearby.

"Dear Ian," it began, "Remember how you told me to watch your apartment while you were bouncing around Europe? Well, I'm sorry to say, Ian, that I guarded it through a flood, a water shortage and an electrical outage, but I just couldn't fight off that nasty fire."

Early Tuesday morning, April 22, Grand Forks city attorney Howard Swanson called the office of his counterpart in Des Moines. Four years earlier, cities along the Mississippi's middle course had been razed when, after a spring of torrential rains, the river flooded. Floodwaters from the Mississippi covered 400,000 square miles. Fifteen million acres of farmland were underwater for weeks, ten thousand homes were destroyed and more than a thousand levees were overtopped or had softened into mush. Hundreds of towns between St. Paul and St. Louis were inundated, and seventy-five were underwater. Des Moines had been particularly hard hit and, like Grand Forks, had lost its water plant. A quarter of a million people went without a drinking water system for nineteen days.

As the Red River floodwaters continued to hold steady at 54 feet, Grand Forks city officials were discovering that what felt like a uniquely horrifying disaster was actually only the most recent in a series of natural catastrophes. From three record hurricanes on the eastern seaboard to record flooding on the Mississippi River, hundreds of city officials had, in the last three years, struggled with the same tasks Pat Owens, Howard Swanson, Ken Vein and countless others were now tackling.

When Howard Swanson phoned the city attorney in Des Moines that morning, the first thing he said to Swanson was, "Oh my God. We've been waiting for your call."

At about nine-thirty that morning Pat Owens was told that U.S. President Bill Clinton and five members of his cabinet would arrive in Grand Forks in two hours. Clinton wanted to survey the damage and to look at the still-flooding Red River. In early April, when Blizzard Hannah hit, he had seen news footage of people in Grand Forks stacking sandbags in the driving snow.

"I thought that I had bad reception on my television, at first," Clinton said. "It was an amazing thing. I don't recall, ever in my life, seeing anything like this."

Air Force One arrived at the Grand Forks Air Force Base at eleven-thirty. Before sitting down to a roundtable discussion at the base's Enlisted Club, President Clinton, Secretary of Health and Human Services Donna Shalala and other local and federal officials joined Pat Owens on a heli-copter tour of the Red River valley. They peered out of the helicopter win-dows as they flew over the flooded valley—the river was twenty-five miles wide. No one spoke. When they returned to the base, the President began a roundtable discussion with his cabinet, Pat Owens, East Grand Forks mayor Lynn Stauss, Ken Vein, city council members, the three North Dakota congressman, and North Dakota governor Ed Shaefer.

"First of all," the President began "before I left the White House this morning, I authorized FEMA to provide one hundred percent of the direct federal assistance for all of the emergency work undertaken by federal agen-cies in the one hundred forty-nine counties where disasters have been de-clared." This was a gift—the normal reimbursement rate is 75 percent. And this gift was retroactive from the moment that the counties were declared federal disaster areas during the blizzards months before. Clinton also told city leaders that he was asking Congress to approve an additional $200 mil-lion in contingency emergency funds for the Dakotas and Minnesota.

"The only other thing I'd like to say, Madam Mayor," Clinton said, "is that a lot of people are still in shock and have not had time to focus on some of the things which will make the losses most painful—the things that have been lost in these homes, the records of family occasions, the letters from World War Two, the letters from the kids that go off to college, all the things that people will have to come to grips with in the days ahead."

Owens countered: "My greatest worry is that we do not want to lose our citizens at this time. People need to know where their paycheck is com-ing from now, where are they going to live in the future, what are they going to do when they are rebuilding their homes, how can they get their small businesses started?" She turned to James Lee Witt, at that time the head of FEMA, who was charged with helping Grand Forks get back on its feet. "As I was walking with you, a phrase came to me and I wrote it down. It's the phrase from the Bible that says, 'It's my brother. He's not heavy,'" she said. (The phrase is, in fact, the motto of Father Edward Flanagan's Boys Town, in Nebraska.) "The next time you come, you will see a city thriving.

"I would like to introduce to you a gentleman who I have followed for the last couple of weeks. I think he's tired of me because I have been his shadow because I knew he had good direction and I knew he was putting his heart and soul into the community. That is Mr. Ken Vein." Owens turned to Vein, who was sitting quietly, waiting to speak. "And without you, Ken, we could not be at the point we are at right now. We would have lost lives. I just can't tell you how much I value you within our community and within our city employment." Vein, whose face was ashen and drawn, had slept less than ten hours in the last three days. He acknowledged the applause with a weary smile.

For the next hour, city department heads, all with their own stories and agendas, took turns briefing Clinton. Ken Vein told Clinton the water treatment plant was useless, the storm sewer was filled, and only four of the city's thirty-seven lift stations were intact. He also told Clinton of his personal distress about the breaching of the dikes.

The Grand Forks public health inspector warned of the sea of contaminated water surrounding downtown Grand Forks. He suggested that all citizens get tetanus shots. A Grand Forks firefighter named Randy Johnson told of his department's heroics during the downtown blaze, and of watching his brother's apartment building burn to the ground, helpless to save anything in it. Senator Kent Conrad told Clinton he thought rebuilding Grand Forks would require "a Marshall Plan type of effort." Representative Earl Pomeroy spoke about Lisa Hedin, "a very talented young woman who was looking at the topography maps and crying as she said 'there's no high ground.' And really," Pomeroy continued, "that's the shape of the community, as you can see from the air. No component—not the financial, not the business, not the university—is out of the water. It is all hit. So we don't really have a toehold even to begin the reconstruction." The president needed no convincing. The money had been promised.

However, Clinton took care to warn of possible disappointments when the aid request was sent through the federal pipeline to Capitol Hill and, stripped of the living images of the devastation, was presented to legislators as a bald request for money.

"Sometimes in Congress, when something that is so important, so popular like this comes along, other people—for perfectly legitimate reasons—think, 'Well, I've got something I care about; maybe I can tack that on there, too.' And there may be some other agendas that get caught up in this. It's just an irresistible temptation when you think some interest you represent can ride along on the train that deserves to go out of the station in a hurry." It would be important to put a face on the flood. The woman sitting next to Clinton in the Enlisted Club had the face for the job.

After the roundtable discussion, Clinton and Owens spent an hour in the F-16 hangar, listening to the people who had watched their city go under.

"The hardest part," Owens said, "is going to be when people are taken back to their homes, when they see the damage that has been done." Ken Vein had announced that it might take a month before the water and sewer systems would be operational, much longer before they would be back to normal.

"Some parts of the city may never be rebuilt," he said. "There are homes that are floating. The water is eroding new channels."

Clinton's presence touched Owens. As she started the press conference, Owens turned to Clinton, wiped a tear from her cheek and said, "You bring us hope."

"It may be hard to believe it now," Clinton replied. "But you can rebuild stronger and better than ever."

To the crowd, Owens said: "This morning, when I heard the President was coming, I thought: what do I wear?" Clinton reached over and touched her arm.

"It looks good," he said.

"What I wear," Owens said. "Is the heart and soul of my community." Her gift for concise, pithy statements about the flood was beginning to emerge. Sobriquets—based on a constellation of personal traits—began showing up in headlines and articles. *The Plucky Spitfire. The Little Giant. The Five-Foot-One Grandmother.* Knight-Ridder wrote: "Grand Forks

Mayor Pat Owens is barely 5 feet tall, but to the people of North Dakota she's a giant." In an interview with Fred de Sam Lazaro from the Minneapolis PBS station (who himself referred to Owens as "the fifty-six-year-old mother of three"), *Herald* reporter Liz Fedor suggested Owens was motherly.

"In a crisis like this, being a mother, being nurturing is, in effect, what is needed because people need some kind of reassurance that people in power care about them and that we're all going to get through this together," Fedor said. Descriptions of Mayor Owens' leadership seldom failed to mention her sex, her size, or her motherliness.

Inside the deserted and drowned homes in Lincoln Drive, Riverside Park, and Central Park, food was rotting, counters were caked with mud, and planters and dishes were filled with river sludge. The river had entered homes with such force that it had picked up sofas and driven them through walls. Some people would return to their Lincoln Drive homes and find them off their foundations. Some found their houses atop their cars.

At the hangar where she was living with her husband—and three thousand of her constituents—Pat Owens was constantly confronted by desperate homeowners.

"Some people would just tear at you because their animals were in their houses. It was awful," Owens said later. At the base, people pressed their house keys into Pat Owens' hands and begged her to retrieve their pets. "I just made up my mind then. We were in bad shape but we will rebuild, we will come back. Bigger, better, stronger."

Pat Owens started her press duties each day at three-thirty in the morning, after four hours of sleep. When it became obvious that the flood was going to overwhelm the town in a way that made great pictures, and with a central character—Owens—who provided great sound bites, the national press was in town almost as quickly as the federal agencies. In her daily press conferences, Owens told the media that she had no doubt that Grand Forks could rebuild "bigger, better, and stronger."

But the downtown business center was essentially gone, and still underwater. At least four neighborhoods—working-class neighborhoods—were history. The heart of the city—Third and Fourth Streets, which closely parallel the river—was not only submerged in water, it was garbage. The brick buildings were just burned facades now and Owens had ordered the fire department to demolish them before they could collapse. Benches from city parks and green dumpsters floated down the streets. Family pets had drowned, family farms were ruined, garbage festered in the sun, heirlooms were buried in mud—a whole town's history was left in piles of debris. Even the town's printed memory—the newspaper archives—was gone. Everywhere Owens looked, something else was lost to the flood.

Did you ever feel like Grand Forks wouldn't come back?

"I just kept saying we will."

Did you always believe that?

"No."

The Federal Emergency Management Agency (FEMA), with its director James Lee Witt, began canvassing the town almost at once. The first thing they realized was that only about a thousand households had purchased flood insurance before the flood. In a town of 52,000, this was another disaster. In a town on a river that floods regularly, it was almost inexplicable, especially since FEMA had barraged Grand Forks with pleas to enroll in the federal flood insurance program. It was so baffling that FEMA would ask two sociologists to figure out why it happened. In an article published in *Applied Behavioral Science Review,* University of North Dakota professor Ronald Pynn and Greta Ljung of the Institute for Business and Home Safety surveyed nearly fifteen hundred Grand Forks residents. They reported that 94 percent of Grand Forks residents knew about the option of flood insurance; yet few bought a policy. The reason: "The National Weather Service did not predict the river to crest so high."

Was it arrogance? People in Grand Forks had seen the Red flood in many years. The river almost always respected boundaries. Many people, even those living in Lincoln Drive, would say that before 1997, they had never even had water in their basements during flood season. They used this bit of trivia as rationale for choosing not to purchase flood insurance. For others, it was hard to imagine such a humble little river, only yards wide, could grow to such a terrible size. And the dikes, all but one considered "temporary"—though most had been in place for decades—had kept the river in check year after year. The year before, in 1996, the Red had delivered one of its worst floods in ten years, and the dikes had proven strong enough.

In addition, Pynn and Ljung wrote: "People were aware of the availability of flood insurance and understood that their homeowners policy would not cover flood damage, and that federal or state assistance would not make up the difference."

But many Grand Forks residents would forget that fact. When they saw the full extent of the damage to their homes and city, they did not only expect the federal and state governments to make up the difference; they demanded it. This was simply because they blamed the National Weather Service, a federal agency, for failing to protect them. In the court of public opinion, the National Weather Service was already guilty of negligence, and when you're guilty of negligence you pay the damages.

For newly homeless residents, FEMA brought in 311 trailers—twelve by sixty feet and a vivid illustration of the term "government issue." They were set in perfect rows, so many that it seemed "FEMA Village," as it came to be known, extended to the horizon in infinite regression. The trailers were flimsy and thin-walled, but FEMA, and everyone else, believed they were only temporary. Their inhabitants revived an old North Dakota joke: How is a divorce in North Dakota like a hurricane in Florida? Either way, you lose the trailer. No one, however, wanted to hang on to these trailers. They didn't think they would have to. When winter arrived, though, FEMA Village would remain. It would be divided into two courts and, by giving them official names—Princeton Court and First Season—FEMA indicated, contrary to its public stance about the temporary dwellings, that the trailers would be there for a while.

The largest and most expensive FEMA trailer was quickly christened "Red October" by Grand Forks city staff; the city would operate from this trailer for weeks. Red October was one of FEMA's Mobile Emergency Response Support Units, and the city officials were awed by its technology. The trailer was outfitted with more than a dozen computers wired with Internet access, a satellite communications system, a radio system, and forty-eight phone lines. Two of those were dedicated lines—one to the White House, the other to the Pentagon.

On Tuesday, April 23, a week after Lincoln Drive was evacuated, the U.S. Department of Energy announced an action plan to restore disabled power systems in North Dakota, and deployed personnel to help cities get their systems back on line. For many people in Grand Forks whose homes were not in the "devastated areas" and who were trying to live their lives as best as they could, their most vivid memory of this time would be the crushing, bone-deep cold of their unheated homes.

The questions facing the city seemed endless. What about restaurants contaminated by the filthy river water—what was the health department's role? Where would the city council meet now that City Hall was flooded? The backup location was the Civic Auditorium, but it, too, was severely damaged. Maintaining simple civic requirements was proving impossible, and even irrelevant. The idea of Grand Forks as a city—with all the underpinnings and trimmings a city requires—had become ambiguous. It would require a Herculean effort to preserve some semblance of a working government.

In Grand Forks, tensions rose concerning the temporary dike Ken Vein, Lisa Hedin, and city and Corps engineers had built down South Washington Street. The Red had taken city engineers by surprise, again, when its flow shifted from north to west during the flood, and started inundating the dry west side of town. The dike ensured that the water traveled north. But just as Howard Swanson had guessed days earlier, people living on the east side of Washington Street—closer to the river—felt that the dike was forcing the water to pool even deeper on their side of town. To make matters worse, a rumor began circulating about farmers on the outskirts of town opening the floodgates on their land and letting the water atop their crops run off toward the city. FEMA placed an FM transmitter on a now off-air Grand Forks radio station to broadcast information regarding phone lines, electricity, water availability and distribution, and to address rumors that ran through the town more quickly, it seemed, than the river.

Meanwhile, Howard Swanson was finding he had been rushed into a kind of fraternity of attorneys for cities nationwide that had suffered major natural disasters. Swanson reached out to many of them, asking what problems, legal and otherwise, he should anticipate in the coming months.

John Copeland, then the county attorney for Broward County, Florida, which had been slammed by Hurricane Andrew in 1992, warned Swanson of the "carpetbaggers" who were sure to descend upon Grand Forks. In the years following Andrew, heartsick residents of Broward County were defrauded out of hundreds of thousands of dollars by dishonest contractors who either didn't finish work promised but paid for, or whose work-manship was so bad that the homeowner had to hire another contractor to clean up the first one's mess. More questions arose as engineers and city cleanup crews were dispatched to homes in Lincoln Drive, Riverside Park, and Central Park. Could they legally enter private property to collect and dispose of debris? The Corps of Engineers had already organized inspectors to examine and determine the integrity of buildings, both public and private. In Lincoln Drive, some homes had floated off their foundations and taken up new positions in the middle of streets. Others had broken sewer lines, cracked water pipes, and open gas lines, and had to be dealt with immediately.

However, houses were still homes, and now that the river had receded, and relinquished its prizes, the homeowner was again sovereign. And if a man's home is his castle, some were pulling up the drawbridge to keep out anyone, even those who came to help. Many feared their homes would be condemned, and for good reason. The very idea of home, now a most elastic concept, had become even more important than usual; some people clung to what they might lose with a fervor that seemed fanatical.

The water had receded slightly, and that Thursday Pat Owens announced that people could now inspect the homes above water, clean up what they could, salvage what they might, and then return to the shelters. There would be no overnighting. People wanting to see their homes had to pass through a military checkpoint, show identification, and log their visit. If they wanted to drive in, they obtained a permit from the National Guard and displayed an orange pass on the dashboards of their cars. If people hadn't logged out by 4:00 PM, the National Guard Brigadier General sent Guardsmen in after them. Some people had left medication behind in the haste of the exodus. Others were desperate to find pets they had left behind believing that they would be back in a couple days at the most. In many cases, though, the Humane Society and Animal Rescue Service had saved family pets from flooded homes, kicking in doors, grabbing the animals and putting them in sacks for "safekeeping," then loading them onto boats. About two hundred pets were placed with temporary "foster homes." Sometimes the rescuers found the pets dead. One crew, dispatched to find two cats in a flooded home, found one of them clinging to life, but could not find the other. Just as they were about leave in their boat, they saw, through a window of the house, the other cat dead, drowned in a bathtub.

Many people searched through their soaked possessions for documents they would need to present to FEMA in order to qualify for low-interest loans and grants.

On Elmwood Drive, Jim and Mary Lien stepped through the front door of their home for the first time since being evacuated. They had known it was gone, even before they led a caravan of cars full of their teenaged children to Bemidji a few hours after the evacuation orders. Their home here on the south end of Grand Forks had had a view of the Red River until a few months before the flood, when the Corps had told residents they needed to build a dike. Everyone in the neighborhood had agreed to shoulder the cost—about a thousand dollars per family—and in the windy, ice-cold early spring, they built the dike. Though residents worked nearly non-stop and under the guidance of the Corps, Mary would later say she often worried about the integrity of the dike. She and her husband had been the last couple on patrol duty to walk that dike, which had grown soft with saturation by the time the city engineers came by and told them to go home. Within a few hours, National Guardsmen were knocking on their door and asking them to leave, "just for the night." The next time Jim Lien would see his house, he would tell his wife, "it's an absolute fishbowl."

Like many people, the Liens sought shelter far away from Grand Forks. In Bemidji they checked in to a hotel in a casino run by the Red Lake Band of Ojibwe Indians. When they checked out, six weeks and innumerable charged-to-the-room meals later, the total due on their bill would read: thirty-four cents. Residents of the Red Lake, Leech Lake, and White Earth reservations on the outskirts of Bemidji collected clothes and food for the people of Grand Forks. An Ojibwe man who had recently left the hospital gave Jim Lien a favorite shirt, and tribal members took pant and shirt sizes from the Liens and came back with donated clothes that fit perfectly.

When Jim and Mary stepped through the door of their home that first time, though, they felt sick to their stomachs. With her camcorder in her hand, Mary walked through her living room—an unrecognizable pile of soaked, stinking rubble. They did not speak; the only sound was the suck and sigh of their sodden living room carpet each time Jim or Mary took a step. With the camera, Mary inspected what looked like a ransack job.

Books were strewn about the house, warped and swollen, the television knocked off its shelf, and the force of the river washing through the house had somehow stood the piano on end. As Mary walked into the kitchen, she caught her breath and then began to cry. She picked her way over the fallen refrigerator, with its contents thrown about the sludge-covered linoleum, and walked towards the back window. Through that window, she saw the Red River running through her back lawn, lapping against her porch, which itself looked like the boiler deck of a Red River steamboat. "Oh, God," she said.

A few days later they drove to World's Greatest Deals in East Grand Forks, where Jim was an employee. Seeing that the warehouse door had been pulled open, Jim stepped into ankle-deep water and yelled, "Hello?" His voiced echoed through the dank, cavernous warehouse, where everything that used to be inventory was now worthless debris. "Holy shit," he whispered as he looked around at the overturned shopping carts, the ruined televisions and VCRs and floating boxes of granola bars. "It looks like it's a total loss in here," he said. Mary panned the video camera across the street. The windows had been broken out of East Grand Forks Family Medical Center, and burlap-colored curtains snapped in and out of the shattered panes.

The couple tried to make their way towards Jim's upstairs office, and almost stumbled over an upended sofa wedged in an interior doorway. Their yellow flashlights danced over chocolate-colored river water and orange insulation spilling out of walls eaten through by the floodwaters. "Ugh, what a disaster," Jim said as he tripped over a paint can.

Jim and Mary were engaged in a kind of reconnaissance, and across both Grand Forks and East Grand Forks, thousands of other people were doing the same thing. Anything that looked familiar, that had retained some semblance of its pre-flood appearance, was jealously seized.

"That family photograph that I kept behind my desk is gone," Jim said to his wife when they finally made it to his office. "But this other one is still here."

"Grab it," Mary said.

Peg Rogers and her children headed back home from Preston, where they had been staying with relatives. Tim was still in Grand Forks. He had been putting in fourteen-hour days at the telephone plant, then picking his way through downtown after work to their home to clean through the night. When Peg and the children finally arrived, the house was an empty wreck. The life she had left behind was now "out on the boulevard in piles."

Tim was exhausted. He had been part of a near superhuman effort to save the city's telephone system, and had been working around the clock.

"He looked cold, tired, and older," Peg said. "The kind of older that happens when you have been through tough times." Peg surveyed her home. Like most in Grand Forks, she had no heat, no electricity, and no water. When she asked her husband about the bathroom, which was caked in mud, he pointed to a Port-a-Potty that had been placed in the middle of Cherry Street. Just as she looked, her neighbor was emerging from it.

"There's your bathroom," Tim said.

On Maple Avenue, in the war zone that was still identified on city maps as the Lincoln Drive neighborhood, Kelly Straub and her three children saw their home for the first time since evacuating a week before. The pretty yellow house, with its blue shutters and red door, looked like it had been torn through with a wrecking ball. Walls had collapsed, the roof was soaked and sunken, and the garage was just a pile of wood and shingles. After fighting her way through a window—the door was blocked by her antique china hutch, which had been tossed about during the flood—Kelly saw that her living-room couch was now standing on end against a far wall. In her bedroom, she found that floodwater had filled the room, picked up her bed, turned it upside down, and set it back on the floor. She spotted a red shoe on the blade of her ceiling fan; she later found the other shoe lodged under a pile of river-soaked clothes in the basement.

Kelly saw that her antique teacup collection was intact, with not a cup broken, but each one was filled with river water, mud and pebbles collected at the bottom, like coffee grounds. Sludge was caked on the walls as if it had been applied with a paintbrush, and the smell of river bottom and dead fish made her children queasy. Maggots had already attacked the rotting food in the kitchen. When Kelly tried to pull the china hutch out of her entryway, she found her teenage daughter Molly's baby clothes lodged beneath it. With each painful discovery of some much-loved family treasure ruined, Kelly's grief deepened. It would not be long before her grief would more accurately be called rage.

Leon Osborne finally left the RWIC one evening to have a look at his home after employees began returning to work. Driving down Thirty-Second Avenue, one of the city's main east-west streets, he blended in with the traffic of returning evacuees. But as he approached his neighborhood, he began seeing fewer and fewer cars. Soon he was the only driver on the roads.

"You turn on South Washington and go on Fortieth into Sunbeam, and that's where it really hit home. No lights. No sounds. I think even the birds left town. To walk into your home knowing your basement is full of water and you didn't know if you were going to be looted . . . just going upstairs and collapsing into bed, that was very emotional."

At the Grand Forks post office, a week's worth of mail for 25,000 households was sitting in piles, bags, and bins. In the *Herald*, a small local story announced that "the post office will be open from noon to 5:00 PM so customers can pick up mail and drop off change of address forms."

People were now leaving the air force base, and officials from FEMA and other agencies encouraged them to find housing with friends and relatives. The Salvation Army offered to pay for bus, train, or plane tickets. Most of the homeless found temporary quarters in small North Dakota and Minnesota towns like Crookston, Bemidji, Cass Lake, and Fertile.

Immediately after the flood, the meetings had begun in earnest. Daily status reports from various departments—public works, health, emergency management, and so on—were delivered in daily conferences with the mayor, FEMA officials, and other federal employees. In fact, Grand Forks had started to remind some people of an old frontier outpost, with the influx of unfamiliar, often unsmiling faces. A dozen federal marshals, dressed in fatigues with guns strapped to their legs, strode into one meeting in the Red October. One of them wore a cowboy hat. A team of elite U.S. customs officers from Miami showed up to provide security in anticipation of the looting and disorder that often follows disasters, supplying infrared detection technology and night vision goggles for surveillance of flooded neighborhoods. Sightseers had already begun arriving in town, eager to gawk and scavenge. An unusual number of burglaries were reported, though what constituted burglary became unclear as people began piling their damaged belongings on lawns and berms to dry out. Everything looked like abandoned trash.

At the same time, Grand Forks police were supplementing their force with National Guardsmen and police officers from other North Dakota towns. Aerial reconnaissance missions continued day and night, using night vision equipment in the evening. National Guardsmen made their rounds by boat. The city was patrolled by air and water.

Peg Rogers had reluctantly decided to visit the supply warehouse the Salvation Army had opened for flood victims. She was embarrassed.

"It was so hard to take anything," she said. She was standing in a corner with her grocery cart, immobilized by shame, when a woman, an out-of-state volunteer, approached her and asked her how she was doing. "I remember her walking through the store with me and saying 'You will need this and this.' I thought there would be someone else who would need it more." Peg's mother, whose house was still completely submerged in the Red, felt the same way. When a volunteer had called to offer help, Peg's mother had said she was fine; surely someone else needed help more urgently than they did. When she hung up, her daughters laughed.

"Mom," Peg said. "Do you realize that you have no house, no belongings, and no idea of what is going to happen? How can someone have it worse?"

Of the hundreds of city meetings held as the river was receding, one was particularly well attended by North Dakota politicians and other leaders. The meeting between the Chamber of Commerce and the city council's Business and Government Relations Committee was held at the Rural Technology Center—now the city's nerve center—and included North Dakota governor Ed Shaefer, Mayor Owens, and U.S. Representative Earl Pomeroy, along with some *Grand Forks Herald* staff, including publisher Mike Maidenberg, and the National Guard.

University of North Dakota rural sociologist Curt Stofferahn was sitting next to a *Herald* reporter when Maidenberg stood up and said that he thought the city should declare martial law and appoint a "flood czar." Stofferahn turned to the reporter and said: "Do you hear what I'm hearing?" The reporter smiled and said "It's great news." Great for news, he meant. It was not good news.

"We were doing very well without that," Owens said later. "And we didn't want to come across like that because we hadn't had a lot of problems." The suggestion had been made, ostensibly, because people wanted to be back in their homes and other people were already scavenging through the debris, stealing belongings that had floated out of a garage, for instance, and onto a neighbor's lawn.

The debate lasted longer than Stofferahn thought it would, however. Some people wanted democracy temporarily suspended in favor of a kind of authoritarian rule. Finally, a man from a small bank in town reminded the group that they were in Grand Forks, North Dakota.

"We like democracy with a small 'd,'" Stofferahn remembers him saying. "People here want to participate, they always want to vote. You do this, we'll have a riot on our hands. You're depriving them of democracy. You can't do that." The idea of a governor-appointed flood czar from the business community was abandoned in favor of a flood advisory board. Owens created the board out of city council committee heads and three indispensable members of her city staff: Director of Public Works and City Engineer Ken Vein, Director of Urban Development John O'Leary, and Finance Director John Schmisek.

Owens needed Ken Vein. He had been crucial during the worst phases of the flood and had watched his well-laid flood protection plans fall away, useless. Owens needed him to get the water plant working again, repair the devastated infrastructure, and work on future flood control with the Corps of Engineers. John O'Leary would deal with HUD and the money Grand Forks expected to receive from the federal government. Most of the federal funds would come directly to the city for distribution, rather than feeding through the North Dakota state bureaucracy first. O'Leary would need to make the tough decisions about how to allocate this money. John Schmisek would oversee this allocation—and the allocation of other federal and state funds—and work to keep the Grand Forks tax base intact so the city would remain viable. With so many houses destroyed, the mayor was concerned that people might not return at all. The likelihood that damaged or destroyed businesses would rebuild was slight. Schmisek would also have to make sure the money was spent in accordance with the appropriate guidelines set out by the donors—usually the federal government. If, at the end of the spending period, the federal audit determined that money had been misspent, the city would have to pay it back. There would be myriad guidelines, not easily understood or accepted by the people to whom the money might or might not go.

These three men—Vein, O'Leary, and Schmisek—were also installed as "tri-chairs," or co-leaders of the flood recovery. Owens also formed a business redevelopment committee and named Tom Clifford as its head. Clifford, a World War II vet and celebrated former president of the University of North Dakota, was considered non-partisan. The rest of the committee was composed of members of the business community and other local leaders and was charged with getting all elements of community life back on track—luring businesses back to town, making daycare available again, attracting housing contractors to town to replace the housing stock, and so on. And finally, Owens created a Flood Response Committee made up of five of the fourteen city council members, with councilman and NoDak Electrical Cooperative employee Duane Hafner as chair.

They met quietly. The city was still flooded and people were busy trying to figure out how to find fresh water, how to clean out their homes whose soaking remains were becoming toxic, and how to salvage what they could. The twenty-four-hour curfew Owens had declared on April 20 was still in effect and the air force base was still jammed with refugees. Three thousand olive-green cots were lined up in rows with little piles of home scattered about each one. Tattered Ken Follett novels were passed from cot to cot, toothbrushes were shared, socks were turned inside out and worn for another day.

Though the post office was closed most of the day—nearly all of the postal employees had fled town along with everyone else—Pat Owens still received bags of mail each day, delivered to the Emergency Operations Center on campus. She carried each day's delivery back to the base with her in the Hugo's Grocery Store bag she had been using for her briefcase, which she had lost when City Hall flooded. Owens had little time to read the letters, but one evening she returned to the base and pulled a few out of the bag. One letter, written on blue stationery, was from an ex-mayor of San Diego who said she might know someone who could, and would, give Grand Forks a large financial gift. After a few telephone conversations, the ex-mayor took a private jet from San Diego to Grand Forks and told Owens about an "angel" who wanted to donate fifteen million dollars to the people of Grand Forks. But there were strings.

The donor did not want to be identified, and she did not want the money attached to any agency. Her only other directive was to help as many people as possible. It was a nice sentiment, but an ambiguous and ultimately impossible edict to follow. Owens would be responsible for distributing funds which, although very generous, were nowhere near enough to go around. And everybody was hurting. Everybody needed the money.

By April 28, a week after the Red River crested at Grand Forks, more than twenty thousand people in northeast North Dakota were still without electrical power, running their sump pumps off generators. The city of Grand Forks dispatched electrical inspectors to every home in the city to check circuit boxes and to do what they could to repair the electrical infrastructure. In hard-hit neighborhoods, if someone happened to have had his power restored, neighbors might "borrow" the electricity by stringing extension cords between the homes in order to run a fridge or a heater. The Kennedy Bridge was reopened on April 28, reconnecting Grand Forks and East Grand Forks for the first time in nearly a week.

Many elderly Grand Forks residents in particular were having difficulty with the extensive FEMA paperwork necessary to secure immediate-need loans and grants. As Pat Owens was racing from a meeting at FEMA's temporary headquarters to another meeting, an elderly woman grabbed her sleeve and said: "Pat Owens, I need to talk to you."

"I thought, 'Uh-oh,'" Owens said later. "We sat on a bench in the hallway and the tears started to fall, and I said, 'What's wrong?' She said, 'I have to start this paperwork all over again; I'm just too old for this. My home is devastated.' I said, 'Why do you have to start over?'" The woman pulled a piece of paper from her purse. It was her husband's death certificate. He had been cleaning out their basement and had had a heart attack and died a few days earlier.

"I was, at one point, surprised and frustrated that they didn't have a little black book that they could hand us with steps A, B, C and D," Howard Swanson said. "I did expect the federal government, and in particular FEMA, to walk in and take over the situation, to take control of it. They never did that."

But by April 29, the federal government had provided the state of North Dakota with seven military airlift missions—bringing food and medications, nine water purification units (yielding three thousand gallons of drinkable water an hour), fifty dump trucks, ten front-end loaders, fifteen bulldozers, seven thousand blankets, nine hundred sleeping bags, thousands of cots, a communications satellite uplink, a mobile radio van, a video vehicle, an emergency operations vehicle, over three hundred staff members for the Disaster Field Office—and $93.6 million in allocated funds. FEMA provided temporary housing for more than 39,000 newly homeless flood victims, immediately released $57 million for home repair grants, and dedicated about $243 million for infrastructure repair.

Just seven days after the Red River crested at 54.11 feet, 26,605 people had applied for federal disaster assistance. Hardly any had flood insurance and many had lost almost everything. They expected the federal government to reimburse them, to help them rebuild. For many people, that was their only hope. By December, North Dakota disaster victims would receive from the federal government more than $587 million in disaster loans, $389 million in agricultural aid, $130 million for road repair or replacement, $10 million in disaster unemployment aid and $8 million in social, community, and health services. The figures were already dizzying.

The day after the Red River crested at Grand Forks, the *Fargo Forum* editorial cartoonist drew a prophetic symbolist portrait of what Grand Forks would look like in the months following. Uncle Sam, sans hat, stands thigh deep in Red River floodwater, his sleeves rolled up to his elbows. He gazes benevolently at a little man in a rowboat that has lost its oars. Its stern is half sunk, weighed down by a huge bag of "Federal Aid." The man in the rowboat holds his hands, palms up, to Uncle Sam. "Please sir," he says. "May I have some more?"

The end of April brought clean scents on the winds, purple crocuses emerging from the soaked soil, and new green shoots of prairie sweetgrass. The skies were clear and the temperature was mild. Spring had finally arrived in Grand Forks.

Two

7 *Angels and Devils*

Old Testament prophets were obsessed with disasters because they presaged a great change or because they were delivered as retribution for bad behavior, a grave transgression. What, people in Grand Forks wondered, was their transgression, and how would their city change? Grand Forks citizens had already suffered the loss of almost everything material, the possessions they believed comprised their lives, the objects that had been proof of a meaningful life. The documents that mark birth, marriage, and death. Baby albums. The corsage a boyfriend tied on your wrist before a high school dance; the bouquet you decided to keep instead of throwing to your bridesmaids; the wreath that was placed next to that boy's coffin at his wake sixty years later.

In the next months, the flood would continue to plunder. It seemed unsatisfied with mere belongings. It wanted whole neighborhoods, and got them. With their houses emptied and their downtown reduced to blackened brick and ash, the people of Grand Forks were going to have to fight the flood for what seemed the only commodity they still had: their community.

Ken Vein had watched the city's infrastructure and flood protection systems—his domain—collapse under the pressure of the river. The dikes were his responsibility. People were using the word "failed." The word bothered Vein. The dikes hadn't failed; they had been overtopped. While the dikes were not able to hold back the flooding river, that doesn't mean the engineering was flawed, and Vein was quick to point that out to the media. "I'm not blaming anybody at this point," Vein told the *Herald* days after the river crested. "But as an engineer, I feel that protecting the population from a flood, given the right information the right amount of time, is something we could have done." His were some of the first, and gentlest, censures of the National Weather Service. In fact, a tempest was brewing over the NWS forecast—not only in the Midwest media, but nationally. The National Weather Service brass in Washington braced for the onslaught and began to form a plan for damage control, keeping a firm hand over the mouths of its employees, who were themselves bewildered by the criticism.

Meanwhile, the staff of the Grand Forks branch of the agency had been moved out of its offices. Many employees were relocated to offices in Bismarck, Duluth, the South Dakota town of Aberdeen, and Minneapolis. Newspapers reported that although the Grand Forks office was not flooded, "officials were worried about the possibility of losing telephone service and other communications."

In the days immediately following the crest, however, the National Weather Service headquarters' PR machine had not yet grasped just how bad it was going to get in the Red River valley, just how angry people were becoming, and just how deeply it was all going to affect the men and women who had spent the last four months eating, breathing, and dreaming of the Red River of the North.

After deliberating, the National Weather Service allowed its hydrologists and other employees to grant interviews to the press, teaching, as Mike Anderson later put it, "Hydrology 101" four or five times a week. Anderson found himself faced with a seemingly endless line of reporters who had never seen a rating curve, never considered the relationship between discharge and stage. Anderson's challenge was to take a subject that he had spent his whole life mastering and translate its principles and operations into simple English.

"We tried to bring it, literally, down to a non-technical level, which is very hard." In the first interviews with the press, agency employees were unguarded: "It's an act of God," Minneapolis office meteorologist-in-charge Craig Edwards told the *St. Paul Pioneer Press*. "A little bit beyond the capabilities of science."

"This was very personal to us," NCRFC hydrologist-in-charge Dean Braatz said.

After the flood crest, visions of the perfidious rating curve haunted the hydrologists' waking hours. "It was dynamic for a month and a half; you didn't know what you were walking into the next day," Anderson said.

But it was the images of destruction that clicked through Mike Anderson's mind like a never-ending slideshow: the leaking dikes, the people fleeing Lincoln Drive, the burning buildings, the drowned city. "If there had been more time for Sherlock Park . . ." Anderson said later, trailing off. "People were taking their picture albums out and as they're running down the street, water is at their heels. I can only imagine how I would have reacted if something like that had happened to me." He paused, contemplative, saddened. "What they'd been through for four months already, and in previous flood years. And to lay confidence in you as a professional technical person. And it didn't work out."

A year later, the Minneapolis ABC affiliate would run a special half-hour program on the Red River flood, reported and hosted by a veteran reporter named Jason Davis. Davis's concluding comment was that everyone in the Red River valley knew there was going to be a flood "except for the people at the National Weather Service." But the NWS employees remembered the endless warnings: "Severe flood potential." "Flood of record at Grand Forks." "We've never seen this much water in the snow before, we were expecting a serious situation." "They're going to see more water than they've ever seen before in their lives."

"The Monday morning quarterbacking is starting," Lee Anderson (no relation to Mike), the meteorologist-in-charge of the Grand Forks office, wrote in an internal e-mail. "You guys did a great job, but you have to be able to clearly explain that to a lot of uninformed people (i.e. reporters and citizens.)" "Uninformed" was fair. Most of the reporters covering this story were encountering complicated hydrologic and hydraulic principles for the first time in their careers. Even two full years later, after countless stories on the National Weather Service's hydrologic modeling during the 1997 disaster, the *Grand Forks Herald* would characterize a rating curve, a simple graph, as a "computer model." The hydrologists at the NCRFC might normally have laughed off such a gaffe. But these days, everything mattered.

One of the first stories critical of the National Weather Service was an NBC News report by Jim Avila, which ran on Thursday, April 24.

"For many, loss is turning to anger in the flooded streets of Grand Forks, North Dakota," Avila said. "Residents interviewed by NBC News said they were living in fear of the federal agency that was supposed to have warned about the rising river." Avila had interviewed Frank Richards, head of the NWS Hydrologic Information Center. He asked Richards if the National Weather Service was "pleading guilty, with explanation, to a bad forecast." Richards told the reporter he was asking the wrong question.

"Predicting a record event six to eight weeks ahead of time was an audacious statement for scientists who, by their nature, are conservative," Richards said. Yet Avila claimed Richards "concede[d] forecasters are not proud of their efforts."

Internally, the National Weather Service reacted angrily to the story, though officially it maintained its silence. Frank Richards wrote an e-mail to a list of agency employees—among them public affairs officers and NCRFC hydrologists—claiming he was misquoted.

"I can appreciate the consternation this article may have caused," he wrote, "not only at the RFC [River Forecasting Center], but to me personally." He went on to advise those employees involved to be receptive to media inquiries, especially if it directed official federal attention to them. "I can appreciate the frustration (and possible anger) on the part of some staff in our offices because of this article. I share their chagrin, but I continue to feel that especially in these times of tight budgets, that prudent risk, such as contact with the media, has a potential upside. Specifically, we need to highlight the areas where we can do more, given adequate resources."

What Richards was saying was that if the National Weather Service could make a case that the botched forecast was the result of an outdated forecasting system—and many employees would agree that it was—then the long-delayed funding for the new, much sought-after "probabilistic" forecasting system might be sent down the Congressional pipeline at warp speed.

Hydrologists like Mike Anderson and Steve Buan had been forecasting the problematic Red using a fairly old river model. The National Weather Service River Forecast System was developed in 1971. Forecasters calculated streamflows and stage forecasts using one of two hydrologic models available to them, along with real-time, or near real-time, precipitation numbers, snow water equivalents, reservoir stage data, and so on. Although each river is as unique as a fingerprint, the National Weather

Service made only two continuous hydrologic forecasting models available to its forecasters.

The older of the two, the one Anderson and Buan used, is the Antecedent Precipitation Index, a no-frills, statistically based model developed in 1940. Although the model's longevity actually attested to its value, it also illustrated the National Weather Service's tendency to patch up decaying infrastructure instead of implementing an overhaul. (U.S. Commerce Secretary William Daley would concede that what had happened in the Red River valley was "well beyond any operational flood forecast modeling capabilities that we currently have on-line.")

But in the Des Moines basin the agency had recently implemented the new and far superior Advanced Hydrologic Prediction System (AHPS). Largely Web-based, it displayed most of its forecast products in real time on the Internet. Using huge amounts of data—gathered from geosynchronous satellites, automated gauges, Doppler radar, co-op observers, and so on—AHPS produces what is termed a probabilistic forecast; that is, instead of releasing a single-value flood crest number, it provides a range of probability of a flood at a certain forecast point. The range is expressed as percentage values; a 10 to 15 percent chance of a flood of record, for example.

Moreover, the new system can measure and integrate the probability for future precipitation estimates. But the National Weather Service's current model only allowed for two blunt scenarios: zero future precipitation and "average" future precipitation.

The new AHPS had not yet been implemented for the Red River and Upper Mississippi basins, and no one was sure it ever would be. The National Weather Service faced a $27.5 million shortfall in the 1997 fiscal year. And by April 25, the agency's Office of Hydrology had produced a conservative cost estimate of $2.4 million to implement AHPS in the Red River basin. Des Moines had been the first basin to implement AHPS for one reason: the Mississippi flood of 1993. When something went wrong—and went wrong in front of the whole world—money followed.

After the flood crest, Senator Kent Conrad had immediately entered into a detailed dialogue with the hydrologists responsible for forecasting the Red. In a letter to Commerce Secretary Daley on April 30, Conrad wrote: "I'm very concerned about the capability of the National Weather Service to accurately and in a timely manner predict river levels on the Red River in North Dakota."

Conrad asked staff at the NCRFC for a "wish list." Increase support for the USGS gauging network in the flooded area. Add National Weather Service telemetry on river gauges in the flooded area. Enhance the capability of the National Operational Hydrologic Remote Sensing Center located near Minneapolis. Install AHPS for the Red River of the North.

However, when Secretary William Daley responded to Conrad's letter, he took care to remind the senator that "as early as six weeks prior to the floods, we were predicting the potential for record flooding."

If the hydrologists at the NCRFC hadn't heard of Leon Osborne before the flood, there was no escaping him now. His internal forecast of 52 feet was the subject of a number of national broadcast stories, including one on NBC on April 25. Between cleaning up his home and working at the RWIC, Leon Osborne had started giving interviews to the media. He never felt good about it. He sensed that the reporters who visited him were looking for a controversial story.

"We had a reporter from NBC come and do an interview in the facility, and he was not going to leave the facility until he had a controversy," Osborne said. "They were not there to do good journalism, they were there to create a controversy." While Osborne watched the television crew set up its equipment, he told himself he shouldn't have agreed to the interview. He went through with it anyway.

"Finger pointing has begun," Randee Exler, a NWS public affairs officer, wrote in an e-mail to colleagues. An unidentified agency employee wrote: "NBC called this afternoon asking for a comment on Leon Osborne, U of N. Dakota, Regional Weather Information Center, who says that he gave the National Weather Service an accurate forecast and the information was not used . . . I fear that Osborne is using us to gain credit for himself."

In early May, people began moving back into their homes. Eighty percent of the homes in Grand Forks suffered flood damage. In East Grand Forks, only eight homes were untouched by floodwaters; five hundred homes there would be condemned. Digging out from the sludge, people attempted to piece together their domestic geography. Refrigerators were in living rooms. Beds in kitchens. Washing machines on front steps. People found the walls of their homes covered in mold and mildew. The smell of decomposing animal corpses, river sludge caked on walls and dishes, rotting meat in defunct refrigerators, and broken sewers was overwhelming. Many Grand Forks citizens would remember the stench years later as if it were still fresh in their nostrils.

Another odor that was difficult to get rid of was that of industrial-strength bleach. The city had asked everyone with wet basements to clean them with bleach to kill any black mold, which is mildly toxic to those exposed to it. The process could cost hundreds, even thousands of dollars per home. Bleach was also put to other uses—many people tried to salvage clothes, tablecloths, sofa covers, and baby clothes by soaking them in buckets of icy water and Clorox. It didn't always work. All along the streets of the hardest-hit neighborhoods, wet clothes hung limply on laundry lines, over porch railings, and from windows. On East Elmwood Drive, Mary Lien spread what remained of her family's wardrobe on her back deck—a soaked dress, a purple sweater, a white blazer, and a pair of slacks.

Anything touched by river water was considered by the city to be contaminated because of the broken fuel cells, human waste, and other sewage in the water. Whatever could not be easily sanitized was thrown out. In the days and weeks following the flood, homeowners hauled everything from baby clothes and broken dishes to television sets and furnaces to the berm, the grassy area between the sidewalk and the curb. Piles of garbage lined the streets of Lincoln Drive, Central Park, Riverside Park and other riverside neighborhoods, as well as districts farther away. Even wealthy Reeves Drive was a thoroughfare of coughed-up basement rubbish.

The local VFW commander, John Hanson, was deeply wounded by the number of ruined American flags that had been balled up and tossed out along with other debris. In the *Herald*'s May 11 "Flood Notes" section, he begged people to phone him if they had an unsalvageable American flag. "There is a proper procedure," he wrote. "Call."

From nearly every home came the dyspeptic sound of filthy, fetid water gushing from pump hoses snaking from basement window wells across driveways and onto front lawns. Neighbors, together again for the first time in weeks, took breaks to commiserate. Some people were furious that Pat Owens had chosen to evacuate the town—or, in the words of one irate man, had chased him away from his home.

"I'm angry, and I mean royally angry," homeowner Jim Votava told a reporter. "I've got a foot of water in the basement and if I had been here, there wouldn't have been a drop . . . when someone takes charge, they have no mercy." A foot of water. It was unlikely Votava's neighbors were impressed.

One evening between meetings Pat Owens drove down to Lincoln Drive to take a look at the damage. She parked her car and walked through the darkened streets. She listened to the buzz of sump pumps, the heavy splash of mud dumped from a five-gallon plastic bucket, and the periodic slushy thud of a chunk of sodden carpet tossed from a house lit by flashlights and kerosene lanterns. As Owens passed one home, she saw an elderly man sitting alone on his porch. As she approached him, he said angrily: "You didn't get water. You don't know what this is like."

Owens was nervous. "I really do feel for you," she said. "You don't know me. If you did, you'd know that." She took the seat next to the man and asked him to tell her what had happened to him in the flood. For the next hour, the old man talked, and the mayor listened.

Down on Cherry Street, Peg Rogers and her family spent their first full night back at home. The force of the floodwater had blown out all the windows on the first story, and the house still had no electricity, water, or heat. Their second floor, however, had been spared, and Peg and her husband settled in together for a much-needed night of sleep in their own bed. Before turning out the light, Peg told her husband that she was worried someone might break in.

"He rolled over and said 'You have got to be kidding,'" Peg said later. "'There is no heat, no lights, no water, and half our house is out on the lawn. You're worried about someone breaking in? I say if they do, we put them to work.'"

Most people, though, slept elsewhere that night because there was no fresh water and the sewage systems were not yet working. Even if break-ins were unlikely, the warm evenings brought looters and scavengers to the flooded neighborhoods. Scrap metal could be salvaged and sold. Discarded furnaces and stoves could be rewired and sold. Even children's toys were snatched from the berm.

The water had finally receded enough that Peg's parents' home was accessible. It had been annihilated. The water left a ring five feet up the wall—on the second floor. One afternoon as Peg helped her parents dig out, she heard her father yelling. When she ran outside, she saw a couple of gawkers making a slow drive-by survey of the discarded personal belongings.

"This is our home for God's sake," Peg's father shouted at the gawkers. "Leave us alone!"

Because the berms had become repositories for damaged but salvageable personal items—not for trash, as was normally the case—it was hard for anyone to tell what was rubbish and what was a cherished possession. In response to the looting problem, city officials asked homeowners to tag their disposed household items—to paint the word "Flood" or a large X across their dead appliances. People began spray-painting messages for each other on sheets of plywood set against their homes, or across the doors of their condemned houses and garages. On a discarded curbside refrigerator: "Look Mom, I Cleaned My Room." On the side of a severely damaged house: "Next Time the Party Is at Your House." One of the most photographed graffiti was written across a ruined house right under a dike. In huge, neon orange script, it read: "49 Feet My Ass!" The message was meant for the National Weather Service, and Mike Anderson heard it loud and clear.

"You grind out forecasts for years and years and years, and know that they're important," he said. "But when it comes down to going through what we did, I had a completely different attitude—an awareness, I guess—that it's not just another number that goes out. When you get into that previous flood of record number, then you're putting some meat out there. As I learned—as all of us who worked on the Red learned—how long do you hang on to that number? No matter what you say with that number, is that being heard? Is it being substantiated? In the end, though, it's basically the number: forty-nine feet. The guy paints it on his house. 'Forty-nine feet my ass.'"

On Mother's Day, Kelly Straub received a new black and white polka-dotted bikini swimsuit from her three children, Molly, Emily, and Andrew. Because it was such a warm day, Kelly decided to put the gift to immediate use. In her new swimsuit, Kelly sat atop an overturned bucket in her driveway and scrubbed glasses and silverware with bleach. Water had filled her basement, her entire main floor, and part of her second story. An obvious watermark on the roof showed that the river had been as high as "six shingles up." She and the kids were sleeping in a tent on the front lawn so they could start cleaning as early as possible each morning.

All around her, neighbors were falling to pieces. For days, the woman living across the street sat in a lawn chair in front of her home and wept.

"She just cried and cried," Kelly said. "'Oh no, oh no.' Just sat in her chair and pissed and moaned and cried. And I thought, 'She's got fifteen minutes to get over it or I'm going to go over and just knock her off her lawn chair and tell her to shut the hell up.'" Kelly laughed bitterly. "You want to cry, fine," she said. "But keep it to yourself."

Such scenes were taking their toll on Kelly and her children. In fact, as time passed, the more Kelly thought about it, the stronger she felt about staying right where she was. Her neighbors were coming to the conclusion that they would likely never live in the Lincoln Drive neighborhood again, that the city would probably clear the floodplain and buy them all out. The flood had exhausted them. After months and months battling the snow and then the river, most of the Lincoln Drive inhabitants had no more fight left in them. But the flood had the opposite effect on Kelly Straub. It made her stronger and it made her meaner. She decided that she was going to stay put, even if she and her children were the only ones left.

All around her, her neighbors' homes were cordoned off by yellow police tape; they had been condemned and would be torn down. It would only be a couple of months before gaps began to appear in the rows of Lincoln Drive homes like missing teeth.

On May 17, WCCO-TV helicopter pilot Dale Dobesh, who was out at the Grand Forks airport, watched a sleek Gulfstream private jet land on the tarmac, a jet rumored to belong to the "angel" who had promised the city a large donation. The serial number on its tail looked familiar to him. He jotted the number down on a scrap of paper. Two *Herald* reporters also saw it land, and also noted its serial number. They resolved to look it up in the FAA database and discover the donor's identity. They watched as an older woman with carefully coiffed blonde hair emerged from the plane, walked inside the fueling station and was met by East Grand Forks mayor Lynn Stauss. She and her entourage, along with Stauss, disappeared into a motorhome owned by local radio station KCNN to begin her tour of the devastated cities.

"It looks like a war zone with no bodies," the woman told Stauss as they surveyed Lincoln Drive.

The woman was particularly taken with Pat Owens.

Owens later recalled, "She looked at me and said, 'You know, when I saw you on TV, this little mayor in her little jeans, I thought: I'm going to help that little fox.'" Owens, too, was impressed by the donor, whom she called "a beautiful woman" with a "very soft voice."

"She didn't want a lot of red tape," Howard Swanson said. "I was concerned about things such as fraud and auditing and audit trails and it became very clear to me in my discussions with the representative out at the hangar that if this was going to happen, we would have very little paperwork, very little qualifications for people to participate, and it would have to happen very quickly." This posed a problem. With few guidelines—the program description was composed on a laptop computer set on a garbage can in the Plant Services building at the university—the dispersal of funds could easily become arbitrary. The donor wanted her $15 million to go to those who were most immediately impacted—which, from the looks of things, would be those living in Lincoln Drive, Central Park, and Riverside Park.

At a press conference at the hangar ("The donor wanted us to make a splash," said Swanson) Pat Owens and Lynn Stauss announced that their cities had received a gift from an anonymous donor and that each household that had been evacuated was entitled to two thousand dollars. The thousands of evacuees in the hangar cheered, and countless others, scattered across the plains states, likely cheered as well. Money was extremely tight, as many people had dug deeply into savings accounts to floodproof their homes during the winter and spring thaw, and now had to spend even more on basic amenities during their exile.

"So we just started writing checks just then and there," said Swanson. Within hours, base security was forced to close the gates to the base. People had begun streaming in to get their checks.

The "Angel Fund" grew smaller and smaller with each check written—and people grew more and more angry as they saw some residents getting checks and others not. Rex Sorgatz, who had spent much of the last weeks standing in line after line—Red Cross, FEMA, Small Business Administration—saw the queue for the angel money and turned around to go home. Rex, who had lost everything he owned in the flood and fire, said he just didn't have the heart.

The angel's nebulous guidelines made it difficult to judge degrees of loss—and at that point, no one wanted to. Husbands and wives fought over whether to ask for angel fund money. Longtime city councilman Eliot Glassheim, who owned Dr. Eliot's Twice Told Tales, one of Grand Forks' few bookstores, and his wife Dyan debated the ethics while bunking together at a Mayville College dorm, forty miles southwest of Grand Forks. Dyan, a painter, argued that the couple should apply for the two thousand dollars because she was losing money—no one was interested in buying art and it seemed no one would be for a long time. Eliot, on the other hand, felt that he and his wife had not suffered enough.

"If only the poorest of the poor were meant to get it, then I should not," he said later. "If only the most damaged with the greatest flood losses were meant to get it, then I should not get it. As it turns out, because the giver was so vague and so anti-rules, the city was unclear and kept changing its story by the day as to what the intended purpose of the money was." Glassheim was also prescient enough to know that any decisions, public or private, made by public officials during this time would be scrutinized later.

"It would become known—everything becomes known—and give fuel to cynics saying 'Oh, sure, the councilman was the first one to get it.'"

The donor had asked that the language be clear and the bureaucracy kept to a minimum; she wanted the checks in the people's hands immediately, not after some application had been approved. It was also important to the donor that people did not feel that they were begging or accepting welfare. She needn't have worried. When, on a routine helicopter survey flight, city attorney Howard Swanson flew over the Century Elementary School, where angel funds were being distributed, he saw a line that stretched for blocks.

Howard Swanson told the *Herald* that "We're finding people's interpretation of 'substantial harm and need' is broader than we expected."

On May 2, nondrinkable water was restored to the city, but it would be ten more days before the Grand Forks water plant would lift its "boil order." The Coast Guard's Pacific Strike Team arrived to handle the hazardous materials—known around town simply as "hazmat"—that had found its way into people's homes. The Pacific Strike Team, a pollution control force, had cleaned up Prince William Sound after the Exxon Valdez ran aground in 1989. Grand Forks would prove a much easier cleanup task, but the presence of this elite cleanup team was testament to the severity of the contamination in the city. Broken fuel tanks had leaked into flooded basements, agricultural pesticides further poisoned the water, and, in nearly every basement, red oil slicks slid across the floor.

Several elementary schools, one middle school, and a high school had to be condemned and torn down. The last six weeks of classes had been canceled at both Grand Forks high schools—Red River and Central High. The prom, scheduled for the weekend of the evacuations, had also been canceled, much to the disappointment of high school seniors.

On May 3, Canadian Prime Minister Jean Chretien and U.S. President Bill Clinton announced that they believed there must be an accounting for what had happened in the Red River valley that spring. An international approach was needed, they said, to find long-term solutions to flooding in the basin. About five weeks later, the U.S. and Canada would create the International Red River Basin Task Force and appoint members from both countries to investigate the flood. One of the task force's articulated goals was to improve flood forecasting. Two of the questions on its agenda were: "What improvements are necessary to the current flow and stage forecasting?" and "Are the two countries' meteorologic and hydrologic data networks sufficient?" Manitoba's Water Branch—Canada's equivalent to the National Weather Service—had a representative on the Task Force, and so did the U.S. Corps of Engineers, despite having no forecasting responsibilities.

No one from the National Weather Service was appointed to the team.

Senator Kent Conrad knew it would be difficult to convince his colleagues in the U.S. Congress to allocate $100 million to his state. A good number of them already saw North Dakota as a black hole into which millions of dollars in government subsidies disappeared each year. In Congress, many states are portrayed by their representatives as proud-but-needy or as long-suffering-and-deserving. But it would take more than mere need and old style politics to convince skeptical members of Congress to send $100 million to North Dakota.

When Pat Owens walked through the halls of the U.S. Capitol, though, everyone seemed to recognize her and legislators wanted to shake her hand. Conrad had urged both Owens and Lynn Stauss to join him in Washington to lobby and, more importantly, to put a face on the flood. Like children on Halloween night, Owens and Stauss went door to door showing their faces and soliciting support, first in the Senate offices, then at the House.

Initially, the North Dakota and Minnesota congressional delegations had asked for $100 million, but Conrad quickly realized that wouldn't be enough. He called Owens into his office.

"He said, 'A hundred million is not going to do it,'" Owens said later. "We need five hundred million. We all thought he was way out there; we'd never get it."

Film crews from NBC followed Owens down the halls of the Capitol, meeting and greeting congressmen who seemed star struck as they shook her hand. She was immensely popular on the Hill. Normally parsimonious senators seemed willing to open the federal wallet and hand her whatever she wanted: $171.6 million in Community Development Block Grant money for rebuilding; tens of millions for home buyouts and re-location for damaged homes, businesses, and schools. Farmers who lost livestock and that year's crop were also looking for recompense. Two cities needed to be rebuilt, and a massive dike system would have to be con-structed. The mayors were also asking Congress for a series of generous, low-interest Small Business Administration loans for homeowners and small businesses. Owens lobbied hard. As city councilman Eliot Glassheim said: "Her presentation of the situation moved people."

Owens was charming in a simple way that belied her complexity. She was fond of telling the press that she was not, in fact, part of the process. "I'm not a politician," she told reporter Fred de Sam Lazaro of the *Jim Lehrer NewsHour.* "I believe there is a need for people to realize that gov-ernment is open, and that government is people and not politicians." There was value in being a plainspoken outsider, and this style of dia-logue was the currency of her realm. By trying to distance herself from them—lifetime politicians, professional in their approach, polished in their tactics—she was, rather, drawing them to her. And, by professing to have no credentials as a politician, Owens came across simply as the "face of the flood." Her girlhood stories of digging potatoes with her bare hands out of the soil of her father's farm were seamlessly incorporated into re-quests for millions in federal funds.

Pat Owens was, of course, a politician. She performed—she didn't wheedle. Owens was annoyed at her portrayal in the media as vulnerable, diminutive, and motherly. But in the halls of Congress, she traded on those traits. When you're asking for something, seeming vulnerable can be a good device. But it doesn't work when you're trying to lead people, and Owens would find it impossible to shake that image when she returned to her city with $500 million.

Pat Owens tucked into the crook of Bill Clinton's arm: the image was an easily identifiable metaphor for Grand Forks being taken under the wing of the federal government. A video clip of Owens wiping away a tear while she told reporters that her own home was going under was an affirming sign that "Mayor Pat" was not abandoning ship.

"In every big disaster, someone emerges who just becomes the symbol of the future of the community," said Ed Conley, then director of FEMA Region VII. "I don't know that she likes all the attention. She's a very unpretentious person."

In one of a seemingly endless series of meetings with normally reluctant congressmen and women, Pat Owens sat across a table from Ted Stevens, an arch-conservative Republican from Alaska and chair of the Senate Appropriations Committee. A thirty-year Senate veteran, Stevens was notorious for being cantankerous. Before their meeting, Conrad had warned Owens that Stevens would be a tough sell. The congressman was in no mood, in 1997, to give away millions of dollars to a state that had been draining federal funds for decades. But when Owens sat down and asked for his support of the disaster bill, Stevens softened.

"I remember sitting down right beside him and just talking directly to him," Owens said. She told Stevens that her city, at that moment, was teetering on the edge of extinction. "This isn't about Democrats or Republicans," she told him, "This is about our people, and they're hurting." She shared with Stevens the story of growing up in East Grand Forks, farming the land with her father and older brothers, of loving the land and the people who had been ravaged in the flood. Ted Stevens was mesmerized.

"I could see the creases beside his eyes softening, and tears there that did not flow," she said. Kent Conrad could not believe his eyes.

"I've never seen Stevens so warm and so receptive to a message," Conrad said. "It was really her charm that got his attention." Stevens promised to support the disaster relief bill and to do all he could to push it through the Senate as quickly as possible.

It's easy to see why local and national media chose, time and time again, to tell the story of Grand Forks through its mayor. She was petite, which made people feel an immediate need to "protect" her. She was plainspoken and always prepared to dispense an inspirational nugget ("What I wear is the heart and soul of this community") or an endearing reminder of her non-political background ("Sister Adelaide taught me all the ins and outs of the business").

The *St. Paul Pioneer Press* opened its story about Pat Owens' appearance on the NBC Nightly News "American Spirit" segment this way: "Grand Forks Mayor Pat Owens is barely 5 feet tall, but to the people of North Dakota she's a giant."

"Pat Owens wears her heart and soul on a flood-dirtied sleeve," read an editorial in the *Fargo Forum*. In an article in *American City and County Magazine*, which announced Pat Owens as "Municipal Leader of the Year," Owens was portrayed as a blushing, self-effacing farm girl, who seemed genuinely amazed that anyone found her worthy of praise.

"I would come home and sit down and think, 'My goodness, I just spent the day with [President Clinton,]' says Owens. 'My goodness,' she says, 'do you know I was on 'Good Morning America?' Moments later, Owens apologizes, 'I'm sorry. I'm not very interesting,'" read the *City and County* story. And of course, very few lines of copy could pass without reference to her age, height, and motherliness. "Now, with her town in ruins around her," the article continued, "Owens, a 57-year-old, 5-foot-tall grandmother, did what any grandmother would do: she sympathized, she listened, she cried, she hugged."

She had been given monikers, and she had come to be known by them; her accomplishments seemed more impressive because of the personal traits the media celebrated. However, the descriptions of mayor Pat Owens that appeared in newspapers around the country affected her ability to lead. For some on Owens' team, it took a little more effort to take the ex-secretary seriously. For a few, the idea of woman without a college education trying to sort through the tangles of federal money, a severe housing shortage, a debilitated infrastructure, a dying downtown, and a community in danger of losing its population, was worrisome if not outright laughable. What the rest of the world found so charming about Pat Owens the architects of Grand Forks' recovery found to be a liability. In fact, despite the accolades, there was something that Owens found difficult to forget; it lodged in her psyche. No matter how many times she blinked, rubbed her eyes and opened them again, when Owens looked in the mirror, she still saw a former waitress with only a high school education. She wondered if people in City Hall and in the Chamber of Commerce were reminding one another that the mayor was really only a naïve farmer's daughter who carried her dead mother's rosary in her pocket and had never entered a college classroom as a student. Owens wasn't paranoid; people *were* talking. Male members of the business community told her she was "unfocused," that she was an inspirational leader but incapable of putting a city back together.

"I do not like being treated like a child," Owens said. "I may be inspirational because I'm a small female, and because I believe in God and I believe in keeping faith and in putting your heart into things, but that doesn't make it all bad. I can be the one that can lead you through this."

"People said this to me, and I didn't like to hear it because it's a classist and sexist opinion," Eliot Glassheim said. "'She's a little woman, she's only got a high school degree.'" Owens, however, was a tough woman to figure out. Outwardly naïve and unassuming, Owens had more than thirty years of political experience (although some unfairly dismissed it as "administrative" experience). She knew how this game worked. She had watched it from the sideline for decades, and just as benchwarmers often make the best coaches, Owens parlayed her years of observation into practice. Owens knew she was good, and sometimes alluded to it slantwise, by placing her leadership in the context of praise of Grand Forks citizens.

"People would say 'Pat, you're a hero,'" Owens told an *AP* reporter, "but maybe I was a hero because of all the unsung heroes that were working beside me."

Still, there was something vulnerable about Pat Owens as well. One of the first times she broke down in tears was when reporter Don Shelby sat Owens down for an interview. Owens began what had become her usual riff on the heroism of her citizens. Shelby cut her off.

"We don't want to talk about flood-related things," he said. "We want to talk about you; we want to talk about you—Pat Owens—and your feelings and how you've helped pull these people through." Owens started weeping.

North Dakota's U.S. senators, Byron Dorgan and Kent Conrad, were unembarrassed about expecting federal assistance—they had been doing it for years. But East Grand Forks mayor Lynn Stauss was more reflective and, one could argue, savvier, when he portrayed the two cities as supplicants, and appeared to be a little embarrassed by the whole game.

The $5.5 billion relief bill had been working its way through the Senate; $500 million of it was slated for Grand Forks and tiny East Grand Forks, the rest for other disaster-struck areas nationwide. It was an enormous package but burdened by an amendment, attached by the Republicans, which would prohibit a government shutdown if Congress could not agree on a budget. President Clinton had made it clear that he would veto the bill if it contained language that would preclude government shutdowns. Owens visited the Oval Office a few days before the bill was scheduled to land on Clinton's desk, and he assured her that Grand Forks would eventually get the aid.

After sending the bill to the White House, Congress recessed for the Memorial Day holiday. During the ten-day recess, Representative Earl Pomeroy borrowed a UND video camera and walked around Grand Forks, interviewing people who were spending their holiday digging out. He made copies of the tape and sent them to his Republican colleagues.

"We were in hopes that it would be settled by now," one resident told the camera. "In hopes that Congress would have done everything before the recess. But it just didn't happen, so now we're kind of in limbo for an extended period." However, when a reporter told Senate Majority Leader Trent Lott that "folks in Grand Forks have no place to live, no place to send their kids to school," Lott responded that if that were the case, then "FEMA's not doing its job. . . . I believe the record is very clear that help is getting there, and if it's not getting there, the problem is not here; it's there." Clinton vetoed the bill on June 5.

A month earlier, on May 8, the Grand Forks Historic Preservation Commission agreed to oppose a rumored plan to open a floodway through the city. In the zealous declarations that immediately followed the 1997 flood, a colossal new levee system and floodway seemed to be a foregone conclusion. If such a project had been on a referendum in the weeks following the flood, it likely would have passed. Still, even a rumor of such a project was enough to draw the preservationists out of their muck boots and into City Hall.

The rumored flood control plan would take out nearly two-thirds of Grand Forks' riverfront downtown. Five of the city's thirty-five buildings that were "of historic interest" had burned and been demolished during the flood. If the rumored dike and floodway were placed along Fourth Street, another twenty-four would have to be demolished or removed.

In its May 8 announcement, the Commission pushed instead for a diversion ditch that would reroute up to half of the Red River's spring flow around the city. And despite the fact that diversion ditches had been studied by the Corps of Engineers, and rejected by Grand Forks officials in the past, Corps Project Manager Lisa Hedin said the Corps would examine the feasibility of such a project—although she and the Corps doubted that the state could fund it, even with the additional federal funds. At the time the cost estimate of $75 to $100 million was, according to Corps engineers, up to two and a half times as expensive as a dike system. But two years later, when the Corps and the city of Grand Forks finally agreed upon a flood protection system, that early estimate would seem like a bargain.

Meanwhile, the National Weather Service was still trying to figure out what had gone wrong in Grand Forks while simultaneously attempting to boost the morale of its dejected employees. At the end of May, Dr. Susan Zevin, the agency's deputy assistant administrator, visited the NCRFC and the offices involved in forecasting the Red River flooding. Among other things she learned during her trip, Zevin was told that neither Grand Forks city engineer Ken Vein nor East Grand Forks city engineer Gary Sanders had been in contact with the local National Weather Service office or the NCRFC since the flood. Vein would later confirm this, saying: "I'm not denying that there wasn't lots of communication; I'm just not sure what they wanted. There was only one thing I needed from them—what the crest was going to be."

While Pat Owens and Lynn Stauss were in Washington supplicating, homeowners in Grand Forks had been discovering the interminable frustrations of dealing with federal agencies, even agencies that had professed to have cut down the "red tape" considerably in order to make immediate recovery easier.

At a series of public city council meetings at the Chester Fritz Auditorium on the UND campus, Owens and council members had fielded questions from aggravated townspeople. The council convened, appropriately, on a stage. The seats were filled with disheveled, tired Grand Forks residents wearing soiled sweatshirts and old jeans. Before the flood, council meetings at City Hall on every other Monday night attracted a handful of people. But the first post-flood council meeting on May 12, which lasted three and a half hours, drew more than a thousand. They wanted to know where the money was.

"It's right at the tips of our fingers," Owens told them. "But we don't have it in the bank yet." City council president Tom Hagness responded to residents' frustration with a sharp warning.

"We can't bite the hand that feeds us," he said. But the people in the auditorium that night would not be pacified.

"Monday, I had my insurance guy over. My house was a total loss," Vern Sander, a former resident of Lincoln Drive, said into one of the microphones set up in the aisles. "Tuesday I had the FEMA guy over. My house was a total loss. John Schmisek brought up taxes. Am I liable? Do I have to keep paying city tax on my property I cannot live in?" The questions seemed to baffle the council members. "Good question, huh?" Sanders said.

Even more pointed questions came from Marian Hastings, who owned a ruined downtown bakery. She wondered whether the "angel fund" moneys were being unfairly withheld.

"You have money sitting in the checking account. The infrastructure is being paid for by the federal government. Your angel fund supposedly gave money to people that needed it immediately. What is happening to the money in that account? How much is there? How much more red tape, how many more days, how many more weeks, how many more months before you decide how you're going to release that money?"

Pat Owens, who looked haggard and thin in her black and white striped T-shirt, tried to appease the woman. "We need to meet this week," she said, without mentioning the fact that, for the last month and a half, her life had been, essentially, an endless series of meetings. "I'm not exactly sure what's in that fund at this point, but it's been coming in quite steadily, and we will get together and we will see what's in there, and we will let you know what's going to happen with it." It was as if city council members were staring into a crystal ball—but they were as nervous and as uncertain as the people whose fortunes they were telling.

Hastings' tone of suspicion was contagious. It was one of the first symptoms of what rural sociologist and University of North Dakota professor

Curt Stofferahn would later call "flood angst." A number of people, for instance, asked their city council member, point blank, if the city had known beforehand that the river would crest as high as it did. It seemed an odd question. Councilman Eliot Glassheim had to mollify a woman who came into his office convinced that city council members had been given a heads-up and had skipped town a week before the crest. In fact, city council president Tom Hagness suffered $37,000 dollars worth of damage to his home; several police officials lost every possession in their homes; city councilman Art Bakken suffered major damage to the condominiums he owned close to the river. Nevertheless, the rumor persisted.

A few hours after Captain Dale Dobesh jotted down the serial number of the Gulfstream jet that had carried the "angel" to Grand Forks, that same plane touched down at Regent Aviation, a small landing strip in St. Paul. It was May 18. Dobesh had called his news director and told him to send a camera crew to the airstrip to meet the plane.

"When our crew met them, she admitted to being the donor," Dobesh said, "and asked that we honor her anonymity." The "angel" had made anonymity a precondition for her $15 million donation to the city of Grand Forks, and city officials there were determined to honor her request. WCCO, too, decided breaking the story would do more harm than good; revealing the donor's name might discourage other wealthy benefactors from donating if anonymity could not be guaranteed, and Grand Forks needed all the money it could get. The station's news director made it clear that if anyone else broke the story, however, the station would maintain it had the information first, but had withheld it.

At the *Grand Forks Herald* on May 18, however, the newsroom—which was still the classroom in Manvel—was electric with the excitement of a huge news story about to be broken. Someone had run the Gulfstream's serial number through a database and had come up with the jet's registration. The donor also had paid for jet fuel at the Grand Forks airport with her credit card, and the *Herald's* reporters told the airport manager that receipts at the city-owned airport were considered public records. The *Herald* had the donor's name.

Most city officials knew the *Herald* had the information. Reporters had asked them point blank if McDonald's heiress Joan Kroc was the donor. The officials would neither confirm nor deny. But governor Ed Shaefer, mayors Pat Owens and Lynn Stauss, and city council members all begged editor-in-chief Mike Jacobs not to run the story. City attorney Howard Swanson told reporters Ryan Bakken and Mark Silva: "Don't, don't, don't. You do that and you destroy an awful lot of things. This is irresponsible. There is no reason to identify anybody." Their appeals only confirmed to the *Herald* that this was a big story.

On May 19, the banner headline above the fold in the *Grand Forks Herald* read: "Angel appears in GF/EGF." Just below the banner, another headline read: "Angel's wings registered to Kroc." The *Herald* identified the donor as Joan Kroc, who had grown up in St. Paul and returned there often to visit a sister. Captain Dale Dobesh had seen her plane land at Regent Aviation in St. Paul many times, never knowing to whom it belonged.

The community of Grand Forks reacted in an interesting way to the *Herald*'s story. It got angry.

"Sunday night, when we knew we had the story, there was a fair amount of feeling really good about ourselves," managing editor Jim Durkin said. "Monday morning after publication the question was: 'OK, who's going to answer the phone?' People would hear a phone ring and decide they needed to be on the other side of the room." Citizens apparently felt they didn't need to know the donor's identity—in fact they didn't *want* to know. The effect of the *Herald*'s May 19 story was a bit like enlightening a child about Santa Claus—but implying that there would now be no more Christmases. And that was what many people feared. The *Herald* knew that by revealing the donor's name, other philanthropists might choose to pass Grand Forks by.

"We could jeopardize a few million dollars in help," Durkin said. "You consider that, but you put that in the basket and you say, 'Okay, the next guy comes along and gives one hundred thousand to the United Way but only if we don't publish the name.' Where does that stop? We don't get permission to publish stories." Jacobs' newsroom motto was to never hold the news. The angel's identity, the *Herald* maintained, was news.

The day after revealing Kroc's identity, the *Herald* ran a front-page story about the commotion its story had caused. The owner of KCNN radio, Dave Norman, told the paper: "I think there are times when you have to put the community first." Lynn Stauss was typically succinct when he said: "You don't bite the hand that feeds you." Citizens, too, were unhappy with the paper. One resident said that he was afraid the decision would have far-reaching effects. He cited the *Herald's* mission statement, in which it calls itself "the people's paper," one that "protects their interests."

"How did this do that?" the man wanted to know. In the article, reporter Ryan Bakken reminded readers that the *Herald* had not missed one issue, that it had offered the paper free of charge for three weeks and that its building had burned to the ground. Mike Jacobs' last word on the issue was this: "If she really wanted to remain anonymous, she should have driven into Grand Forks in a pickup truck. With a gun rack."

In early June, the National Weather Service was still trying to handle its morale problem. The unceasing bad press was deeply distressing to the hydrologists at the NCRFC in Chanhassen and the forecasters and meteorologists in Grand Forks. Ed Johnson, the chief of hydrologic operations at NWS headquarters, was concerned enough that he contacted a mental health expert in California for advice on helping his employees get through this. The expert's written response, which contained three pages of "Trauma Recovery Guidelines," began: "You all have encountered a stressor outside the realm of usual human experience."

The same could be said of nearly everyone up and down the Red River valley, but the anguish felt at the National Weather Service was different. Its employees were being blamed, in Mike Anderson's words, for "making a whole town disappear."

The initial damage assessment was made a few days after the flood— $775 million. This was a conservative guess. The 1997 Red River flooding ranked as the country's eighth most expensive natural disaster since 1903 (ranked first was the 1993 Mississippi flood, second was 1972's Hurricane Agnes). The final damage estimate in Grand Forks would be $3.5 *billion*. The National Weather Service made sure to provide this estimate to Senator Kent Conrad, a supporter of the new AHPS forecasting system, hopeful that the information would persuade the appropriations committee that implementing the system in the Red River valley would have a positive cost-benefit ratio.

For the National Weather Service, though, things just got worse and worse. On May 4, the *Grand Forks Herald* landed what the NCRFC's Red River crew felt was a sucker punch. The headline was plastered above the fold in wartime font: "An $800 Million Oversight." In the article, the *Herald* blamed the National Weather Service for the disaster. The Corps of

Engineers, the article reported, not only had the tools to correctly predict the flood crest at Grand Forks, but *did* correctly predict it; the National Weather Service just didn't know enough to ask for it. The *Herald* maintained that the Corps, for its part, didn't contact the National Weather Service until it received an April 18 fax from the Pentagon warning that the crest would be much higher than the NWS was predicting. Further, the *Herald* reported a split within the Corps itself, with the St. Paul branch believing the NWS prediction, and the Washington brass believing in its own higher estimate.

The *Herald* held the reputation of the National Weather Service in the Red River valley in its hands, and the article was rife with errors that cost the hydrologists sleep at night. For instance, the reporter, Monte Paulsen, wrote that the faulty rating curve was generated by the National Weather Service's computer model. He was wrong. The rating curve was, rather, a U.S. Geological Survey document fed into the National Weather Service's computer model, not generated by it. It was a significant, if seemingly subtle, mistake.

Paulsen wrote that "whereas the National Weather Service merely extrapolated its existing rating curve, the corps [sic] went out and measured the shape of the river channel above 48 feet."

"As with most articles in the *Grand Forks Herald*, and others, the writer's use of the words dealing with technical issues is awkward and, in this case, just plain misleading," Corps engineer Richard Pomerleau later maintained. "Historical flood profiles were constructed from high water elevations recorded throughout the city, including one from 1897 at the DeMers Bridge. Once calibrated, the model was then run with higher discharges up to and including the five-hundred-year flood."

The model Pomerleau mentioned had been designed as part of a Corps feasibility study that posited a Grand Forks surrounded by a series of ring dikes, and fed hypothetical flows through a hydraulic river model. In other words, the Corps hypothesized. The model could not truly predict what would really happen, because it was based on imaginary topography.

If the North Central River Forecast Center in Chanhassen, Minnesota is Mount Olympus, then the Grand Forks National Weather Service forecast office is the Oracle at Delphi, interpreting and relaying data from the "gods." The small granite building on the west side of I-29 is one of the Na-

tional Weather Service's newest forecast offices, just a year and a half old
in 1997. This new office is located on Technology Circle—whose parking
lot offers evenly spaced outlet boxes and extension cords to drivers whose
engine blocks die in the North Dakota cold.

Gregory Gust, a warning and coordination meteorologist with a most
appropriate name for both his personality and his vocation, is an energetic
man built like a football player. His voice has the resonance of a stage ac-
tor, and he seems to be the star of the Grand Forks office. Gust had watched
the events of 1997 unfold from his post at the Glasgow, Montana forecast
office before he joined the Grand Forks team in the midst of the post-flood
media storm. He was immediately incensed on behalf of his new colleagues.

"That's the problem with people in media who catch half the sentence
and only figure out a quarter of what that means and only relay ten percent of that in the article," he said.

Working in the cubicle across from Gust, quiet hydrometeorologist
Lynn Kennedy would soon begin spending a good deal of his time inte-
grating data into the new hydrological prediction system that everyone in
the office then hoped was only one congressional session away from receiving full funding.

Each morning since the flood, Kennedy and Gust, along with service
hydrologist Michael Lukes, had picked up the *Grand Forks Herald* and
read about their alleged incompetence. East Grand Forks mayor Lynn
Stauss continued to criticize them; North Dakota Representative Earl
Pomeroy told the *Herald* that "the inability to get realistic flood numbers
certainly hindered the communities' ability to prepare." But it was Monte
Paulsen's May 4 article—charging the government with the absence of interagency coordination and charging the National Weather Service with
costly, lazy mistakes—that was the most painful to the staff both at the
Grand Forks office and the NCRFC.

"They talk about lack of interagency communication," Kennedy said.
"I have never talked to so many different people from so many different
agencies at so many different times than during that whole January
through the end of April." The important miscommunication was not between the National Weather Service and the Corps of Engineers; it was,
instead, between the National Weather Service and the city of Grand Forks.

During the flood, the Grand Forks branch office had been temporarily
relocated to Bismarck. Lynn Kennedy, whose family was now split up

among various towns across the state, had returned to the reopened Grand Forks Office after two weeks in Bismarck to find that their administrative assistant had lost her home, and that most of his co-workers had suffered major structural damage to their homes. Kennedy, a robust, soft-spoken man who wears tinted glasses, accompanied warning coordination meteorologist Jim Bellis on his first visit to his flooded home.

"You open the front door and look down the steps and the water is at the top step of his basement," Kennedy said. "He had just refinished it three months before. It wasn't as if we were sitting three thousand miles away and didn't care about what was going on. We had houses to clean up, too." When Kennedy returned to his own home, he found that it too had not been spared. "I came back to a house that had two feet of sewage in it, no heat, no electricity, and I had to work a shift here and clean up my house. I mean, I'm not giving you a sob story but we were impacted too," Kennedy said. "We didn't want it to flood. We cared."

In its earlier ruminations about the Red River at Grand Forks for a 1994 flood protection feasibility study, the Corps developed a hydraulic computer model with actual topographic information—the slope and grade of the riverbed, for instance, which determines the river's rate of flow. The model was calibrated to historical flood data which, for the Corps, consists of measured discharges and high water marks, identical to the National Weather Service's calibrations. This historical data forms the skeleton of the model, though, not the body. This is where the Corps and the National Weather Service part company.

To see how proposed dikes will hold up against severe floods, the Corps runs "larger discharge events" through its model. The point is to calculate the effect these floods would have on existing or imagined structures. In the Corps' models, whole areas of the floodplain could be removed from the equation. For example, the Corps could excise the Lincoln Drive dike from the model and draft a scenario in which the river ran past the neighborhood unimpeded, rather than flowing through the channel squeezed between two dikes, as it had been doing since 1958.

As part of their package of would-be's, could-be's and what if's, the Corps drafted a rating curve—the same kind of hydrological graph the National Weather Service used in its model when determining a river's flow and volume. The Corps needed a rating curve for the same reason the National Weather Service needed it: to convert discharge to stage.

Mike Anderson and his crew had based their flood crest prediction on one rating curve; the other was part of the Corps' dossier for Grand Forks—the rating curve that was filed away in St. Paul until the day Patrick Foley dug it out. How did these two curves differ? The difference is like the difference between a historical document—or a textbook, perhaps—and a historical novel. In one, the information is verifiable. In the other, the portrait drawn is based on history, but not constrained by it. And while unfailing accuracy is expected and required in the former, it might appear in the latter sporadically. The *Herald*—and everyone else in Grand Forks, it seemed—had accepted the novel rather than the textbook.

NCRFC hydrologists Mike Anderson and Steve Buan kept close tabs on the *Herald* and other newspapers in the Red River valley. Anderson saved every article mentioning the National Weather Service or NCRFC until he had accumulated boxfuls of clippings. Most of what he read hurt.

Dr. Roger Pielke, Jr., a scientist at the Environmental and Societal Impacts Group at the National Center for Atmospheric Research in Boulder, Colorado, also clipped a newspaper article about the botched flood forecast in Grand Forks and filed it. Pielke is an environmental sociologist as well as a meteorologist with a degree in mathematics and a Ph.D. in political science. The precision of mathematics and the human mechanics of political science led Pielke to study the relationship of scientific information to decision-making—the way people use science in their everyday lives.

A week after filing the article, Pielke received a phone call from someone at the National Weather Service, asking him to join what the government was calling a "Service Assessment Team." In Washington, the National Oceanic and Atmospheric Administration (NOAA), the parent agency of the National Weather Service, was in the process of assembling a disaster survey team. The team was composed of members of the USGS, the National Weather Service (from offices in Silver Spring, Tucson, Sacramento, and Las Vegas), and the Corps of Engineers. NOAA wanted to include a scientist from outside the federal government, and Pielke was one of only a handful of scholars studying the sociology of science. Pielke was intrigued by the way the community of Grand Forks used science to make

critical decisions—or had failed to use science. He agreed to drop everything and join the team.

"People were a little shell-shocked," Pielke said of the NWS employees
with whom he spoke. "Many of them had tremendous damage and property losses themselves. They were profoundly affected by this event. At the
same time that they were being criticized by their community; they had
suffered a disaster." However, by instructing employees not to respond
to the media reports, the NWS officials had forced those deep emotions
into a dark place. Every once in a while, an employee would hint at the anguish going on behind closed mouths. The day after the Red crested at
Grand Forks, a story came across the *Associated Press* wire with the headline "Flooded Town Angry at Officials." In the article, NCRFC hydrologist-
in-charge Dean Braatz noted that one of his own forecasters had lost his
family home in Grand Forks. "We've got a lot of emotion on our staff here,
too," he said.

Headquarters directed employees to tell reporters that the National
Weather Service's official response to the 1997 Red River flooding would
be its Service Assessment and Hydraulic Analysis, due in a few months.

Although Pat Owens was cited in the National Weather Service's list
of its post-flood critics, she had actually taken a political risk to avoid
placing blame on the agency. She was a leader with a minority voice on
that issue.

"I'll be the last one to stand there and point a finger at them," Owens
had told an AP reporter, somewhat testily, during her daily news briefing at the University of North Dakota on May 5. "I think now is the time
to move on." But it would be some time before anyone would be willing
to move on from this topic. In fact, as reports began circulating of western North Dakota farmers calling the now federally subsidized people of
Grand Forks "greedy whiners," a general opinion began to form on a loose
understanding of the laws of liability: the National Weather Service's failure to provide an accurate and timely crest prediction meant the federal government had been negligent, and the guilty pay for the damage—
all of it.

In Chanhassen, the survey members interviewed the NCRFC hydrologists
who had struggled with the flawed rating curve in the weeks leading up to
the flood.

"It was very intense and there was a lot of criticism going on but we were down in the weeds," Pielke said. "The first thing that we wanted to get was what exactly occurred, what info was released, to whom and how. What words were used, why they made the decisions they made." The more the survey team talked to the National Weather Service hydrologists in Chanhassen, Fargo, and Grand Forks, the more convinced they became that, in fact, those responsible for forecasting the Red River flood of 1997 had had to do it with one arm tied behind their backs—they didn't have adequate tools to forecast this flood.

8 The Value of Home

On May 21, 1997, Edward Johnson sent a polite e-mail to Leon Osborne asking if he could visit Osborne's Regional Weather Information Center. Co-leader of the National Weather Service Assessment Team, Johnson worked in the NWS's Kansas City regional office. He asked Osborne for a general description of the model he had used to come up with his nearly accurate crest number. After his initial round of interviews with the media following the flood, Osborne had tried to keep a low profile. But several factors had drawn national attention to him: news of the North Dakota congressional delegation's confidence in Osborne's crest number, the rumored split between Corps of Engineers brass in Washington and its St. Paul district regarding that number and, most importantly, the fact that Osborne's number was closer to the observed crest than the National Weather Service's. Osborne usually chose not to comment. Privately, however, he was troubled by news stories claiming he had notified the National Weather Service of his 52-foot crest prediction and had been told to "shut up."

"Never once did I get a telephone call from the National Weather Service that said 'Osborne, be quiet,'" he said. Yet Osborne was overwhelmed by regrets. "Why wasn't I out there challenging the weather service? Why didn't I attempt to work closer with the National Weather Service? Why didn't the National Weather Service attempt to work closer with me?" He was angry that his scientific methods were being denigrated by some in the scientific community. Paul Todhunter, a UND professor of geology, told the *Grand Forks Herald,* "It's hard to imagine anything [Osborne] did might stand up to a scientific engineering review. You certainly wouldn't use their method to second-guess the weather service, which has spent millions of dollars developing their system and has decades of experience running it.

That would be like conducting your own poll at the mall and declaring it more accurate than the Gallup poll."

A subgroup of the National Weather Service survey team—several hydrologists from Maryland and California—visited Osborne at the RWIC. The conversation was polite; Osborne patiently diagrammed how he came to his 52-foot crest prediction, and the team members listened intently.

"It was very interesting," Osborne said later. "When the meeting ended and the recorders are off and they're breaking up, they made a few off the record comments that really made one give pause; they thought 'Gee, that was a really neat way you did this.'" When the National Weather Service's report was released in August, however, there was no reference to Leon Osborne, the RWIC, or its more accurate crest prediction.

A number of Osborne's former students were now NWS employees in North Dakota and Minnesota. A year before the flood, when the agency was considering relocating its Fargo forecast office to Grand Forks, Osborne had been a great champion of the move, and collaboration between the two offices—mostly in the sharing of co-op reports and other precipitation data—was very much hoped for by both sides. After the flood, though, things changed.

"There was tremendous friction with the National Weather Service," Osborne said. "There was nothing near the camaraderie we had prior to 1997."

The National Weather Service, for its part, did not know what to make of Osborne and his prediction. The NCRFC hydrologists seemed genuinely bewildered when they learned of Osborne's crest number. Mike Anderson, for example, said he hadn't even heard of Leon Osborne by name until after the flood.

"Nobody ever said to us, on a conference call or in an e-mail or anything like that, 'I heard that Leon Osborne said that the river is going to . . . ,'" Steve Buan said. Then, firmly: "That never, ever came up. If it had, we would have done something about it."

However, other NWS employees wanted to lash out at Osborne and the media that had elevated him to the status of oracle. This was particularly galling to a large contingent of distressed NWS employees who saw Osborne as a researcher, an academic with the luxury of hypothesis, the flexibility of theory, and the freedom to make mistakes. In internal communications—the National Weather Service, for the most part, chose not to discuss Osborne's forecast with the media—Osborne's harshest critics were the National Weather Service Washington public affairs team (the cleanup crew) and staffers from other river forecast centers. They were, like Greg Gust, angry on behalf of their colleagues.

They weren't the only ones; many in the Corps of Engineers were angry, too. But they, like their federal colleagues, chose to stay mostly silent about the bad press. The *Herald* tried unsuccessfully to interview Colonel John Wonsik, the chief engineer for the St. Paul district, for its many stories on what was now being called "the oversight." Editor-in-chief Mike Jacobs wrote in an editorial: "To say that Wonsik's staff rebuffed the *Herald*'s reporter would be an understatement." Jacobs also said that Wonsik had been irked by the *Herald*'s May 4 article, and that the colonel had said as much in a letter to Senator Kent Conrad on May 16. The *Herald*, however, did not choose to publish the letter it referred to.

On June 11, Pat Owens was in a meeting at City Hall when her cell phone rang. It was a staffer from Senator Conrad's office.

"It's been passed," she said. "The President will sign the bill in the morning." Owens drove home and called Lynn Stauss, and the two began packing for a redeye to Washington. As Owens ran out to her car—"with a piece of pizza between my teeth"—her cell phone rang again. Conrad's staffer said Clinton had decided to sign the bill that evening, without a ceremony.

"But call Clinton and thank him," she said. "He'll appreciate that." When Owens called, Clinton was in physical therapy—he had hurt his knee a few weeks before—and she left her cell phone number with a member of the White House staff. Owens and her husband decided to take a ride through Lincoln Drive while they were waiting for the President to call back.

"Mr. President?" Owens said, when the call finally came.

"No Pat, this is just Bill." She laughed.

"I wanted to thank you on behalf of all our people," Owens said. "For sticking with us and coming through to help so we can recover as a city." As she sat in her car on a deserted Lincoln Drive street talking to the president of the United States, Owens felt as if she were observing herself from a distant point. "Who am I?" she thought, and then answered herself: "A farm girl."

On June 12, the White House officially announced the signing of the disaster bill that had wound its way through Congress, burdened with pork-barrel spending and special provisions. At a Washington, D.C. news conference three days later, HUD secretary Andrew Cuomo, flanked by Pat Owens and Lynn Stauss, announced that the bill provided, in total, $500 million to towns affected by flooding in the Upper Midwest. Expedited assistance of $50 million would be forwarded to Grand Forks immediately, and $60 million more was headed to communities in Minnesota, South Dakota, and smaller towns in North Dakota. CDBG funds had a few strings attached: tasks such as building rehabilitation, infrastructure improvement, homeowner assistance, clearance and demolition, and "economic development activities" were encouraged, but only if completed in the context of flood mitigation.

Flood mitigation is a broad, imprecise term. FEMA, the kingpin of disaster mitigation, defines it as "sustained action that reduces or eliminates long-term risk to people and property from natural hazards and their effects." It is almost always a painful process to someone. Kelly Straub and Jim and Mary Lien were about to discover just how painful it was going to be.

By the time Kelly Straub finally moved out of her wreck of a house in the Lincoln Drive floodplain in September 2000, she and her four children had lived there illegally for more than three years. She spray-painted two messages on her house for the city of Grand Forks to ponder. The first: "Do Not Tear Down. Die If You Do." The second, embellished with plastic picnic tablecloths that looked like American flags: "Let the guilty pay, it's Independence Day."

"The flood dug the hole and the city's just pushing people in," Kelly said at her new home on Eighteenth Avenue. "Just picking them off and dumping them in the hole."

Kelly, a school nutritionist—"Let's be real here, I'm a lunchroom lady"—is a lively, often acerbic woman with red hair and freckles. At the time of her fiercest battles with the city, Kelly was a recently divorced single mother of three—with one on the way. She's unguardedly expressive, tending toward raucous, and is deeply in love with her children, to whom she speaks as if they were fellow bar patrons. Her middle child, Molly, a serene fifteen-year-old with lank brown hair and glasses, regards her mother with amused detachment. When discussing a Grand Forks city council member who had recently told a Seattle alternative weekly that women were "throwing themselves" at him, Kelly looked at Molly and said: "That's you and me, honey. Molly, you slut! Quit it." Molly just smiled and nodded slowly.

Kelly's eyes are a translucent blue; but sometimes, for brief moments, it seems the life drains out of them, replaced by an unforgiving coldness. This is rage. Her old home on Maple Avenue—and though she wasn't living there anymore, it was still, unquestionably, her home—was a three-story yellow house that used to be surrounded by other houses, other families. In the summer of 2000, it was the only house still standing in the Lincoln Drive floodplain. It was a baffling sight; in its dilapidated, miserable state, it seemed like a squatter's cabin, with the wide-open, deserted former neighborhood its played-out homestead.

At the time of the flood, most of the homes in Lincoln Drive were worth between $40,000 and $75,000; many homeowners had paid off their mortgages. When the Red River spilled over the lip of the Lincoln Drive dike, these houses became simply river debris. When the people of Lincoln Drive returned to their neighborhood, they found nothing was rooted anymore—not trees, nor gardens, nor swing sets, nor homes, and least of all, their lives.

Kelly Straub was determined to keep her family in Lincoln Drive, even if she had to be the only one brave or stubborn enough to defy the city's orders to keep out.

"We had moved nine times in six weeks," Kelly said. "And I decided if I'm moving again with this many kids and cats, I'm moving home." Someone from the city driving by Kelly's home saw the tent pitched in her front yard and snapped a photograph. "Are you living here?" Kelly remembers the person asking.

"Yeah, I am."

"You can't live here."

"Yes, I can." That exchange was the first, and quietest, of countless shouting matches between Kelly Straub and the City of Grand Forks.

Within a week of this confrontation, Kelly and her three children moved from the tent to a trailer outside of their home in Lincoln Drive. It was an act of civil disobedience. The city had forbidden anyone from living down in the fishbowl because it was, according to city and state health inspectors and anyone with reasonably good sense of sight and smell, not fit for human habitation. Kelly's home was a putrid mass of mud and maggots. On one especially difficult day, Kelly scooped up some mud the Red River had deposited in a corner of her living room and smeared the word "Survivor" on the south wall of her living room. A *Grand Forks Herald* photographer, cruising for a shot, came by her home a few days later. Kelly was digging out, dressed in rubber boots, heavy work gloves, and a dust mask. The photograph that appeared in the next day's *Herald* was of a smiling redhead trying to keep her balance atop a broken rocking chair while she reached over upended furniture to fight a stuck window. The word "Survivor," scrawled on the wall in mud, appeared just above Kelly's outstretched left arm.

But few in City Hall saw Kelly Straub as anything other than a whiner, a troublemaker who was getting way too much media attention. City attorney Howard Swanson wanted Kelly out of her home immediately and she refused.

"I wasn't doing it to punish anybody," Kelly said. "But these kids needed to work through the cleanup and what happens to all their stuff, what you can save, what you can't. You know, they needed to have some kind of closure. And I did too."

Kelly Straub's stubborn occupation of her Lincoln Drive home put Grand Forks city officials in a delicate position. The neighborhood had been declared uninhabitable, yet Kelly was insisting on staying. To make matters even more sticky, three children, all under the age of sixteen, were living near squalid, sewage and water-soaked homes where toxic black mold was flourishing in dark, moist pockets of debris. For reasons that still remain unclear, the city did not officially condemn Kelly's house, but city attorney Howard Swanson did condemn the children's playhouse, according to Kelly, a total of six times. (Swanson refuses to discuss his dealings with Kelly Straub or other individual homeowners.) If the Straubs left to run an errand, they might return to find the little yellow and blue playhouse, its roof collapsed by the flood, surrounded by yellow condemnation tape. The children would dutifully roll up the tape and place it in the trash can.

"The whole city's devastated and he has to take the time to harass me," Kelly said of Swanson. "I don't care what he wants, he's not getting it. If he's that desperate, the next year we were going to tie a big red bow on [the playhouse] and dump it in his front yard."

Legally, Howard Swanson had to concede that the city had no right to force Kelly out of her home unless it was condemned. But Corps engineers had deemed Kelly's home structurally sound, so there was no basis on which to condemn the home. They could only plead with her to consider her children's health.

Dragging Kelly Straub out of her home kicking and screaming—and that, she promised, was the only way she would go—would be a public relations nightmare. To many people outside city hall, Kelly's mulish attachment to her home was poignant; she was a fighter. To most Grand Forks city officials, however, she was proving to be an embarrassment.

Pat Owens visited Kelly at her home in early June 1997 and begged her to leave. Kelly refused. An hour later, Kelly says two representatives from social services appeared and told her that if she did not vacate her home, the city would take her children because they were in an unsafe environment.

"I said, 'You know what, you take my kids and I will take myself and any media I can possibly come up with—and now it's a lot—and you will find me standing on City Hall's steps. It's gonna be ugly. You don't want to take my kids.'"

People who had lost property and suffered damage in the 1997 Grand Forks flood found themselves trying to unravel a tangle of federal guidelines, provisos and prohibitions; if they had one loose thread in their hands, there was no telling where it would lead, if it could be extricated from the knot at all.

The cleanup and mitigation was not simply a matter of knocking down condemned houses, carting the debris to the dump, and constructing a new levee system in place of the old one. Homes—and all the emotional ties that bind people to them—would have to be cleared from the floodplains of Lincoln Drive, Riverside Park, and Central Park. The flood had delivered an incontestable rationale for a massive levee and floodwall system, and better floodplain management. The homes near the river would have to be torn down or relocated and the people living there would have to find new neighborhoods.

When the city of Grand Forks agreed to work with the U.S. Army Corps of Engineers on a new levee system, it had to also agree to clear the floodplains. If the federal government was to foot half the bill, the flood protection plan the city chose had to have a cost-benefit ratio of at least one to one. The Corps had to shape its project plans to satisfy this federal requirement. The city also had to agree to prohibit any kind of construction in the "hundred-year floodplain"—forever.

The federal buyouts, administered by the Grand Forks city council, would take place in phases. The city would first buy, then tear down, the "totaled" homes nearest the river—totaled, by definition, meant that damages amounted to at least half of the home's pre-flood value. Although the buyout was termed "voluntary," very little was voluntary about these "phase one" buyouts. The city would not let homes be rebuilt or repaired if their damage totaled more than half their value. It simply would not issue the permits. Homeowners could take the buyout or not. It really was just a question of whether the homeowner wanted money for the house. The home was coming down.

Then there were the homes that were now in the footprint of the proposed dike, and those numbered about two hundred. Some had suffered substantial damage, but some had not. Damaged or undamaged, they, too, would have to come down. The buyout process was, according to the city council members responsible for administering it, touch and go.

During the Mississippi floods of 1882, a reporter from the *New Orleans Time-Democrat* rode the packet *Susie* up the river from New Orleans to survey the damage. He saw cattle standing impassively in floodwaters up to their nostrils; at one farmhouse he watched frantic farmers evacuating hogs from temporary quarters in a back bedroom to a waiting skiff. But mostly the reporter noted with astonishment the cool obstinacy displayed by homeowners along the flooded banks.

"After weeks of privation and suffering," he wrote, "people still cling to their houses and leave only when there is not room between the water and the ceiling to build a scaffold on which to stand. It seemed to be incomprehensible, yet the love for the old place was stronger than that for safety."

More than one hundred years later, this sentiment was unchanged. No one was looking forward to the buyouts, called the Voluntary Acquisition Program by the federal government. Grand Forks city council members, themselves new to the federal appropriations game, were faced with making tough calls with limited information. When homeowners received what seemed like absurdly low offers from the city, they felt betrayed.

Most people on the Grand Forks city council wanted nothing to do with the buyouts. Even though nearly all of the council members still say that the city was extraordinarily generous to Grand Forks homeowners, it was clear that whoever had to administer this federal program would be seen as a bad guy. For the Grand Forks buyouts, there would be three "bad guys": Art Bakken, Sam Martinson, and LaVerne Babinchak, the buyout committee appointed by Mayor Pat Owens.

"Nobody wanted to do it," Bakken said later. "I got most of the jobs no one wanted to do; I don't mind doing them. I don't care what people think. I don't care if I'm reelected." A small, stocky, white-bearded man who wears his collars open to show off the weighty gold medallion around his neck, Bakken is also the owner of Pro Transport & Leasing, a Grand Forks trucking company. On the city council he represented the sixth ward, a district between Interstate 29 and South Washington Street that had suffered very little flood damage, and therefore would be relatively unaffected by the buyouts.

Sam Martinson, a Korean War vet, former fire captain, emergency medical technician, graduate of the National Fire Academy, and self-proclaimed "tough Norwegian," was not a player in city politics when close friend Pat Owens appointed him to the buyout committee (he would later become a city council member). He had been a Grand Forks realtor for more than thirty-two years and seemed in a good position to understand the often ineffable emotions that people felt about their homes. He had spent a career trying to make people happy; putting families in new homes, getting the best price for people who wanted to sell. These transactions were always voluntary. It would prove to be a whole different ball game when the sale was compulsory and the buyer set the price.

Finally, LaVerne Babinchak joined Art Bakken as the committee's second representative of Ward Six, the section of the city that had come through the flood unscathed. A slender woman with dark, narrow eyes and a bright flash of peroxide-blond hair, she had been a council member since 1994.

Because federal money was used to clear the damaged homes from the floodplain, federal rules had to be followed. There were many frustrations.

For instance, the few people who had listened to FEMA's earlier pleas to buy flood insurance found themselves almost penalized for having done so. Any money a homeowner received from a federal flood insurance policy was shaved off the city's buyout offer. Those who hadn't bought flood insurance, still received the house's full city-assessed value. With a policy like this, it would be hard to convince Grand Forks homeowners to buy flood insurance in the future.

Things weren't easy for the council, either. People in Grand Forks often circumvented the city permit office when they remodeled their homes. The city of Grand Forks, like any other city in the country, wanted to be apprised of residential improvements so property taxes could be appropriately increased.

After the flood, homeowners showed up at the tax assessment office with photographs of the home improvements that had been completed prior to the disaster. They offered the photographs as proof of increased value—the only proof, in the face of a ruined house. When city tax assessor Mel Carsen tried to match these photographs with a tax permit on file, he rarely found a match. The permits weren't there. It was an embarrassing situation for everyone. The homeowners were asking the city to bail them out, furnishing evidence of tax evasion as proof of their home's value, and the assessors would have to admit they had been duped. In the hectic months during the buyouts, city assessors were omnipresent. They were not, however, clairvoyant, so buyout offers were based on the city's most recent assessments. And if there was no record of remodeling since the last assessment, no amount of professed good faith could count as evidence for it. The flood had wiped out the proof. And without proof, it would be difficult to get the city to pay what homeowners felt was the fair price for their home.

The process seemed interminable. Any homeowner on the wet side of the dike or whose home's damage measured at least 50 percent of its value was living in limbo, suspended between a homecoming and a good-bye.

"A lot of people think everything is hunky-dory here now," Pat Moen, one of Kelly Straub's Lincoln Drive neighbors, told a Minneapolis reporter who had returned to Grand Forks in December to see how the city was recovering. "It's not; far from it. They're still messing around with this buyout. We're all still soaking wet, and to look at it, it's gonna be awhile before anybody's dry."

Early that winter Jim and Mary Lien received the city's buyout offer for their East Elmwood home. It was far less than they had expected, far less than they thought their home was worth. After weeks of deliberation, the Liens decided to appeal the city's buyout offer. These appeals had to be made at a city council meeting. The Liens were the first people to ask for an increase, and those in Grand Forks who had been too afraid to voice dissatisfaction with their own offers watched the proceedings very carefully.

Like the growing number of Grand Forks residents who knew they needed to sell their home to the city, the Liens had hired an independent assessor to produce an appraisal and see how it stood up next to the city's assessment. The city had offered them $158,300 for their home. The private appraiser they hired, a Grand Forks woman who had worked with the city before, said it had been worth $200,000. The city was, itself, working with an independent appraiser because of the state of the city's tax records (whole boxes of them were being freeze-dried in Bismarck). The city's appraiser was from Fargo, where homeowners were penalized for building on the floodplain, so he had shaved nearly $32,000 from the city's last tax assessment of the Liens' house. In Grand Forks, however, there was no such penalty, and the city missed the appraiser's error.

In Jim and Mary's case, Mel Carsen and his staff said they had not known the Liens had remodeled, and were unaware of the value of those improvements. The Liens, however, were adamant that the nature of their remodel job had not required them to notify the city of the improvement; Jim Lien had marched down to the city permit office during the job just to make sure. He said he had been assured he did not need a permit to strip the inside of his kitchen and outfit it with new cabinets, which was the extent of the improvements.

An open, spirited woman with a streak of black humor, Mary Lien was still nearly paralyzed with fear before appearing in front of the buyout committee. In fact, she was mortified, because that night in council chambers, in front of her neighbors, television cameras, and newspaper reporters with pens poised, Mary would lay out her private finances, including her mortgage burden, and then ask the city for $41,700 more for her house.

North Dakotans treasure their privacy. Initially a condition forced upon them by their isolation, it has become a birthright. But the work of disaster recovery meant that one's private life was split open like an apple and any bruises or wormholes could be examined by anyone who cared to look. Others, seeing their own lives would be laid bare if they appealed the city's buyout offer, chose to keep quiet. But the city council would speak up, and in the Liens' case, decide the couple was being greedy for seeking more money.

"We were made to feel like we were trying to put something over on the city," Jim said. The buyout appeals committee acceded to Mary's claim that the city's hired appraiser from Fargo had made a mistake in dropping $32,000 from the assessed value of their home. Despite the assessing mistake, the city's second offer was only ten thousand dollars more than its first offer. The Liens tried to stand firm; they insisted their home was worth $200,000. After much debate, the cameras rolling, the pens filling the lined pages of reporters notebooks, the appeals board finally offered the Liens $195,000.

This was $5,000 less than the Liens said their home was worth. It was also $36,700 more than the initial offer. The Liens were not happy. Their existing mortgage would have to be paid out of the buyout settlement, and so would the down payment on any new house they might find that was reasonably priced. An inflated housing market meant that the average price of a home in Grand Forks had leapt from just $67,000 before the flood to $80,000 six months after. Two years later, the average price of a home in Grand Forks would be $100,000. In addition to their mortgage, the Liens were paying monthly rent for a small apartment they had felt lucky to find. Nearly all their possessions had been lost in the flood, including essentials like shoes, clothes, and bedding for themselves and their six children. They had also spent thousands of dollars killing the black mold spores in their home as the city had ordered, had spent thousands of dollars trying to patch up their home before learning that they would be compelled to sell, had three children in college and Jim had just lost his job only a few years away from retirement.

And while that extra $5,000 was, as Mary Lien would put it, "so important," the more Jim and Mary thought about it, the more certain they felt they needed to get that $5,000 from the city for reasons that went beyond the merely monetary. It was now a matter of principle.

On January 5 the Liens appeared before the buyout appeals committee to make another plea to the city for the $5,000. Their request was rejected. About two weeks later, the Liens made their final appeal during a city council meeting. LaVerne Babinchak, and the other buyout committee members had had enough.

"We are not going to allow families in this community to dictate to this council," Mary Lien remembers Babinchak saying.

"If you're going to attack every family like we feel we've been attacked," Mary responded, "you're not going to have a city to govern." City council president Tom Hagness told the couple to take the $195,000 offer.

"It's more than I would have given you," he said. Jim and Mary were stunned and humiliated.

After these council meetings, council members sat in the chambers and wondered at the behavior of people like the Liens.

It seemed irrational, this attachment to a structure built of sheetrock, concrete, brick and mortar. But the idea of leaving home, of clearing those neighborhoods like a scythe cutting wheat, was not just a concept anymore; it was reality. Council member Duane Hafner, a cheerful and robust electrical engineer with NoDak Rural Electrical Cooperative, could often only shake his head.

"I would sit in the meetings and we would talk afterwards; how can so-and-so be so attached to their house? It's just a house," he said later. "If I could sit and reason with you that I'm going to offer you ten percent more than your house is worth, you'd say, 'Hey, I think I'm going to do that.'"

It would be a couple more years before he would understand the sorrow that led many homeowners to haggle over relatively small amounts of money. "When it's jerked away from you, unwillingly, it's a whole different psyche. These people had no choice. They woke up one day and they didn't have a house. You lose just about everything you have; they were fighting to keep what they could."

Peg Rogers recalled the pain of watching her parents' Lincoln Drive home being torn down. Four years later she could still remember exactly how long it took—twenty-two minutes.

"It seemed that a home filled with laughter and dreams and hopes could not be torn down so fast," she said. She also remembered—and would always remember—standing with her children outside their home, watching the Corps of Engineers load their ruined belongings into a garbage truck, then watching the truck drive toward the dump with its cargo—the remains of the Rogers' lives.

Art Bakken, however, was not moved. "People only hear what they want," he said. "You can tell people one thing, but they hear another. We sat through our appeals hearings and you could tell them exactly what we were doing and why; they didn't care." Bakken, and the rest of the city council, had grown frustrated with residents' demands, especially when many of them justified their requests for more generous buyout offers by admitting to earlier dishonesty.

But while Bakken seemed gruff and coldly unsympathetic to many people who went through the buyout process, he had actually gone out of his way during the flood to help those same people. When city residents—specifically those in Lincoln Drive, Central Park, and Riverside Park—were first allowed back into their neighborhoods, Bakken and his workers assembled cleanup kits, complete with rubber clogs, Dylex and other cleaning supplies, and distributed them to the people who needed them. Bakken's trucking company also helped FEMA and other relief organizations deliver food and water. Art Bakken considered that behavior simple common sense. When it came to the buyouts, common sense held that you got exactly what your house was worth, according to city tax records. "The program is meant to get you through a disaster; it's not meant to make you as well or better than before," Bakken said. "The problem with government aid is that you lose sight of the point you start from—the point you started from, 'Please help us a little bit' to 'Help us with everything.' The further and further you get into it, the greater the greed gets." The Liens might say the view from Ward Six—from the dry part of town—was rosy.

On the night the buyout committee denied the Liens the last $5,000 they asked for, Mary told the city council that it had abandoned Pat Owens' promise of "compassion and humanism." Later she would say the flood was "one of the most debilitating events of our lives" and that the celebrated Dakota ethic of good-neighbor compassion had deteriorated almost as soon as the river receded.

"We experienced being alone," Mary said. "Something never noted in our community. Everyone was engulfed in their own personal disaster."

9 *The Mistake*

Meteorology is the rock star of the earth sciences. Geology is a patient science, one in which great leaps of faith are made, but it wears a worn tweed suit with patches on the elbows and has a nervous cough. Biology, its taxonomic estate crowded with families, keeps its eye to the microscope, turning a cold shoulder to the public. But meteorology—and the complementary disciplines of hydrology and climatology—stops traffic. It gets the most face time on television, it sprawls across entire back pages of newspapers around the country, it is sanctioned to interrupt national programming, it has its own cable channel.

And yet visiting a National Weather Service forecast office or river forecast center is somewhat like going backstage at a rock concert: the scraggly-bearded roadies grumpily testing microphones, the frantic caterers making sure the buffet table has enough gluten-free products for the drummer, the weary, abused road manager who preps his band for the audience. The glamour belongs to the messengers—the television meteorologists. The message, however, has been significantly manipulated by the time it hits the airwaves.

The forecast seen on a local newscast bears little resemblance to the forecast produced in the offices of the National Weather Service. Here, information passes through a kind of sieve—the possibility ranges, the margins of error, and the caveats are almost always left out of the televised reports. Only the most clear-cut, comprehensible information is presented to the viewer. There simply isn't enough time in a three-minute weather report to cite the effects of ice action in a thawing river, the two- to ten-percent margin of error in a flood crest prediction, the effect of the current snowpack on flooding, and numerous other micro-factors. And, as the National Weather Service would discover in post-flood community meetings, the public wants concrete single-value numbers they can count on, absorb with as little effort possible, and use to pencil in their weekend plans. A barrage of hydrological factors will only confuse. As a result, a certain number can begin flashing like a neon light, and each time that number appears, it burrows deeper and deeper into the viewer's mind, until it becomes truth.

Perhaps one of the most frustrating aspects of federal meteorology is also one of its greatest successes—the public seems to think that, while the day-to-day forecasts might prove unreliable, making fodder for neighborhood conversation, the National Weather Service doesn't get the big weather events wrong. Its users tend to invest the agency with a kind of divinity. It can seem like a monolithic institution, composed not of humans but of robotic gods manning the ticker-tape machines that spit out forecasts.

It would be tough to overestimate the importance of the NWS, and weather prediction in general, to the river community of Grand Forks during a winter of such mythic proportions, and a flood that was, according to Frank Richards, the head of the agency's Hydrologic Information Center, an "act of God."

But the rating curve, perhaps the simplest tool in Mike Anderson's toolbox, came to bear a heavy burden. As time passed, blame was ascribed to elements that had not been identified earlier, elements that had become apparent only after months of scrutiny.

By far the most important variable in the 1997 Grand Forks flood was a loop—as neat as girl's hair bow—on the rating curve, caused when the river does not fall in the same pattern in which it had risen. Mike Anderson and Steve Buan momentarily suspected a loop in the rating curve as they scrambled for answers the night of Thursday, April 17.

"But okay," Anderson said, "what do you do with it? Where's the loop?" The loop was invisible—it could only be seen *after* the event when someone at the U.S. Geological Survey took the actual flood numbers from that event and drew a graph.

A looped rating curve is a difficult concept to explain to the public. It's especially difficult for a group of people used to working in what seems like a shadowy private club with its own argot. Every once in a while, though, they are compelled to stumble out of that club, squinting into the bright sunlight of the real world, and put into intelligible terms "what went wrong."

The National Weather Service told the North Dakota congressional delegation that "extrapolation of the rating curve did not account for anomalous behavior of the stage-discharge relation at levels higher than any previous observations." Mike Anderson could explain it better.

Four years after the flood, Anderson stood next to a whiteboard in the conference room of the NCRFC, picked up a red marker, and began to draw the Red River of the North the way most good hydrologists would: in terms of its slope.

"The Red River drops a foot a mile from Wahpeton to Grand Forks," he said as he began moving the red marker across the whiteboard in a mild downward slope. "You're going from Wahpeton to Fargo, you're going down, down, down, down, down . . . and pretty soon you're doing this." Anderson now dragged his red marker across the board slowly, drawing what appeared to be a heart monitor's flat line. The Red's course at Grand Forks had, in essence, reached the bottom of the fossil lake Agassiz and would run quite some time before heading up its north beach. "Big change," he said. "This can easily cause a lot of backwater. If the water isn't leaving as fast as it's coming in, it's going to start to back things up."

This is important because most flooding rivers rise and fall following the same pattern. "Say the river's rising," Anderson said. "At twenty feet it's flowing at, for the sake of argument, say two thousand cubic feet per second; when it comes back down and reaches twenty feet again, the volume of that river is two thousand cubic feet per second just a straight line, no guessing whatsoever." Mike Anderson had just described what the USGS rating curve for the Red River at Grand Forks looks like—what every USGS rating curve looks like: a single-value rating curve which, like most basic mathematical curves, is a "best-fit curve." Each point on the graph represents an actual measurement of the river's discharge and stage made at some point in time by the USGS, usually over a period of record (in Grand Forks' case, 117 years of measurements); the USGS differentiates between those measurements made as the river was rising and those made as it receded. But the river's height (in hydrology, the word "height" is used rather than "depth" to describe a flooding river) is usually the same for any given rate of flow, regardless of whether it is rising or receding. Put another way, a flood usually behaves in the way a baseball thrown straight up into the air appears to do; it goes up and then follows the same path down. That's what the Red River had done in 1997 at six of its seven forecast points, too. But at the fourth forecast point, Grand Forks, the baseball had stopped in midair, hovered, shot out horizontally, then continued falling (Fig. 4).

"It didn't follow that same curve back down," Anderson said. It took its own curve, its own path." The deviation the river took from the USGS rating curve, that is, from the path the USGS thought the Red would take, from the path the Red should have taken—had always taken—created a loop on that curve. The loop, unforeseen and invisible until after the flood when all the data had been analyzed and a new curve had been drawn, created a $3 billion controversy.

"The NCRFC uses a logarithmic technique for extending rating curves," hydrologist-in-charge Dean Braatz wrote in a paper for the National Hydrologic Warning Commission a few months after the crest. "However it does not adequately reflect the stage discharge relationship in complex hydrologic situations such as was observed at Grand Forks in 1997." When, early on, the computer model received river data that indicated a 49-foot

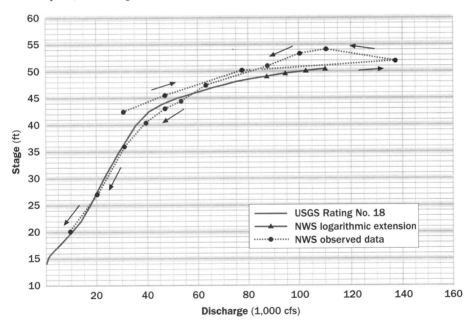

Fig. 4.
Looped rating curve at East Grand Forks, 1997 flood

crest, it stuck there because it had nothing else to refer to, and the model, teetering on the boundary of history and present, became unreliable. The rating curve went off the top of the graph paper into thin air.

The National Weather Service compared its data to the highest historical flood levels, and they did not have on file any hypothetical curves that charted hypothetical numbers. There was no feasible way for NCRFC hydrologists or other team members to draw rating curves for every possible hydrologic scenario that could produce a catastrophic flood—unless federal appropriations had funded a office for Red River basin research, which was not the case.

"They didn't deal in worst-case scenarios," Lynn Kennedy said.

Why not?

"The nature of the business. They're purely scientific and they're looking at facts that they had, and at what the facts could produce." Being purely scientific, in the world of the National Weather Service, means operating on verifiable data. Human judgment is a vastly inferior mode of operation, even if used sparingly. This is why, when Blizzard Hannah hit and no data arrived from the remote sensing pilots, the recon team, or the co-op observers, the Red River of the North flood was still, to the NWS, going to be a 49-foot flood. Leon Osborne could improvise when information channels closed: he filled in data gaps with his best educated guess. And as a meteorologist, Osborne could hazard a pretty good guess. At the National Weather Service, though, an educated guess wasn't permitted.

In 1997, the space between where the rating curve left off and the necessary human judgment began was not wide, but to people in Grand Forks, everything that went wrong during the flood could be traced to that one gap.

When it comes to the Corps of Engineers, you love them, hate them, or don't care about them; and if you don't care about them, you don't live near a river. This army of engineers, with ranks like lieutenant general, major general, command sergeant major and brigadier general, is also an army of civilians—only three percent of Corps employees are army soldiers or officers. In that way, the Corps is an unusual organization—a nonmilitary federal agency made up of private citizens, each of whom is accorded military habiliments. Every Corps engineer wears on his or her uniform the *Essayons* button—a small gold button minted with the image of a marine battery surrounded by water, bathed in the rays of a glowing sun and presided over by an eagle. It seems a declaration that controlling nature does not necessarily require a war waged against it. The word *essayons*, after all, means "let us try."

The agency's cheerful audacity, best illustrated when it offers to straighten or reroute a river, is almost charming. Not to everyone, though. John McPhee, that great documenter of the contests between men and nature, wrote about the Corps' attempts to handle the Mississippi near Baton Rouge, where it longs to relinquish its channel to the Atchafalaya River. Some people, he wrote, would "come to suggest that there was about these enterprises an element of hauteur."

Lisa Hedin, the project manager for the St. Paul district office and for the Grand Forks Flood Control Project, tried to appease heartbroken Reeves Drive residents who found their homes were on the wet side of the new dike line. She told them the Corps could straighten the Red's channel behind Reeves Drive and spare their homes. It was a classic Corps proposition. It was so expensive that the engineers hadn't considered it viable. Hedin was simply saying she could get it done.

The Corps of Engineers had been in Grand Forks for more than ten years trying to convince citizens they needed a more extensive flood protection system.

In the feasibility studies the Corps had drafted for various flood protection systems there, the agency calculated a hydraulic effect the National Weather Service had not: the damming effects of the bridges that cross the Red at Grand Forks. It was essentially an engineering detail, caught by the mind of an engineer. The Corps had even mentioned the damming effects on a flood in an agency newsletter that circulated in January of 1997.

"City bridges, particularly the Burlington Northern Railroad and DeMers Avenue bridges, obstruct flood flows at higher stages." After the flood, editorialists, city leaders and residents seized this fact, revealed by the *Grand Forks Herald*, as more proof of the National Weather Service failure to protect the city. As it turned out, these effects were not what "blew" the forecast—the presence of the bridges added only two-tenths of a foot of elevation to the crest at Grand Forks. But still, it was another factor the Corps had foreseen that the National Weather Service had not.

The Corps' feasibility study, the one that contained the rating curve that appeared to have "predicted" the actual flood crest, contained these elements: a map of Grand Forks and East Grand Forks, the Red River flow-ing between them, a projected flood, and the number 54 feet. It mattered little that this draft was completed in 1995, took no current weather data into account, and was not a response to the weather events of the winter of 1996–1997. Patrick Foley used only the study's rating curve to compare the Red's real-time rise that spring. None of this seemed to matter. What seemed to matter was that the Corps had a number that matched the 1997 crest at Grand Forks, and that the National Weather Service had not.

"Well, that's bogus," Greg Gust said three and a half years after the flood at the Grand Forks forecast office. "It's a non-issue, because the Corps did not have another rating curve for this river, for this location, for this dike, for this time."

What Gust was suggesting was that the feasibility study that so excited the critics was drafted for a nonexistent city—an engineer's city, existing in the realm of theory only. This extant river flowing by a nonexistent city in a parallel, engineer's universe had also flooded. This city looked like Grand Forks and stood on the banks the Red, but was surrounded and protected by a ring dike, something that the real Grand Forks did not have.

Gust suddenly stepped forward and pointed toward the city that lay a few miles beyond his extended arm. "There's no Grand Forks that ex-ists like that," he said." It was simply a model for a fictitious entity that doesn't exist. There is no city of Grand Forks in 1997 that has a ring dike around it with the specifications that were in the model that the Corps were playing with." Lynn Kennedy and Michael Lukes nodded gravely. "It's like me turning around today and saying, 'Gee, I wonder what would happen if we had three inches of rain on the current snowpack and what that would do,'" Gust continued facetiously. That kind of theoretical con-templation had no place at the National Weather Service; it was akin to daydreaming.

But Corps engineers bristle at the suggestion that they are daydream-ers. After the flood, they found themselves in a delicate position; while they didn't want to say they their rating curve had correctly "predicted" the 1997 Grand Forks flood, they also didn't want to say it couldn't have.

"The Corps rating curve could have been used in the National Weather Service model," Lisa Hedin said. "But the unpredictability of the flood with regard to snow, rain, cold and warm temperatures—there would have been insufficient time, equipment and materials to raise the emergency levees any further." This seemed to be the party line at the Corps—the data was correct, the rating curve capable of being operational, but there just wasn't enough time. And who would have thought to use a Corps rating curve from an old feasibility study to question the National Weather Service's million-dollar data? However, Hedin made one very important point that was echoed by the authors of the NWS's Service Assessment and Hydraulic Analysis: "It is possible to use hydraulic models in engineering studies to produce a rating curve for hypothetical flood control works or hypothetical flood events." Perhaps the National Weather Service was beginning to realize that "daydreaming" might not be such a bad thing after all.

A small article in the May 12 *Grand Forks Herald* written by a stringer named Mark Angeles mentioned that the daydreamers up north—the NCRFC's counterparts in Winnipeg at Manitoba's High Water Planning and Development branch of the province's Natural Resources Department—had produced "scenarios" of what the Red River might do.

"We always prepare for the worst," Larry Whitney, a PR man at that Winnipeg office said, "and we actually prepare a forecast that we call worst-case scenario." The way Canadian officials had prepared for the 1997 flood season was to use a range of scenarios. There seemed no shame in this in Winnipeg, especially since it worked. However, this was not an option that the National Weather Service was willing to consider.

"The more numbers you get into the mix," NCRFC hydrologist Dean Braatz said, "the more confusing it gets."

And yet the hoped-for new system, Advanced Hydrologic Prediction Services (AHPS) would produce more numbers for both the hydrologists and the customer to work with. In November of 1997, the National Weather Service Office of Hydrology finished its proposal for AHPS implementation for the Red River of the North at the NCRFC. It requested a complete overhaul of the Red River system. The models would take the Red's complexities into account—its tendency to retain backwater, its almost nonexistent slope—when it produced a forecast. The current model simply shoehorned a generic river model on the strange Red. This new calibrated model would take everything into account, even the vegetation growing on the river's banks. It also would produce a model sophisticated enough to handle information gaps and bad data.

As part of what the National Weather Service called a "seamless suite of user-friendly products," the NCRFC and Grand Forks office hydrologists would maintain and update an extensive Web-based system that anyone could access to see a huge range of numbers, based on probability. The user could decide what level of risk he was willing to live with, instead of relying on a single National Weather Service number. AHPS was almost holistic, in approach, and yet extremely advanced. It seemed just what people in Grand Forks—hydrologist and citizen alike—needed.

In September of 1997, the National Weather Service began holding "Red River Post-Flood Community Meetings" in towns up and down the river's course. In Grand Forks, Mike Anderson entered hostile territory.

"I was the forecaster that put out the forty-nine feet and walked into a situation like this," he said. "I basically laid it out on the table: We had the discharge nailed ten days ahead of time." Anderson went on to do his best to explain the looped rating curve and the backwater effects, while Richard Pomerleau discussed the effects ice jams had had on the river during the flood. At each post-flood meeting in the valley, the hydrologists broached the idea of issuing flood crest numbers as a range, a probability. Each time, the resounding response was that the emergency managers, the mayors and the townspeople wanted "single value, best estimate." They wanted a single number. The hydrologists from the NCRFC were disappointed, and deeply frustrated.

"They're looking for a number, and I totally support that," Anderson said. "But it's difficult just to give a number. These are things that we, as an agency, are trying to work out to make it simpler for our user to understand. To get rid of the technical jargon, and yet get something out there that is usable: You got a ninety percent chance of reaching flood stage, you got a fifty percent chance of getting a couple feet above flood stage, and you've got a ten percent chance that it's going to get to the flood of record." He paused. "Well, when we hand that to the user, especially on the Red River, now they're saying, 'What are we supposed to do with this?'"

The new hydrologist-in-charge at the NCRFC, a brittle Chicagoan named Daniel Luna, was more to the point: "They don't like it because the onus is on them to look at the data and say 'What risk are we willing to live with?' They want a number. We all like numbers," Luna continued, bitterly, "because then, if it fails, we can point a finger at someone and say 'You told me this.'"

The National Weather Service made itself understood best when it spoke in plain language: most of the flood insurance policies purchased in the Red River valley in 1997 were purchased not when the outlook crest numbers were released, but on March 19, the day after Dr. Elbert "Joe" Friday held a national press conference warning North Dakotans and Minnesotans of "more water than they've ever seen before in their lives."

Roger Pielke was not surprised. In his conversations with the NWS hydrologists manning the computers during the spring of 1997, he found that, like the townspeople, the agency's employees also had exaggerated confidence in the accuracy of their predictions.

"Their idea that the model would automatically extrapolate gave an improper sense of precision in their estimate," Pielke said. "At a minimum, there is a lot of uncertainty in the choice. It's pretty clear in hindsight there's no single rating curve that can be right. Inherent uncertainty wasn't appreciated by anyone, including the people issuing the forecasts." In addition, Pielke found that the National Weather Service's distillation of a complex numerical and statistical hydrological forecast down to a single number—something the agency felt was a service to a public who tuned out when forecasts got diffuse and number-heavy—resulted in a misleading forecast. "The National Weather Service knows better," Pielke said. No one, it seemed, was going to win this battle over blame.

After the 1997 flood, the National Weather Service's main failing—its ironic flaw—was built like an O. Henry plot twist. The certainty it and its customers ascribed to its products was a testament to its greatest strength: its accuracy in previous floods. But now it was almost as if the agency had to undermine that reputation in order to save it. To emphasize the uncertainty inherent in prediction would seem to cast doubt on the agency's abilities. Yet Roger Pielke believes that was exactly what the National Weather Service had a moral obligation to do.

"I have argued in many settings that it is indeed the responsibility of the National Weather Service to ensure that its products are both useful and properly used," Pielke said. "Technical skill is only a benefit insofar as it can be translated into useful knowledge for decision making."

However, the question National Weather Service asked one another— "What part of 'record flooding' did they not understand?"—eerily echoes a post-flood comment from the U.S. Weather Bureau (the National Weather Service in its formative years) following the 1927 Mississippi flood. After a spring filled with unprecedented rainfall, huge amounts of water in the Mississippi's tributaries, and flow fluctuations, the Weather

Bureau stated "there was needed neither a prophetic vision nor a vivid imagination to picture a great flood."

On December 11, Commerce Secretary William Daley announced that he would award a silver medal for outstanding work in river forecasting to the Grand Forks forecast office and the NCRFC for their work during the spring flooding. The announcement shocked, and then incensed, many in Grand Forks. The NCRFC had correctly predicted flood crests for nearly every forecast in the Red River and Mississippi River basins in 1997—except for Grand Forks—so it could be argued that it deserved the award. Regardless, it was widely believed, in Grand Forks anyway, that the announcement was mainly a morale booster.

"Good for whose morale?" Leon Osborne wanted to know when he learned of the award. "The NWS's morale, or for the public of Grand Forks? Did those people wear that badge of honor around Grand Forks? No. Did it really have the morale boost they expected it to have? I don't know." Councilman Bob Brooks was less contemplative: "They shouldn't have even accepted the award."

Like the city it covered, it seemed the *Grand Forks Herald* had been suffering dark moods. The *Herald* had been around since Grand Forks' grimy frontier days; at 117 years old, it was one of Knight-Ridder's oldest newspapers. Along the way, it had snuffed out competing papers, so that for decades it had been the only daily in town. It is one of only three sources for local news, the others being Grand Forks' tiny ABC affiliate WDAZ, and KCNN radio. In spite of losing its office, archives, and printing press, the *Herald* continued to publish without missing one issue. As a result, the paper became a kind of lifeline to evacuees who had no idea what was happening to their neighborhoods.

The journalism that came out of the 1997 flood was impressive and valuable, if occasionally self-congratulatory. ("In a weird sort of way Grand Forks is now the *Herald*," Mike Jacobs told a reporter just after the flood crested. "It's the tangible part of Grand Forks, and we just really feel like it's important.") The photojournalism was particularly striking. But most importantly, the *Herald* performed a crucial public service.

Like any good newspaper, the *Herald* kept its eye to the keyhole when it came to city business, especially now that so much federal money was involved and the tasks at hand were so consequential. It made stars of the city council members. At a certain point, however, when rebuilding was well underway, the tone of the *Grand Forks Herald* noticeably shifted.

Editor-in-chief Mike Jacobs was angry. He had written an editorial on April 17 scolding people for listening to "rumors" of a higher crest. He had, in many ways, defended the National Weather Service's honor in those hectic days of the flood fight. His own house was damaged, along with the houses of hundreds who had heeded his advice to ignore rumors of a higher crest. The *Herald*'s editorials, and even its news coverage, were so critical of the National Weather Service that NCRFC employees began to bristle any time the *Herald* was mentioned. For a city desperate for a scapegoat, Jacobs had found one.

Mike Jacob's editorial on May 5, 1997, the day after the "$800 million oversight" article appeared, twisted a knife already plunged deep into the heart of the NCRFC.

"Disappointment, not anger, is the emotion of the hour," Jacobs wrote. "That two agencies of the same federal government, studying the same river, failed to share their separate conclusions; that officials of one agency waited so long to express that their conclusions about the river were different, and more ominous, than the conclusions the other agency published; that local officials weren't able to use the information that federal agencies had developed to make plans to fight the rising river; and that thousands of people have suffered."

Jacobs' emphasis on the word "disappointment," juxtaposed with the word "anger," was tactical. By affecting resigned disappointment rather than overt anger, he delivered a blow that was keenly felt in the NCRFC offices. Jacobs was like an imposing yet reserved father who reacts to a major transgression by telling his child: "I'm deeply disappointed in you."

Jacobs concluded his editorial: "There is no point in pointing fingers or assessing blame." The faux-conciliatory conclusion, however, conveyed the blame more effectively than an outright accusation would have. As lagniappe, Jacobs had printed, on a back page featuring the artwork, poems, and thoughts of Manvel schoolchildren, the work of seventh-grader Michael Docker: "You wonder if the National Weather Service equipment is malfunctioning, or if they just can't predict a flood if it hit them." Although Jacobs advised against finger-pointing, he continued to publish editorials about the mistake. The day after his "disappointment, not anger" editorial, he followed up by calling his readers' attention to the National Weather Service–Corps controversy in an otherwise unrelated editorial on looting, titled "Ethical Scavenging—It Can Be Done." "True, there is dismay federal agencies didn't talk to each other . . . [which] might have prevented some of the flood's damage," he wrote.

A few weeks later, in his editorial chastising the Corps' Colonel J.M Wonsik for declining numerous interview requests but then complaining about the *Herald*'s "$800 Million Oversight" article, Jacobs wrote: "Col. J.M. Wonsik is too defensive by half . . . at the time the article was published, the *Herald*'s editorial board expressed disappointment that the two federal agencies had failed to coordinate more closely on flood predictions. That same disappointment remains." The headline: "More disappointment from the Army Corps." In closing, however, Jacobs wrote: "The *Herald* has no interest in assigning blame for the Red River flood . . . there's no time now for recriminations. Let's move on."

Although the National Weather Service had no official reaction to the *Herald*'s stories and editorials, in the NCRFC offices a storm was brewing. Even employees as far away as the Kansas City office and personnel at headquarters in Silver Spring were indignant. Angry e-mails circulated from office to office, commiserating with the Red River crew; public affairs officers took breaks from damage control to fume about a "negative" article or television report; every article the *Grand Forks Herald* published that mentioned the National Weather Service was circulated via e-mail.

Yet the hydrologists who were being criticized had been gagged. They could not defend themselves—the agency didn't want them to. Following the federal line, the National Weather Service brass felt it was best to ignore most of the criticism. It was a tough rule to follow, most particularly for employees stationed in Grand Forks. They had to live among their critics; many of them had grown up with those who now blamed them for ruining many lives. Some had to drive by the "49 Feet My Ass" sign on their way to work.

On January 6, 1998, a National Weather Service public affairs man, Patrick Slattery, scheduled a meeting with the *Grand Forks Herald* editorial board. Slattery planned to fly up from Kansas City, "get in some rehearsal time" with three employees from the Grand Forks office, and "finally come to a peace agreement with the *Herald*."

On the morning of January 15, Patrick Slattery, Lee Anderson, Wendy

Pearson, and warning coordination meteorologist Jim Belles sat down with six members of the *Herald*'s editorial board: opinion editor Tom Dennis, columnist Ian Helms, city editor Julie Copeland, reporter Doreen Yellowbird, and editor-in-chief Mike Jacobs. In a post-meeting memo, Slattery wrote that "the most vehement critic of the National Weather Service has been Mike Jacobs. Through the course of the conversation, it was revealed that Mr. Jacobs is one of the Grand Forks residents who did not buy flood insurance and subsequently lost his home to the flood. It's obvious that he remains angry and wants to blame someone other than himself for that loss. His anger/bitterness became evident a couple of times during the meeting, as it has in the editorials he's written. I found it interesting that Mr. Helms lost all his possessions in an apartment house fire during the flood, but he seems to hold no animosity."

The session may have been emotionally loaded for the National Weather Service employees, but for the *Herald* staffers, it was just another meeting.

"I remember a fairly straightforward editorial board meeting," Tom Dennis said. "I remember Jacobs making the point at the meeting that there are other number predictions in a weather forecast that are taken at face value, so it was understandable that he and everybody had taken forty-nine feet in that way." Normally, Dennis said, an editorial board meeting results in a story in the next day's newspaper. When he searched the archives years later, however, he found no story had been published regarding the meeting.

The Grand Forks forecast office staff spent some time explaining National Weather Service operations and flood forecasting procedures to the editors and reporters sitting across from them. When asked why no one from the NWS had responded to the *Herald*'s post-flood editorials, Slattery explained that the service assessment team was the agency's tool for determining how well—or how poorly—it had performed. Opinion editor Tom Dennis invited Lee Anderson to write an editorial; the *Herald* promised to run it ("a course of action I recommend against," Slattery noted in the memo). Despite what seemed like a productive meeting, Slattery couldn't help but comment that Mike Jacobs seemed to be "the only one of the *Herald* group to adhere to preconceived notions, turning mostly a deaf ear to what our group had to say."

In mid-April, the *Grand Forks Herald* was awarded the 1998 Pulitzer

Prize for service. The *Herald*'s staff heroics during the flood were noted in the Pulitzer citation, as well as the paper's "sustained and informative coverage, vividly illustrated with photographs, that helped hold its community together in the wake of flooding, a blizzard and fire that devastated much of the city, including the newspaper plant itself." Mike Jacobs represented the *Herald* at the ceremony and accepted the medal from Columbia University president George Rupp with a smile. Overlooked was the *St. Paul Pioneer Press*, which had made the *Herald*'s continued publication possible. Staffers from the Twin Cities daily had volunteered to send the *Herald*'s copy electronically to the *Pioneer Press*'s printing facility, facilitate the printing, and load thousands of papers into the belly of a chartered plane, which made an early-morning flight to Grand Forks every day for more than two months. Because the Pulitzer committee gave the *Herald* its award for service, rather than for excellence in reporting, some in the Twin Cities thought it might have been appropriate to split the honor between the two newspapers.

The day the *Herald* won the Pulitzer, Lee Anderson wrote Jacobs a letter of congratulation. There is no record that anyone at the NWS sent a similar note when Jacobs received another large honor: the American Society of Newspaper Editors gave him a "Distinguished Writing Award" for his editorials following the flood.

10 *To Rebuild a City You Must Take It Apart*

In the warming summer of 1997, everywhere residents of Grand Forks turned, they saw red-jacketed Corps engineers. The Corps, which had almost immediately identified an extensive levee system as the city's best flood control option, was under pressure by homeowners who were rumored to be in danger of losing their homes to the new dike. The immediate post-flood fervor—during which everyone seemed in favor of a massive dike project to keep the Red from ever invading the city again—had waned. It had waned when it became clear that homes would be sacrificed to the new dike. The Corps had not yet publicly tagged the project with a positive benefit-cost ratio, but it was clear to many people that a diversion channel was at the bottom of its list of options; it just was not feasible, economically or environmentally. Those homeowners who had suffered minimal flood damage, but who were in the footprint of the proposed dike, were becoming more vocal, their complaints more strident, and their criticism more accusatory.

The problem for the Corps of Engineers was not that their language was too complex—it was that their message was one that many citizens did not want to hear. Clearly, the area needed a new flood protection system as soon as possible. In August, Pat Owens and East Grand Forks mayor Lynn Stauss had asked the Corps of Engineers to develop a major flood protection plan. The request was only the latest volley in a long exchange between the cities of Grand Forks and East Grand Forks on the one hand and the Corps of Engineers on the other. This match had been going on for more than ten years.

In the mid-1980s, when the Corps was working with the city of East Grand Forks—at the city's request—to design a system to protect it from a catastrophic flood, the Corps had balked at suggestions that the Red River be diverted as drastically as it was in Winnipeg. In its feasibility studies, the Corps had determined that a diversion ditch was far too expensive to seriously consider. It had instead favored a citywide dike and floodwall system that would have protected the city from a 49-foot crest. With a cost-benefit ratio of 1 to 1.70 (or $1.70 saved for every dollar spent on the project), the project seemed like a go. Congress approved funding for the project, and the Corps presented it to city officials from both sides of the river.

Both cities rejected the plan.

"Part of it was just about money," Lisa Hedin said. "But some of it was because of the engineering realities; the levee had to be set back quite a ways and in East Grand Forks that would have cost them about a block and a half of downtown. Well, they weren't willing to do that in the mid-eighties; but after '97, they had already lost two blocks of downtown."

At a January 7, 1998 luncheon at the Grand Forks Holiday Inn, the Corps presented dike alignment blueprints to local and federal leaders. Lisa Hedin had recommended using three kinds of hydraulic structures: clay dikes, concrete floodwalls, and a mechanically stabilized earth wall. The Corps envisioned a set of levees and floodwalls set back from the river, turning the city of Grand Forks into a tiny planet with three rings: one of earth, one of clay, and one of reinforced concrete.

The estimated cost: $360 million. The Corps' project would protect the city of Grand Forks from a flood equal to that of 1997, which according to the Corps was a 210-year flood event. (The USGS designates it a 118-year flood event; such frequency numbers, both agencies agree, are useless, but people like numbers, as the National Weather Service had discovered.) Under even the most hopeful and accommodating of the Corps proposals, large chunks of many Grand Forks neighborhoods would find themselves on the wet side of the new dike line. The homes there would have to be destroyed or moved.

"The fact that anyone was allowed to build in Lincoln Drive, Central Park, and Riverside Park is a crime," Ken Vein said. "We then had to live with those sins." In the weeks and months after the flood, homeowners who had lost everything stopped Vein in the street to beg him to build the dikes high enough to keep the river out of the city for good. Never again, they said. Vein heard those pleas in his sleep, took them as orders. Making sure the river never again overtopped the dikes seemed to Vein, as an engineer, a point of honor.

As often happens in river towns, the oldest, prettiest homes were built on high ground, affording homeowners a view of the water. While Lincoln Drive and Central Park were working-class neighborhoods, Reeves Drive and Riverside Park were home to Grand Forks' most beloved houses. Reeves Drive was by far the most affluent neighborhood, with homes that were relics from the Dakota boom years. The houses on Reeves Drive—home to the Grand Forks aristocracy—stood on either side of the street like monuments. The architect Joseph Bell DeRemer also designed a number of homes in the riverside neighborhoods; he lived in what was Riverside Park, where he would pluck a blossoming bachelor's button from the garden each morning, push it through his buttonhole, and head off to work. It was Reeves Drive, however, that was a museum of DeRemer masterpieces.

On paper, the Corps' flood structures would slice through Reeves Drive, leaving half the museum pieces on the wet side of the dike and half on the dry side. Among the threatened homes were a number of old Queen Anne homes, a Dutch Colonial, and a Cotswold cottage with a shingled imitation thatch roof. Nearly all of the homes lining Reeves Drive had historical importance in the eyes of the State Historical Society in Bismarck. Gayle Clifford, then the society's president, was married to Tom Clifford, one of the most powerful men in Grand Forks, former University of North Dakota president and chair of Mayor Owens' business redevelopment committee. She was entirely opposed to the sacrifice of any historic home in the city. "In Europe they save everything," she told the *Herald* in early 1998. "They never consider tearing down a place like this." She and her husband lived on Reeves Drive.

Reeves Drive was problematic for the Corps, even without the public pressure to draw the dike alignment around it, because two federal mandates were diametrically opposed there. The U.S. government expected the Corps to keep those mandates on separate and equal footing: viable flood protection and historic preservation. Often these goals are incompatible. Six Reeves Drives homes that had been deemed eligible for National Historic Register listing were in the footprint of the dike.

About two miles downstream from Reeves Drive, the residents of Riverside Park were slowly beginning to accept that their entire neighborhood was likely going to be sacrificed to keep the town dry. The St. Anne's Rest Home on the north end of Lewis Boulevard was another important landmark—freighted with emotional weight for many people in the city, especially older people. Before the rest home was turned into a retirement home it was St. Michael's Hospital and Nurses Residence. Many people in Grand Forks had been born there; many people had said their last goodbyes to loved ones there. Pat Owens was born there in 1941. But the picturesque former hospice and hospital was in the line of the proposed dike.

In the months—weeks, even—following the flood, the Corps and the city found themselves under great pressure to make some decisions, and to make them quickly. At those first public city council meetings at the Chester Fritz Auditorium, people—many still dressed in flood clothes donated by the Salvation Army—had demanded that the city give on-the-spot approval to an extensive, costly dike system that had been immediately drawn up by the Corps and city engineer Ken Vein. That early plan would demolish or relocate 650 homes and 135 businesses. Certain people wanted quick answers to the dike question: the people whose homes were located in the devastated areas of Lincoln Drive, Riverside Park, and Central Park, but whose homes' damage measured less than 50 percent. They wanted to know if it was worth their while to dump money into rebuilding. An inviolable dike line would tell them whether their homes would be on the wet side or the dry side.

But another camp did not want decisions being made under the gun—mainly the vocal Reeves Drive crowd whose minimally damaged homes were also on the wet side of the proposed new dike line. The most vociferous of the Reeves Drive homeowners was a man named Hal Gershman. Gershman owned a chain of liquor stores called Happy Harry's—big red barnlike warehouses scattered around town. At that tense first public city council meeting on May 12, Gershman had approached the microphone and dispensed a bit of well-timed, well-articulated hyperbole: "Our city has been through three catastrophes: a blizzard, a flood, and a fire. We are about to have a fourth: the wrecking ball. Demolishing large parts of downtown and our neighborhoods in order to make a dike will destroy the architectural character of this community, drastically shrink our tax base, and forever alter the sense of who we are."

Gershman advocated an alternative that most of the city's engineers, along with all of the Corps engineers, believed was simply unfeasible. He wanted that diversion because it would "allow us to stay closer to the river."

At the urging of Reeves Drive residents, the Corps began work on a study of the alternative. It later found, through collaboration with a private engineering firm, that the channel would have to be nearly twenty-three miles long, a half-mile wide, and thirty feet deep. It would require the sacrifice of nearly 3,000 farm acres and 7,332 habitat acres. The diversion would have a dire effect on water quality. It would also degrade 649 acres of wetland because of the necessary lowering of groundwater elevation.

But it would save six homes.

"It's very hard for us to come in and say, 'We've really looked at it hard and these are the two hundred homes that have to go for the rest of the city and here's why they have to go, here's the engineering principle behind why they have to go,'" Lisa Hedin said. "People say you've *got* to find another solution."

To many in Grand Forks, sacrificing huge amounts of farmland for an enormous diversion was an appropriate solution; there seemed to be so much of it in the surrounding area. There was, however, only one Riverside Park neighborhood, only one Reeves Drive. "You could argue that farmland has a greater emotional value because these are century farms, and your great-grandmother came out here and planted this peach tree," Hedin said. "You could debate the emotional value forever."

There was more: the project would take an estimated thirteen years to complete and would cost nearly $450 million. To a federal government watching its pocketbook, a small North Dakota city did not warrant a project of the magnitude of a Winnipeg diversion. The government would not pay for it. It was that simple.

City engineer Ken Vein either made a mistake at this point, or he didn't. He publicly agreed with the Corps of Engineers. The relationship between private engineers and Corps engineers has, historically, been rocky; the animosity spilled over during early efforts to confine the Mississippi. Vanity has always played a part. In the late nineteenth century, civilian engineer James Eads battled with Corps chief Andrew Atkinson Humphreys over how to contain the Mississippi south of New Orleans. It was not only a battle of ideas, but also a battle of two colossal egos. The better idea proposed by the better engineer, Eads, won the day. The Corps had been shown up, and Humphreys, bitter and embarrassed, considered Eads a lifelong enemy. It is only recently that private and civic engineers and Corps engineers have learned to work together, but cooperation is still tenuous.

In this case, however, the civilian engineer found he agreed with the Corps. James Eads had said his opinions were "impersonal, a question of science, efficiency and truth," and Vein seemed to consider his own to be the same. Still, many in Grand Forks suspected collusion. To agree with the Corps meant that you, like the Corps, cared more about hydraulics than humans; it meant that you would rather see a permanent dike on the banks of a river than a pretty house there with a garden; it meant that you would prefer to hem in the river and obliterate all river views rather than allow a community to gather near the banks.

But to be in bed with the Corps in its dealings in Grand Forks also meant that you didn't want to see the Red River flow through the streets of downtown again, and that you were willing to take drastic steps to be certain that it would never again happen. The recommendation to go with the Corps' proposal—an endorsement, really—would not have come as a surprise to anyone with an engineering degree. But, understandably, the people in the footprint were determined to find any alternative plan that would spare their homes. The Corps had made it clear that while a flood-wall was certainly feasible theoretically, economically the city would take a hit, because a floodwall was not part of the U.S. government's plan. If it were built, the city would have to pay for it—all of it. Ken Vein felt the city would be better protected if the homes were removed from the footprint anyway. While some people suspected Vein was simply power-hungry, the engineer said it his moral obligation to choose what he believed to be the most viable plan.

"We were vulnerable, we were scared. Some people never forgot that, said never again," Vein said. "I couldn't and didn't want to see anyone have to suffer those kinds of losses again. I didn't want to stand face to face again with people who would ask me, 'What am I supposed to do now, where am I supposed to live?' They were asking tough, appropriate questions. But engineers primarily work in a factual world; this was an emotional situation."

It was disturbing to Vein that emotion had crept into his professional life; the edges of his two worlds—private and professional—were bleeding into one another. Vein's discomfort was made more acute when the city council hired a Seattle engineering firm to examine Vein and the Corps' research and to identify dike options that might possibly save some homes along the dike lines. Despite the months Vein and the Corps had spent on riverbank stabilization tests and soil tests, in endless meetings, and in tough confrontations with distressed homeowners, the city seemed to be telling Vein: we don't believe you.

The Seattle firm of Shannon & Wilson began exploring riverbank stabilization options in early 1998. The independent engineers were slated to hand the council a report later that year. Corps engineers, including project manager Lisa Hedin, were cordial and provided Shannon & Wilson with all appropriate paperwork, but privately they were as offended as Vein was.

"It didn't make our team all that much happier, at least initially, to say 'You know what, these folks are coming in from out of state and we want you to lay everything out on the table for them, let them look through your papers,'" Lisa Hedin said. "It indicates a huge lack of trust."

On May 22 Ken Vein called the office of Shannon & Wilson and told the firm to halt its technical review of the Corps' research. He did not tell anyone outside the engineering department that he had ordered a stop to the review. He later said he had wanted to buy some time to tinker with the Corps' proposal before Shannon & Wilson presented its findings to the council.

Two months went by before anyone noticed that Shannon & Wilson was no longer on the job. When the firm's absence was finally noted, and the story came out that Vein had not consulted anyone before sending Shannon & Wilson back to Seattle, Pat Owens says her advisers told her, point blank, to fire Vein from his position as tri-chair of the flood recovery effort. Instead, she met with a group of Vein's critics and tried to pacify them. She promised to talk to her city engineer.

"People thought Ken was demonstrating too much power and being arrogant," Owens said. "I'd try to smooth it over, but he didn't like being questioned. I asked Ken to move it a little faster." Vein countered by saying he was disappointed that the mayor had met with his critics. He told her he didn't feel she was supporting him. "I said, 'Ken, you were supported,'" Owens recalled. "But it was at a standstill and people were urgently needing an answer."

The August 3 city council meeting was crowded with angry homeowners whose houses were in the footprint. Owens then proceeded, in the words of the *Grand Forks Herald,* to "pour political retardant on a firestorm" by apologizing to the city—ostensibly on Ken Vein's behalf. Vein sat in the front row, fuming.

"I'm sincerely sorry if we broke down trust with you," Owens said. Former city council president Tom Hagness, who had recommended the firm, told the council and the audience that he was disturbed that Vein had taken the initiative to delay the firm's research. He turned from the podium and looked Vein straight in the eye. "We'd worked well together," he said. Shannon & Wilson provided hope for residents in the footprint, Hagness concluded. Vein might have thought the hope offered by the firm's research was false.

"It kind of wears you out," Lisa Hedin said. "If you're not an engineer, and you don't trust the Corps anyway, you don't trust the federal government for whatever reason—whether you think the flood predictions were wrong in '97 or you remember back to '79 when the levees were going up on the other side of the river from Oslo and you were unhappy about that, or your parents lost some land outside of Valley City when the Baldhill dam was built in the fifties . . . for whatever reason, you decided you don't trust the Corps."

Most Corps projects are met with deep suspicion and some resistance in the communities in which they are constructed. When Lisa Hedin goes anywhere in her red Corps of Engineers jacket, she knows she's going to get an earful from someone, whether it's a Minnesota farmer from Hastings who's angry that the Corps didn't prevent the Mississippi from flooding his crops or a veteran who wants to vent about the Corps' work in the Everglades.

"We don't go around saying, 'Boy, we're just running a little low on levee work, we haven't done a good levee in a long time. Let's think where we can build one,'" Hedin said, then laughed. "I would speculate that it was people thinking either we were trying make more work for ourselves, which is sort of illogical because if that were true we would have supported the diversion which was another four hundred million dollars. Or that we were just sort of . . ." she paused. "Arrogant, maybe?"

In 1998, the National Oceanic and Atmospheric Administration, or NOAA, had requested a budget increase of $4.2 million to start implementing the new Advanced Hydrologic Prediction System in the Red River valley, among other river basins. When the 1997 flood occurred, the National

Weather Service had been in the midst of a $4.5 billion modernization program, but it had been proceeding slowly. The AHPS was only one component of the agency's proposed National Disaster Reduction Initiative, a program designed to modernize forecasting techniques and equipment in order to prevent millions of dollars in weather-related damages. NOAA predicted that the implementation of AHPS alone would "provide the national economy $600 million a year through fewer flood losses."

While the agency's ultimate goal had always been to implement AHPS in all major river basins, the Red River basin had been fairly low on the list. The events of 1997, however, changed all that. The North Central River Forecast Center was now considered the highest priority. As the NCRFC waited for word on funding, it had spent the year patching what it could with limited resources. Its hydrologists had modified the forecasting system: it now warned forecasters more explicitly when the model automatically extended a rating curve. They had also integrated the Corps' hydraulic analysis of the Red River at Grand Forks—including engineering details like the presence of bridges—into its forecasting model. Other NCRFC employees had spent many months recalibrating the Red River forecasting system with updated historical data.

In March of 1998, the President's budget provided $5.5 million for weather and flood forecasting improvements. It had come at a steep price.

All over Grand Forks, streets were being cleaned up, debris was being removed, businesses were refurbishing. But something else was shadowing Grand Forks through its recovery each step of the way. Grief.

"Like a watery ghost," *St. Paul Pioneer Press* reporter Nick Coleman wrote when he visited the city one year after the disaster, "the flood has divided Grand Forks into one city of the hopeful and healed, and another city of the bitter and tormented."

It seemed Lincoln Drive was home to many of those bitter and tormented. Lincoln Elementary School had been so ravaged that the city had torn it down almost at once. In its place the city planned to build a school it would call Phoenix. The name was, to some, ironic. That's because the person who had loved that school most, the person who had spent the most time there, the person who had considered it "home" even more than his own Lincoln Drive house—that person would not return to work there when the new school opened.

Harlan Thompson was Lincoln Elementary School's janitor. Sixty-four years old and unmarried, Thompson had made the school the center of his universe. "He knew the kids by their first names," Coleman wrote, "knew which kids needed a winter coat or a pair of mittens, knew how to make sure they got them without making a big deal out of it." Thompson was considered a kind man by neighbors, "a saint," in the words of one Lincoln Drive resident. The house he lived in was heavily damaged, but what he lost there could not compare to what he lost when Lincoln Elementary was slated for demolition. His friends in Lincoln Drive soon noticed Thompson couldn't drive across any of the city's bridges without weeping.

On August 17, three days before the city of Grand Forks began tearing down Lincoln Elementary School, the *Herald* reported that Thompson had "died unexpectedly" the day before. Everyone in Lincoln Drive knew. Harlan Thompson had hanged himself in his home.

Just a few blocks from what used to be the elementary school, Nick Coleman found Kelly Straub's neighbor Judy Haney in her garage, sorting through year-old debris. The house next to the garage was a ruin, and Haney wasn't living there anymore. She just visited it every single day to cry over it and to pick through the remains of her Lincoln Drive life. The day Coleman visited Lincoln Drive, the city had planned a "day of remembrance" to mark the one-year anniversary of the flood. Some people had planned to attend church services. Others wanted to climb atop the dikes and hold a vigil. In East Grand Forks, city officials planned to set off fireworks. But when Coleman asked Judy Haney how she was planning to commemorate the flood, she told him, "I'm not celebrating any anniversary of the flood. It's too painful." For her, as for Kelly Straub and many of the holdouts in Lincoln Drive, the flood wasn't over.

"The city says, 'Judy, get over it! Judy, get on with your life!'" she told Coleman. "But this is my life. My life was here, in this house, for twenty-nine years! I'm not ready to 'get over it.'" Like so many in Grand Forks, Judy was in counseling for depression. The grief in Grand Forks was hidden behind closed doors, barely perceptible in the faces of some people, merely a vague feeling that chilled people who visited Grand Forks. Yet at times it was crushingly manifest. One day, Judy had arrived at her counseling appointment to see an ambulance idling just outside the office. A woman had slashed her wrists in the psychiatrist's office.

Judy Haney had also watched Kelly Straub battle with the city over the buyout of her home, and had decided that she didn't want to sell, either.

She clung to Kelly, asked to be led and supported. Judy's husband, however, was exhausted, and begged his wife to sign over the house to the city. She couldn't do it.

"My husband wants to get it over with, and I don't blame him," Haney said. "But what's the hurry? We have nothing to lose. We've already lost it."

Kelly Straub, meanwhile, had been tipped off about the Federal Relocation Act. City officials, at times as confused as anyone regarding the federal guidelines and provisions, had failed to inform people living in the "devastated areas" of one of the many federal programs offering financial relief. Kelly decided to visit John O'Leary's office and ask for information.

"They didn't know what I was talking about," she said. "John O'Leary finally just told me to leave, that I was causing a ruckus. And I said, 'I'm not causing a ruckus, I just want information on the Federal Relocation Act. I qualify for it; I cannot afford a $150,000 SBA loan.'"

The Federal Relocation Act—part of HUD's Uniform Relocation Assistance and Real Property Acquisition Policies Act of 1970—provides financial assistance to households displaced by publicly financed projects like dikes. Now that Lincoln Drive was slated to become an uninhabited floodplain—a greenway—Kelly Straub and her family could now be defined as an affected household. The law requires the government to refer the displaced homeowner to "comparable and suitable replacement homes" after the home in question is purchased by HUD. If a "comparable and suitable" replacement home exceeds the amount HUD paid for the present home, the agency is required to pay the difference. It seemed like a nice deal, yet Kelly Straub had not heard of it until, she says, a Corps of Engineers employee told her: "Don't move yet."

Kelly Straub's holdout was not merely symbolic—although ultimately, that was her main motivation. She wanted a fair price for her home.

Like the Liens, she had had her home appraised, and that appraisal placed the home's value thousands of dollars higher than what the city had offered. Kelly wanted the additional money; she didn't think it would be possible to start again with anything less.

"They wanted to buy your house for tax-assessed," Kelly said. "My house was tax-assessed at $42,000 but it was appraised at $65,000. I got $40,000 insurance. The city wanted now to come in, buy my house and my two lots for $2,000. I said, fine, keep my flood insurance money, but then you give me the $65,000 that my house is worth," Kelly said. They wouldn't do it. Then they went up to $22,000. Nope, I'm sitting on it. Until they put that last piece of dike in, I'm Eminent Domain, I'm Federal Relocation Act. That's all I was waiting for. If I had to wait until I was a hundred years old, I would do it. I told them, it's not about the money now, it's the principle of the thing because you are just screwing everybody."

After her visit to O'Leary's office, Kelly applied for relief under the Federal Relocation Act. Soon after, she and other citizens filed suit against the city of Grand Forks and FEMA, claiming city officials were "bullying residents into selling their homes for unfair prices."

"We just wanted to get back on our feet and live the rest of our lives," Kelly said. "You won't let me use my insurance money, you won't let me rebuild here and you now want to yank my property from me. I don't think I was being unreasonable by saying you can't do that. And if you do, then make it possible that I can afford to begin again. That's all people were asking for. You're completely devastated to begin with and then you've got all these . . ." Kelly scowled, then said venomously—"*officials* running you into the ground."

The *Herald* article about Kelly Straub's lawsuit carried a subhead: "Thorn for the city." Soon after that, Kelly began telling her neighbors about a run-in she said she had had with city attorney Howard Swanson on the steps of City Hall while he was escorting FEMA director James Lee Witt around town. Kelly narrates like a play-by-play announcer: "The bigwig from FEMA is coming to hand all this money to the city. The kids and I are sitting on the curb; Howard Swanson was taking questions; I asked him one; he called me a bitch." The question she asked of Swanson: "Does this FEMA money come to *us* now or are you going to pocket that too?"

Swanson refuses to discuss Kelly Straub or any other homeowner who may have had a problem with the city. After her characterization in the *Herald* as "the thorn in the side of city officials," and after her alleged run-in with Howard Swanson, Kelly became even more popular down in Lincoln Drive.

"I got key chains that said 'I can go from zero to bitch in 2.5 seconds' and I got T-shirts that said: 'I'm not a bitch, I'm *the* bitch and to you that's *Ms.* Bitch.'" Kelly Straub was no longer the "doormat" that she says she was before the flood, no longer just the lunchroom lady dishing out school slop. She was a thorn; she was a bitch. She was angry, and getting angrier. It was as if she had appropriated the fury of her neighbors, who were too exhausted to protest.

"Most people reach that point; they block it out. You tried to discuss the flood and say 'Look, these are your options.' 'No, I don't even want to hear it.' They just go through the motions until four years later, and their feet are stuck in mud and they can't figure out why they are crying all the time and why they can't get themselves out of bed and they work their asses off and don't make enough to cover their bills." Kelly paused. "That is what it's like here now. The city wants all of us to believe we've recovered and we're the perfect little city because it makes them look good." But privately, Kelly was feeling the strain of cleaning up her home, watching her friends crumble around her, keeping up a brave—even defiant—face for her children, and now for her neighbors.

"There were days when I'd get off the phone and crack. And you just cry and cry and cry and cry and then you get mad. I can honestly say, if it wasn't for the kids and me being absolutely financially tied to this flipping city, I would have been gone in a heartbeat. But they've lost everything; they lost their bedroom, all their belongings, their house, then they see their school being ripped down and all their neighbors and their friends are being separated and moved. You needed to try to find one thing that pulled them through." The pretty yellow house in Lincoln Drive was all Kelly thought she and her family had left.

Yet, one by one, everyone else there was selling to the city. Even Judy Haney, a few months after telling Nick Coleman that she wasn't going to sell, turned over her house to the city.

The city wasn't giving up its fight to get Kelly to sell. She received notices from the city with increasing regularity. "The first one scared the bejesus out of me," she said. "They'd say, 'We need to get into your house.' And I'd say, 'What if I don't let you in?' They'll take me to court. But see, that's where I was smart. I'd already realized that they couldn't get into my house because it was *structurally sound*. They'd threaten and threaten, but not once have they dragged me to court.

"So for years, for three years, I would get phone calls or a notice from the city saying that if I didn't mow my yard that they were just going to start mowing my yard for me and fining me and so on. So I called them back and said 'All right, you assholes, you hook up my power and my water because

I'm still paying taxes on that place and I am still a city resident and I'm in city limits. I want all that back." The city refused, but Kelly's story got around, and people started mowing her lawn for her.

University of North Dakota associate professor Curt Stofferahn, who after more than a year was still living in an ice-cold, thin-walled FEMA trailer, was having trouble finding a new home, especially now that home prices had skyrocketed.

"I couldn't find anything. You were buying a third less house for third more price." The city had to scramble if it didn't want a major population loss. In late 1997, the city had entered into a partnership with a private nonprofit group called Grand Forks Homes, an eight-person committee whose members were appointed by local churches. The nonprofit had been organized in the sixties during the urban development movement, and most of its projects had been low- and moderate-income homes or housing for seniors and the disabled. Charged now with replenishing the low- and moderate-income housing lost in the flood, Grand Forks Homes seemed a reasonable partnership option. Federal funds—specifically, HUD Community Development Block Grants—were set aside for the project; the city also borrowed from the Fannie Mae federal mortgage assistance program. The loans were to be repaid with the proceeds from the sale of homes in the new developments, which were given the unfortunate name of First and Second Congressional Subdivisions.

The city purchased barren, isolated lots on the undeveloped outskirts of town, west of I-29. At the time, there was no supermarket, no school, and no daycare facility in sight. Grand Forks Homes worked with local contractors and construction began. But the project was unpopular even before the first Caterpillar showed up. Many people were uneasy with city government involving itself in the commercial housing game. Pat Owens and John O'Leary felt the city had no choice.

"Private builders weren't interested in taking the risk," Owens said. "So somebody had to step in." All through the winter of 1997–1998, the hard, cold earth off I-29 was torn up by construction crews. As the homes were built, many Grand Forks residents drove by to have a look. They didn't like what they saw: the impersonal, gray-cast, suburban-style subdivision was a far cry from Lincoln Drive, Central Park, and Riverside Park. What the city hadn't seemed to fully realize was that it needed not only to build homes, but to rebuild neighborhoods. It tried to do this through very small gestures, gestures that ended up seeming misguided; for instance, the city decided to name the subdivision's streets after the abandoned streets in Lincoln Drive. West Plum intersected West Lanark. It struck many observers as morbid.

When people returned from their reconnaissance trips out to the Congressional building site, they shared their opinions with neighbors. The homes are cheap-looking, they said, they're "cracker-box houses." Word got around. When all 193 homes were completed, Grand Forks Homes listed the prices: the homes ranged from $105,000 to $147,000. An average Lincoln Drive home had been bought out at about $70,000 to $80,000. The new homes were out of reach of the people for whom they were built.

The houses stood empty for months; the months became a year. By February 1999, only twelve homes had sold. Curt Stofferahn had decided to buy one; he bought the second cheapest at $101,000. In August of 2000 he still had no neighbors.

"Where I live now," he said, "there are only five houses that are occupied out of about two hundred. It's pretty lonesome out there." The organization did what it could to draw people to First and Second Congressional: it offered free snow blowers and lawnmowers. It promised to give away a model home as part of a publicity campaign it launched with a local radio station, but nothing seemed to work.

Not much was heard from the John O'Leary while the Congressional fiasco unfolded. It didn't matter. It was as if his name were stamped on each vacant home in both subdivisions. Residents considered the project a failure, and it was widely believed to be O'Leary's brainchild.

"Everyone was saying this is going to be an albatross," Stofferahn said. "To move the houses, they had to offer an incentive to move in." The city and Grand Forks Homes tried out a number of incentives. They lowered prices by an average of $17,500 per home (much to the vexation of the few who had already paid full price); a month later, only thirty-one of the 193 homes had been sold.

The Congressional subdivisions stood mostly empty through the winters of 1999 and 2000. The soil was hard and rocky, the bare yards of most of the homes were speared by red "For Sale" signs, the wind whistled between the houses and prairie snow blew in thin mists, like quiescent specters, across the streets with Lincoln Drive's names. If residents of this new subdivision looked east, toward I-29 and the city of Grand Forks, they would not see the Red River. But just a half a mile from the entrance to the subdivisions, across a broad expanse of undeveloped prairie, situated on Technology Drive, they would see the Grand Forks offices of the National Weather Service.

During the winter of 1999–2000, seventy-seven acres of ugly, frozen land—worth more than a million federal dollars—lay vacant. That it was ugly was not an issue, nor was its proximity to I-29 (it abuts it). It was the purposelessness of the site that most bothered people, a lack of moral worth. Downtown, most of the blank sites that had been carved out of the rubble at least had yellow work permits posted somewhere nearby, a promise that something would appear in its place in the near or not-so-near future. Not so on the seventy-seven acres on Thirty-second Avenue. When people drove past that long stretch of flatland, they could almost see the apparition of what was supposed to have been built there, and what the city had spent over a million dollars from the flood coffers trying to lure to that spot: an Amazon.com distribution center.

The city's urban development director, John O'Leary (who declined repeated requests to be interviewed for this book), had masterminded the negotiations. Enticing a corporate giant to Grand Forks—bringing seven- to nine-dollar-an-hour jobs for at least three thousand people—seemed like a reasonable rationale for dipping into the city's block grant funds. Their chances of success, O'Leary often publicly stated, were good, but he couldn't reveal any details initially, not even the name of the corporation. In fact, only a small, elite group of Grand Forks city officials knew of any concrete details; the city council had to vote "blind" when it came to appropriating federal funds for the project. *Who is it?* the council asked. *We can't tell you*, was the reply.

John O'Leary was the lead talker in the dealings, telling undecided council members that what he was calling the "distribution center" would add tax revenue equivalent to that of two hundred new homes. This was the equivalent, too, of the potential tax revenue of the nearly two hundred empty homes that stood just a stone's throw from the Amazon site.

John O'Leary is a tall man with slightly stooped shoulders, a fair moustache, and a high forehead. He is described by people who have worked with him as "brilliant," "creative," "innovative," "instrumental in bringing Grand Forks back," but also as having had "a history of transgressions." O'Leary was aloof, and serious about his task. But there were political and psychological games played in the context of the recovery.

The city's urban development department is interlinked with a regional economic development corporation—a fairly unusual arrangement. The Grand Forks Regional Economic Development Corporation (EDC) was not a part of city government and was not constrained by city code. Free from the bureaucratic fetters of city government, the EDC could operate independently, engage corporations in deals, take part in capitalist sport. However, it was also charged with communicating details of Grand Forks' economic development activities to then–North Dakota governor Ed Shaefer.

John O'Leary was a longtime EDC board member. In fact, he was a good friend of its newly retired director, Dick Olson; they had worked closely together on a number of projects, and it seemed to go without saying that O'Leary would replace him. To be at the helm of both the city's urban development department and its economic development commission—that was the closest one person could get to absolute power in a city like Grand Forks. And indeed, the aims of urban development and economic development often dovetail.

It didn't matter. Despite O'Leary's history with the EDC and his connections in the corporate world, his application for the directorship was passed over in favor of a man named Mark Krauseneck. The man who made the decision was local banker John Snustad, and this would not be the last time he would hold O'Leary's professional fate in his hands. The decision was a blow, but O'Leary didn't complain. Landing the Amazon distribution center—the biggest economic development in Grand Forks in decades— would be poetic justice if O'Leary and Urban Development alone were the engine behind it, leaving the EDC on the outside looking in.

"This all took place without ever seeing anyone from economic development involved in it," Bob Brooks, an early critic of the Amazon plan, said. "John just moved ahead with it. My criticism of it all along was that we shouldn't be going into a deal of this magnitude if we're not all playing together. I don't see economic development people here. If we're not together as a group working on this thing, we shouldn't be involved in it— I don't care what the potential is for it."

But John O'Leary pursued the Amazon deal feverishly, with help from a tight inner circle of advisors, including city council president Doug Carpenter. Carpenter, too, took little trouble to include Mark Krauseneck and the EDC in the Amazon deal.

Despite the fact that Amazon was slated to lose $400 million that year, O'Leary remained optimistic that local banks would step up with loans to fund the warehouse, which was expected to cost $30 to $35 million to build. O'Leary promised the city council that the company was interested, and that if Grand Forks went after the deal aggressively—if it used $1.25 million in HUD funds to purchase seventy-seven acres of undeveloped land near I-29—they had a very good chance of landing the deal. There was just one stipulation: the company wanted the dealings to remain confidential.

A closed meeting in City Hall was unheard of in Grand Forks, and the *Herald* was particularly offended at being on the other side of a closed door. When the board members emerged from the chambers, they tried to assuage the reporters standing outside, who were demanding answers.

"Doug Carpenter opened the doors up," city council member Duane Hafner remembers, "and of course there was tons of press there, the camera is in his face and they're firing all these questions at him. He was trying to explain what was going on."

Eliot Glassheim remembers the gist of Carpenter's statement: "We're trying to do a deal with a major company, we can't tell you what, we can't tell you where, it could be very good for Grand Forks, it could bring thousands of jobs."

"And he said to them," Hafner said, pausing for emphasis: "'You'll just have to trust us.'" A week later the city council approved the allocation of more than two million HUD dollars for the project, going on half-blind faith. Bulldozers rolled onto the site the next day.

A local attorney named David Thompson was the most vocal critic of the Amazon deal. He told a Minnesota Public Radio reporter that there simply hadn't been enough public input, that development officials, like O'Leary, were hiding something, and that "if we're going to spend a lot of money to bring someone in here to provide jobs, and we're going to pay millions of dollars to that entity to generate jobs . . . then those jobs ought to be real good jobs." Jobs that paid seven to nine dollars an hour were not "real good jobs" by Grand Forks' new standards, with housing prices skyrocketing. On the other hand, there were others who had different reasons for not wanting those jobs in Grand Forks.

"Some people didn't like Amazon coming in with a lot of seven-, eight-, nine-dollar jobs," Glassheim said, "because it would put upward pressure on the hotel industry, grocery, entertainment, all the good old boys in Grand Forks who were paying bottom wages—who didn't want economic development to occur on the bottom level."

In early January 2000, a letter was anonymously slipped through the *Grand Forks Herald* mail slot. Sent to John O'Leary and dated November 23, 1999, it had been signed by a number of Grand Forks bank presidents. In the letter, the presidents spoke of their concern about Amazon's lack of profitability and the "value of the facility as collateral," meaning the warehouse being proposed as part of the deal. David Thompson took responsibility for giving the letter to the *Herald*.

"Someone unknown to me dropped it off this morning," Thompson told the paper on January 5, the day before it published the letter in its pages. "I don't know where it came from. To me this letter identifies what an extreme risk the project is. They should have just come out and said that there is no interest among local lenders." Thompson was half right; although there was interest from local banks—a number of the banks' presidents were members of the Mayor's Committee on Business Redevelopment, for example, and had a genuine interest in seeing Grand Forks get back on its feet—they were scared. As a result, O'Leary and Urban Development had to start looking for private investors to foot the bill for the 770,000-square-foot warehouse Amazon needed.

When John O'Leary had presented the Amazon plan to city council in November 1999, Bob Brooks wondered aloud where Mark Krauseneck was. "I want to see economic development up here beside us," Brooks said later. "Next meeting, they still weren't there."

"The relationships didn't build; the new guy, they kind of left him on the outside," Pat Owens said later. The "new guy" was Krauseneck, and he had come into the Amazon deal midstream. He had also taken a position O'Leary wanted. Bob Brooks took O'Leary aside and asked him why Krauseneck was being kept in the dark. "He said, 'He doesn't know how to do this stuff.'"

O'Leary told Ken Vein, Eliot Glassheim and Duane Hafner, among other city leaders, that he kept Pat Owens abreast of every development in the Amazon deal. "He would say, 'I sent her memos, I talked to her on the phone,'" Hafner said. "I just don't think she could get it all sorted out."

"O'Leary said he briefed her," Glassheim said. "'You're the mayor, you're going to spend a major amount of money in Grand Forks.'" If O'Leary briefed her about the Amazon deal, Pat Owens didn't remember.

Owens was tired. Though the Grand Forks mayor's job is supposed to be a part time, Owens had been working eighteen to twenty hours a day for three years. She woke up each morning before six and checked on her ninety-three-year-old father at his East Grand Forks farm. Her days consisted of myriad briefings, conferences, interviews, and private and public meetings. She had to keep track of the daily developments of the EDC, the Downtown Development Commission, twelve city departments, the Flood Response Committee, the city council, and other smaller civic and charitable organizations. While monitoring these activities, Owens had also to temper petty political bickering, had to try to mend broken professional relationships (O'Leary and Krauseneck's, for example) that were hindering city business, and had to answer pointed questions from an increasingly adversarial press. She was also expected to understand the intricacies of the infrastructure redevelopment, to untangle FEMA and HUD guidelines regarding appropriations and Community Development Block Grants, to expertly assess the city's accounts, to provide educated and quotable opinions on the city's uncertain economic future, to comment on which private and public sectors most desperately needed subsidizing, and to pacify homeowners now on the wet side of the proposed dike. Meanwhile, she watched with growing unease as the people of Grand Forks became more and more unhappy with the decisions made by Ken Vein and John O'Leary. Publicly, she was being accused of giving them free rein.

Most of what Owens was told by her flood recovery tri-chairs drained away, leaving only vague impressions, imprecise recollections, and sometimes complete surprises. She would later say many aspects of the Amazon deal took her by surprise.

In January 2000, Amazon.com shocked Grand Forks by announcing that there would no distribution center built in Grand Forks. In its official statement about its decision, the company seemed to indicate that it had not ever seriously considered a move to Grand Forks. "Essentially," an Amazon.com spokesman told the *Herald,* "[the City of Grand Forks] had been in the process of gathering information, and we've been trying to help them so that if we do go out and look for additional capacity, Grand Forks will be the first."

Governor Ed Shaefer blasted the city for blowing the deal, saying it seemed to have no clear economic plan. He was particularly angered by the fact that he had not been kept abreast of the Amazon deal, and said it was "unusual for the state to be kept outside of such a large-scale economic development project."

John O'Leary was in trouble. Though generally acknowledged to be a capable—even a talented—urban planner, O'Leary's actions were seen as imprudent, possibly even overly ambitious. People who already blamed O'Leary for the Congressional subdivisions debacle now considered him a failure. And if O'Leary was failing, so was Owens. She had granted Vein and O'Leary temporary decision-making power in the weeks following the flood. That had been the easy part. Taking the power away from O'Leary and Vein would be more difficult, but that was exactly what Owens was being asked to do by council members and citizens. Vein and O'Leary were running loose, people said, and Owens was afraid to rein them in.

"We *were* running loose," Vein said later. "If we didn't propose something, though, nothing would have gotten done." Owens found herself pressured to fire John O'Leary, or, at the very least, to publicly reprimand him. Just as she chose not to criticize the National Weather Service's performance following the flood, Pat Owens elected to ignore the calls for O'Leary's head.

"I didn't feel it was appropriate to take these people, when they were doing the very best that they could, and beat them publicly just because people wanted me to," Owens said. Privately, though, Owens wondered if the city had moved too fast on the Amazon deal. "I wasn't as keen on putting that money into it but I wanted to hear it all because there were jobs." The city was a little over a year away from the March 2001 deadline the federal government had set for full allocation of the federal funds; in other words, the money the city was given to rebuild could not be stashed away in a municipal mattress. It had to be used within three years.

A few days after Amazon announced it was not coming to Grand Forks, Doug Carpenter appeared on a local radio talk show and rather angrily insisted that he and O'Leary had kept Krauseneck informed but that Krauseneck "doesn't return his phone calls" and that if communication between

Grand Forks and Ed Shaefer was poor, it was Krauseneck's fault. The state's economic development director, who was also a guest on the show, said that it wasn't the governor's job to "babysit a city."

The combined effects of the closed meeting, the secrecy, the public spats between city officials, and the lack of accountability created a deeply suspicious, resentful constituency—one that was already offended by the buyouts and the Congressional subdivision fiasco. Owens felt she had to make some gesture to show that she had O'Leary under control, so she appointed a task force to look into the Amazon deal. O'Leary's dealings would be investigated.

"She never defended the Amazon deal," Eliot Glassheim said. "Then she appoints a committee to investigate O'Leary. The governor had just badmouthed the city of Grand Forks and said publicly, who has this money, what are John O'Leary's dealings? And Shaefer was being briefed by Krauseneck who never liked the deal, who never went to bat for it, who was in a jealous fight with O'Leary who had run for the position he got. John was not overjoyed with him either; John is not blameless. But this new guy coming in did everything he could to undermine the Amazon deal."

When Owens appointed what she called the Economic Development Review Task Force, she asked it to provide recommendations for improvement, "not to place blame for the Amazon project." Her constituents saw Owens' action as an attempt to assess accountability. But the very act of appointing an investigative committee was an affront to John O'Leary. It also indicated, in the minds of many City Hall insiders, a lack of support. To make matters worse, Owens asked John Snustad to head the investigative committee—the same John Snustad who had passed O'Leary over in favor of Mark Krauseneck when appointing the EDC chairmanship.

Ken Vein watched Owens' handling of the Amazon deal with growing unease. He was still smarting from the vicious criticism he had faced for his plans for the dike project. Owens' decision to appoint the investigative task force reminded Vein of how Owens had "poured political retardant on a firestorm" by apologizing to the city for *his* behavior. The work he and his staff had done to restore the city's infrastructure seemed to have been forgotten.

"I don't mind not getting credit," Vein said. "I just don't like getting discredited."

"There were times when I felt [O'Leary and Vein] made some mistakes, because they had so much to do, and we'd have to take a different path," Owens said. "If I didn't agree with them, I would take them behind closed doors and talk it over. That was looked upon as not being supportive." But Vein felt Owens had abandoned him when he needed her most.

If historic preservationists were the kind of folks who are into tattoos, many of them might opt to have "Section 106" inked onto their biceps. Section 106 of the National Historic Preservation Act of 1966 is perhaps the most important precept in the noisy world of historic preservation. It requires that federal agencies allow the Advisory Council on Historic Preservation an "opportunity to comment on all projects affecting historic properties either listed in or determined eligible for listing in the National Register." To nominate a building for historic preservation—or even simply for eligibility, since both carry great weight—any individual may fill out a nomination form and submit it to a state review board composed of professionals in the fields of American history, architecture, and archaeology. This board then makes a recommendation to the state Historic Preservation Office. But the criteria are intended to quantify the un-quantifiable. "Quality of significance" is one; the structure in question must be associated with events "that have made a significant contribution to the broad patterns of history" and that "embody the distinctive characteristics of a type, period or method of construction that represent the work of a master, or that possess high artistic values, or that represent a significant and distinguishable entity whose components may lack individual distinction." It is a brilliant, broad-brush stroke. But what, exactly, are "high artistic values"? The boundaries of such concepts are difficult to determine, and they matter because Grand Forks found itself hamstrung by these boundaries when it tried to reimagine and rebuild a viable, economically sound downtown. The federal government likes downtowns, and when it uses its own money to rebuild an American city, one of its main requirements is that the city's downtown be rebuilt.

But what about the Boomtown Building, for example, links it with events that have made "a significant contribution to the broad patterns of history"? As an unspectacular general store and, later, an unsuccessful laundromat, the answer is likely that it contributed no more to the broad patterns of history than a Taco Bell will be seen to have contributed in fifty years—when it, too, will be eligible for federal funds in the form of historic preservation dollars. However, it was part of old Grand Forks—and there was precious little left of the town citizens remembered. The Boomtown Building was old and familiar and it had survived the flood and so it was worth holding on to.

Grand Forks had not been a pretty city to begin with, but its downtown had at least provided a kind of visage that could represent the city's longevity and its respect for its history. It also offered an alternative to the anonymity of the pervasive mall culture. The idea of rebuilding downtown seemed like a given; and, in the initial rush of solidarity after the flood, Pat Owens had promised her constituents that Grand Forks would rebuild "bigger, better, stronger." Downtown was her stage—this collection of still-gutted buildings, empty windows, and construction holes. This was what she was expected to resurrect.

"We worked very closely with the historic preservation offices of both states," Corps project manager Lisa Hedin said. "And Grand Forks had the historic commission and we talked to them, tried to balance impacts of historic and cultural properties versus flood protection. But there are people up there right now who do not believe we should be building this project. They really don't. They think the impact is too great, that the need doesn't really exist." Hedin finds this almost impossible to believe. "They think there are other ways of doing it. I mean, they really honestly think this."

"Historic requirements did take away from other programs," Ken Vein said. "But that's just the way it was."

The center of commerce had been creeping out towards I-29 for years. The Columbia Mall out by the interstate was a sleek, popular new retail hub with a number of anchor stores; the Southwinds mall on South Washington was derelict. The few restaurants operating in the historic downtown were really defiant gestures of faith rather than the result of good business decisions. The coffeehouses downtown seemed to survive because of their proximity to Grand Forks Central High School. But for all intents and purposes, downtown Grand Forks had been migrating west toward Columbia Road and South Washington Street, roads which had once been thoroughfares with car dealerships and fast-food restaurants. By 2000, South Washington had become a dividing line, a commercial corridor lined with Taco Bell, Dairy Queen, Cenex, Hardee's, Holiday, Firestone, McDonald's, and an out-of-business Sears. There is traffic here, too many stoplights, convenient turn-offs into the mall and into the gas stations. Grand Forks' economic locus has been drifting away from downtown for so long that its first mall has already become obsolete and unfashionable; only the new mall on Columbia Road, even further west of downtown, is au courant. Columbia Mall is like most suburban malls across the country.

Within four years, one of the new mall's anchor stores, Target, would vacate its sprawling retail space in favor of a new location less than a mile away and mere yards from I-29. Everything in Grand Forks seemed to be racing towards the one road out of town.

When the flood washed through downtown, stripping it of any beauty it may have retained, it seemed like an opportunity to rethink the concept of downtown Grand Forks. Yet Grand Forks' wings had been clipped by the federal government, the very entity which was making redevelopment possible.

"We were told that in order to have a city that would remain economically viable we needed a downtown," Owens said. "Downtown is being renovated because of historic preservation." That mandate came from HUD; when Grand Forks received $171.6 million in Community Development Block Grants (CDBG) from HUD, it was with conditions. Pat Owens and John O'Leary were told that in order to receive the money, the city would have to commit to building a "corporate center" to encourage reinvestment in downtown and to rebuild the city's tax base. Perhaps more importantly, abandoning the historic, unmistakable downtown center for a sprawling, fluid commercial district whose form pushed against the conceptual boundaries of a downtown, would compromise the city's "sense of place." In Grand Forks, as in hundreds of small cities, the significance of downtown was psychological rather than commercial.

"Downtowns are where towns can still be identified," North Dakota's Society of Historic Preservation Architectural Historian Rolene R. Schliesman said. "For instance, pick up a historic photo of a city streetscape. 'Oh, there's the old Opera House—this is Grand Forks.' It's far more difficult to identify a town from a photo of the strip malls, chain stores, seas of asphalt parking lots, and signage clutter—it could be Grand Forks or a Minneapolis suburb. No sense of place, no sense of hometown."

While lobbying Congress for federal funds, Pat Owens had been told that if she expected to get the money, she had commit to rebuilding downtown. "A city has to have a downtown," she remembers being told by more than one member of Congress. "The Feds gave us three million from the Department of Commerce and said 'You need to put something in place.'" That something would be the corporate center—the hundred-thousand-square-foot Grand Forks Financial Center.

The Grand Forks Financial Center is a sleek complex built on the corner of Third Street and DeMers Avenue. Its presence, designed to lure businesses back downtown, had a slightly depressing effect, despite the city's best efforts. In 2000, it had three tenants: the First National Bank and two law firms. Because it appeared stark and unoccupied, and because it was built on downtown's main drag, the corporate center was in danger of becoming what urban planners call a "white elephant," a large, very visible and very vacant building that depresses the blocks around it. City councilman Bob Brooks has a favorite, and locally famous, saying about downtown Grand Forks: "Before the flood, we had a run-down, outdated, vacant downtown. Immediately after the flood, we had a devastated, vacant downtown. Today we have a brand-new, vacant downtown."

One needed only to stroll through downtown once to understand why no one seemed to want to be there; it was depressing. It summoned memories of disaster. It reminded people of just how badly they had been beaten, and regardless of the expensive disguise it now wore, it was ailing. By August 2000, three years after the flood, with the Grand Forks Financial Center in place, the Empire Theater newly renovated, and the county office building sparkling, downtown was still as silent as a morgue. It had become a place urban theorist Jane Jacobs might classify as "a pitiful gesture against the ever-increasing sums of public money needed to combat disintegration and instability that flow from the cruelly shaken up city."

Italo Calvino writes of a mythical city in *Invisible Cities:* "Whether Armilla is like this because it is unfinished or because it has been demolished . . . I do not know." Nothing more pithy and precise could be said about Grand Forks. Like Armilla, Grand Forks was tacking between "unfinished" and "demolished," and it seemed it would be some time before it knew its fate.

11 *Flood Angst*

In the leanest years, when droughts regularly turned corn stalks into pillars of dust and wiped out harvest after harvest, North Dakota farmers often canvassed the prairies near their farms and collected buffalo bones. The grasslands of North Dakota were littered with those bleached and broken skeletons. When he had reaped enough, the farmer bundled them and put them on a train headed east for the sugar refining factories. There the bones would be made into carbon black, used in the manufacture of ink and paint. In this way, many farmers avoided starvation during drought years.

The history of this state is of farms failing, of squatters rushing in and rushing out, of speculators drawing immigrants to the plains with the promise of land and of those immigrants fleeing when their cattle wasted away and their crops never materialized. It continues today: seventeen of the fifty U.S. counties with the greatest population loss in the 1990s were in North Dakota. The history of North Dakota is, essentially, a narrative of failure and flight.

The city of Grand Forks is crowded on North Dakota's eastern border in what strikes one as a posture of petrified near-escape, but most of the city's inhabitants are, as rural sociologist Curt Stofferahn put it, "at most, two generations removed from their rural roots." Because newcomers are so rare, they are often seen as gatecrashers or, at best, lost. For so long, this state's lot was cast by rich, anonymous outsiders with a railroad tie in one fist and a federal farm subsidy in the other. With the state's memoirs full of exploitation by and dependence on eastern bosses (to many North Dakotans the East begins in Minneapolis), radicalism and suspicion became stubborn characteristics of an emerging "Dakota personality." Those who made their homes on the plains became, as North Dakota historian Elwyn Robinson puts it, "loyal members of the self-conscious minority."

"We are left with the residue of the residue of the residue," Father William Sherman, a Grand Forks Catholic priest and professor emeritus of sociology at the University of North Dakota said. "If you're out here, you're at the end of the world. At the bottom of this is the sense that the weak ones have left and the strong ones remain. 'We're the best'; they say it aloud. 'Somehow this land and this way of life will carry us through.' I honestly think there is a kind of personality that's developed over the years, that toughness, resilience, confidence in the future cut in and became part of their psyche. I sense we have a different kind of American here."

People in Montana like to tell a joke about North Dakota. Question: What's the capital of North Dakota? Answer: About a buck twenty-five. In the last twenty years it's been a pretty good bet that things will go poorly in North Dakota. Except for a brief infusion of wealth in the early 1970s, thanks to the Soviet grain crisis, the state has always been poor. Bruised by the mechanization of farming, which funneled single-family farms into a pit of debt, and the depletion of natural resources like oil, North Dakota did not share in the maypole economy the rest of the nation was dancing around during the 1990s.

Instead, during that decade, dying North Dakota communities were selling plots of land in exchange for a single dollar bill. Population dwindled, and instead of being left to fade away, tiny towns facing extinction were handed federal money to stay alive. In one of the emptiest states in the union, the federal government spends about six thousand dollars more per capita in subsidies than the national average. But farm subsidies and retirement benefits don't keep young people here from heading to the nearest urban centers: Minneapolis, Omaha, Denver. They call it brain drain: the exodus of young, educated people to areas with more promise and opportunity. "You know you're a North Dakotan if at least fifty percent of your high school graduating class live and work in the Twin Cities," the old joke goes. Meanwhile, everyone who stays behind is getting older.

Rex Sorgatz worried about this, even as he joined the drain. When he was editing the *High Plains Reader* with his friend Ian Swanson, Ian liked to joke that he was the only person between the ages of twenty-five and thirty-five still left in Grand Forks. After Ian moved from town, Rex wrote him a letter: "Ian, please come back and live with us. I say that not as a friend or a colleague, but as a young person in this town that needs more young people." Yet within a year, Rex himself would leave Grand Forks for Fargo and, later, Minneapolis.

"There's no one in Grand Forks who is young and happy," Rex said a few years after he left Grand Forks for a job in information technology in Minneapolis. He reflected for a moment. "Or even young." The city, he said, wears you out. When he was preparing to leave for Fargo, he tried to think of reasons to stay in Grand Forks. He made a quixotic decision as he packed his car: if he could find any book by Roland Barthes in a Grand Forks bookstore—excluding the university's, which might have copies left over from a required reading list in semiotics—he would stay. But Dr. Eliot's Twice Told Tales was the only other bookstore in Grand Forks at that time, and Rex had its every shelf memorized. "I can still remember where every book is in that store," he said. "If you needed a copy of *Taming of the Shrew*, you remembered where it was." He found no Barthes at Dr. Eliot's, so after packing his car, Rex drove away from Grand Forks with the subdued anticipation of a newly graduated English major heading toward new places with better bookstores.

Though often discussed in terms of natural phenomena, disasters are largely social products, a kind of pathology in the everyday sociology of a community. A natural process—a flood, for example—only becomes a disaster when human lives are affected, and human lives are affected by a natural event only when those human lives and the force of nature intersect, as in a floodplain.

The problem in Grand Forks was that few were aware of, or wanted to admit to, the city's vulnerability to a flood. They simply didn't believe it. The land around Grand Forks was littered with the imagery of destruction: bloated cattle and hog carcasses, sewage-clogged streets, ten-foot-deep holes where homes used to be. Even Mayor Pat Owens became a flood icon, inseparable from the disaster.

In a flood, loss does not occur all at once. And perhaps there is something almost merciful in losing everything at once. The first Christmas after the flood, people in Grand Forks discovered the flood was still robbing them. Every holiday season Peg Rogers' mother had made krumkake for her children, and then for her grandchildren. These thin Norwegian cookies are made with a mold called a krumkake iron. That Christmas, when

Peg's mother remembered that her krumkake irons had been lost in the flood, she was inconsolable. One of Peg's friends found an old iron in her garage and offered it as a substitute. "We told Mom it doesn't have the old memories, but we can create new ones."

During the first weeks following the flood it seemed the act of telling one's personal flood story comforted the wounded. Accounts of lost houses, dead pets, ruined family heirlooms were shared in the shelters, in FEMA lines, in grocery stores. Everyone listened, and when it was their turn, reciprocated with their own story of heartbreak.

In the beginning, the damaged people of Grand Forks believed the flood had been an instant, terrible leveler. People from the working-class neighborhoods, for instance, were quietly amused to see folks in the wealthier neighborhoods sprinting outside when the Red Cross food truck pulled up to the curb, and eagerly taking their ration of hot dogs. But mostly, the comfort in the commiseration took the form of laundry lists of loss. And after the garbage had been cleared away, the definition of loss expanded to include intangibles—security, trust, hope.

The University of North Dakota had already assembled an oral history interview team to gather flood stories. But flood fatigue had set in—that bone-deep exhaustion people would still feel years later. One interviewer approached a man at a picnic.

"What do you think about the flood?" the interviewer asked.

"I try not to."

"How do you not think about it? What do you do to not think about it?"

"Well, one thing I do is I try to not talk about it. If I do, I try not to dwell on it for very long because I feel we have to move on. It's over and done with and there's nothing we can do about it now except to make sure that it doesn't happen again," he said.

"Did you lose a lot?"

"I lost my business and half of my home. But as long as my family's all together and no one was hurt, we'll go on."

"There is no help for you, was there? For business?"

"Very little," the man said. "Very little. So what do you do? Just close it up. Smile. Go on."

"No wonder you don't want to look back," the interviewer said. "There's nothing to look at."

"Nothing to look at," the man said.

Life began to change in Grand Forks in more ominous ways as well. Mental health centers all over the Red River valley reported huge increases in chemical dependency referrals and outpatient mental health visits. Many centers had six-week waiting lists. In March 1998, a Minneapolis television station reported an "epidemic of domestic abuse" in Grand Forks. That same year, requests for temporary protection orders in Grand Forks rose by eighteen per cent from the preceding year. The Grand Forks 911 call center reported a 44 percent increase in the number of domestic abuse calls. "We've heard victims had to get back [with their abusive partners] because they had nowhere else to go," the director of the Grand Forks Community Violence Intervention Center told the television station. The crisis center had added ten counselors to their staff to handle the increase in cases.

Kelly Straub remembers the day when her children, always good at sharing, fought over a pencil.

"'I'll buy you a new pencil,'" she remembered saying to her oldest, Emily. "'Well this is *my* pencil,' she said to me. All of a sudden, everything was 'mine.' You have to really have the patience to work it through. But if you are an adult who is completely whacked out and now you have two little ones fighting over a pencil, it's easier just to crack them across the side of the head and say 'knock it off!'

"You've got these parents who are so highly medicated now they can't even think of taking care of their kids. People are exhausted. They are absolutely wiped out. Most people, if you say flood, they start crying. You can barely get your life together, kids are committing suicide like crazy, you can't deal with every single day getting a call from the city or a court order from the city to move out of your house. You just can't do it." Kelly paused, a dark smile on her face. "Just makes you want move here, don't it?"

While Straub believed the suicide rate had shot up in Grand Forks, statistics had shown that it had not; however, sociologists believe that it takes roughly four years following a disaster for the emotional impact to fully manifest itself. In 2001, the International Joint Commission Red River Board found that the suicide rate in areas directly affected by the 1997 flood had, indeed, increased.

"My mother always told me, 'You can't get angry at an inanimate object. You get angry about the tractor, but don't get angry *at* the tractor. Get angry at your father.' She was right."

Curt Stofferahn, rural sociologist and former FEMA trailer inhabitant, was finding the changing social dynamics of Grand Forks both fascinating and demoralizing. It became his laboratory. "There's a real strain of civility," he said. "We see the lack of respect. Lack of trust has been endemic since the first part of the recovery. I mean the charges they level against Pat, against council members, elected officials were not 'North Dakota nice.' If you listen to any of the talk radio shows in the last three years, at times it was just vile—vile, vindictive, and vituperative." As a sociologist, Stofferahn felt lucky to have all of this in his own backyard—hypotheses could be tested here, behavior studied, human responses logged. The problem was, he was in the same petri dish with everyone else in Grand Forks. He himself was a living example of how catastrophe damages the human spirit.

Stofferahn, a thin-lipped, angular man with a ready smile and a dimple in his right cheek, works out of a spare, neat office in a brick building on the University of North Dakota campus. In the summer of 2000, he still had boxes of flood-related newspaper clippings stacked in the corners. In one of the cartons Stofferahn had filed a *New York Times* article for which he had been interviewed, and in which he had said about North Dakota: "There's a real concern that we're probably seeing the last generation on the land." Stofferahn grew up on a farm in the Red River valley, and before becoming an associate professor and director of UND's Social Science Research Institute, held the job title of agricultural strategies coordinator at the North Dakota Economic Development Commission. He has spent most of his academic career studying the sociology of rural communities. Now his interest was in the people of Grand Forks, his neighbors, and how the flood had changed them—and him.

"I think that anyone who went through this was angry at different times," Stofferahn said. "I was angry. I was angry and my anger got deflected back internally through personal relationships. I guess as a sociologist, you're fascinated by the social and political dimensions of it but my anger was directed internally toward the sociology department and into my personal relationships.

"During that time I lost my father, broke up with a girlfriend, lost a house, had trouble in the department, trouble with the university. It was a mess of a year. All the decisions you had to make were just enough to push the point where you had to find a place to vent, and a significant target would have been the mayor and elected officials." Stofferahn has coined a term for what he saw happening in Grand Forks: flood angst.

Flood angst could also apply generally to the five stages of grief transposed to a disaster-affected community: denial, anger, bargaining, depression, and acceptance. But in Grand Forks, the first among these was anger, and it seemed an exceptionally virulent strain. Kelly Straub, for example, would, four years after the flood, still call Pat Owens "evil."

"You know what Pat Owens was? She was a puppet on strings," Kelly said. She also accepted as fact—as did Jim and Mary Lien—that the city council, city engineer, and mayor had had advance warning of the severity of the flood and chose not to pass it on to their constituents.

"They needed it to be so bad in order to get the funding," Kelly said. "You see what I mean? You need to have a disaster that is worth billions before government steps in and helps you out. If they would have told people, floods coming, plan on water, people would have moved crap out of their house like crazy. They would have gone to high ground. You weren't warned; nobody was told of anything. Except for—did you know every single council member did not have a single drop? And they will swear up and down that it's everybody else's fault. Everybody else's fault." Kelly Straub looks you in the eye when she says this; she is dead earnest. Kelly is not, by far, the only person in Grand Forks who believes that the city conspired to hide information that even hydrologists Mike Anderson, Steve Buan, or anyone else at the NCRFC did not have. It was a conspiracy, they believed, to allow a disaster of such magnitude that federal government would be obligated to step in and help them resuscitate a dying city.

Like any true believer, Kelly will not be convinced otherwise, even though a number of council members actually suffered major damage. After post-flood council meetings Art Bakken and his wife drove over to their condominium, pumped fetid river water out of their living room, ripped up their ruined carpet and sheetrock. "They forgot that we were one of their citizens," Bakken said.

Eliot and Dyan Glassheim spent cold evenings dragging soaked carpet out of their basement, and trying to dry out the bookstore. The flood seemed to have weakened people's memories.

Did the public in Grand Forks want to see people punished? Curt Stofferahn laughed at this question and said, "You mean humiliated? They wanted to see some heads roll. Whether or not the punishment was appropriate to whatever imagined crime they perceived had been committed was immaterial." Pat Owens had run up a long rap sheet of "imagined crimes": mismanagement of funds, bad decision making, weak leadership, secrecy, and spotlight hogging. To make matters more confusing, one person's crime was another's decoration.

Pat Owens' talent for consensus building—most admirably demonstrated in Washington—was considered a debilitating personal weakness by many, and a serious detriment to the city's recovery efforts by almost everyone with whom she worked. What she did in Washington was make friends with everybody. But a true leader in tough times cannot be friends with everyone.

Owens had united the city by force of personality. In the aftermath, she built coalitions by "being a good listener." But people also wanted her to make the tough calls. Although many of Owens' critics said she was indecisive, they seemed not to realize that she was powerless to make the decisions they wanted her to make. It simply wasn't in her job description.

"We have a strong mayor type of government," Ken Vein said confidently. Former city council member Duane Hafner, on the other hand, said equally confidently that "Grand Forks government is weak mayor, strong council. The reality was that Pat didn't have a whole lot of power."

Professor Robert Kweit wrote a pamphlet titled *A Guide to Grand Forks City Government,* in which he calls the city's political structure a "weak mayor/strong council" system, and the formal powers of mayor "limited." A Grand Forks mayor may preside over city council meetings, but can vote only if there is a tie; she can veto actions of council; she can exercise limited powers to appoint and remove department heads. This, according to Kweit, makes the mayor weak.

"The effectiveness of a mayor with weak formal authority rests on the ability to work informally with others and to persuade others to support public initiatives," Kweit said. Others not directly involved in the reconstruction, too, saw consensus building as the only realistic way to govern in the aftermath of a disaster. Chuck Haga, a former *Grand Forks Herald* reporter now with the *Minneapolis Star Tribune*—and a kind of favorite son— wrote only days after the Red crested in Grand Forks: "Consensus building will be vital because some public decisions could hit individuals hard." Liz Fedor, the *Herald*'s political reporter, told Fred de Sam Lazaro of the *Jim*

Lehrer NewsHour that Owens' "ability to be a coalition builder positions her perfectly now to be mayor in this rebuilding effort."

Yet those whose lives had become entangled in the frustrating process of rebuilding a city found that consensus building discouraged quick decisions and left citizens in the lurch, their lives in a state of stasis. Vein and others felt Owens, as the primary practitioner of this type of leadership, was becoming an ineffective leader. Vein preferred the kind of approach then–Minnesota governor Jesse Ventura took. Make decisions now and don't bother to ask questions later. Consensus building, Vein seemed to be saying, was for sissies.

"You'll never come to an agreement," Vein reflected four years later. "We needed *consent* building. Through strong leadership, you develop recovery plans. You just don't question."

What is consent building?

"Going out and determining what is best overall. Working to get people not to disagree. Many people will not agree; but they won't talk against the project."

How is consensus building different from "consent building"?

"It takes longer. It's lengthy and time-consuming." When asked what kind of leader would have been ideal for Grand Forks during the recovery, Vein again pointed to Jesse Ventura. "He's straightforward. You don't argue with his leadership. People know where they stand." By mentioning these three traits—a straightforward manner, a style of leadership that rendered most actions unquestionable, and a clear-cut pecking order—in direct contrast to Pat Owens, Ken Vein was implying something he was too reticent to state explicitly: Pat Owens had failed.

"There's no doubt that we led her rather than her leading us," Vein said. "It was too complex for her."

Could anyone have, or even be expected to have, facility with the intricacies of public works, civil engineering, and federal funding loopholes—simultaneously and without prior experience? Vein thought for a moment.

"No," he said. "No one could have. But we'd almost beg her to come [to meetings]. She was too busy meeting with the public. She dealt with the public; that was what was so natural to her. She didn't have the capacity or the ability to understand the HUD programs. She didn't support John [O'Leary] if he was controversial."

What should she have done?

"Let things go enough to let good people do their jobs."

Is it true that the tri-chairs did things behind Pat's back?

"It wasn't done behind her back," Vein said. "It's just that her back was turned."

Yet John O'Leary had been quoted in an *Associated Press* article in April 1998, saying that Owens was "intensely involved in all aspects of flood recovery, sometimes attending meetings that run past midnight." O'Leary also recounted a story that suggested the mounting pressures were taking their toll on the mayor. The reporter wrote, "He recalls one late-night meeting when Owens, working on almost no sleep, picked up her cell phone to call another city official with a question. That official was sitting directly across the desk." In fact, the title of the article encapsulated the effect the shifting alliances, the political jealousies, and the citywide despair were having on Owens: "Mayor said job was easier when town was underwater."

"I love her like a sister," Duane Hafner said years later. "But the reality is that Pat was a secretary of the mayor for twenty, twenty-five years; got elected because she was popular. She's a consensus builder and became mayor and all of a sudden she's hung with a disaster she wasn't prepared for. She's a part-time mayor and didn't have a whole lot of management experience."

Do you feel she supported her staff fully? That she stood behind them when things got ugly in the media?

"I think she tried," he said. "I don't think she was real successful. I can tell you that Ken felt he was not supported in certain things, and Pat would turn around and say to the *Herald*, 'I had no idea about such and such' when he had told her the night before about it and she had said go forward with it. I don't understand that part of her," Hafner said. "To be honest, she wasn't in the circle of knowledge all the time because she was off somewhere; she'd go to Denver, she'd go to Washington; she'd be all over. She couldn't be in the middle of what we were doing and still do those things. And that's fine. But I think if she would have said from time to time, 'Ken Vein, John Schmisek, and John O'Leary are running the recovery,' and said that's okay, she'd have been a lot better off. But people expected her to be the leader and the reality was that she couldn't be what some people wanted her to be. I don't think any mayor could have."

Was Hafner talking about personal limitations or the limitations of the job?

"I think both," he said. "When people would pressure her to do something different or change things, she should have said 'You know, this is what's set up, these are the leaders, and I support that—and I don't know everything, I *can't* know everything.'" Hafner paused for a moment. "All she had to do was to say that."

But it seemed impossible to make everyone happy. Council members were angry that Owens had let the reins on the John O'Leary and Ken Vein slacken, and O'Leary and Vein were offended when she tried to tighten those reins. Her constituents, meanwhile, saw their mayor jetting off to distant cities to accept leadership award after leadership award, and saw her tri-chairs running wild in her absence.

Most people, even Ken Vein and John O'Leary, found it nearly impossible to believe Owens betrayed people purposefully. Moreover, Owens rarely spoke of Ken Vein in anything less than glowing terms. She considered John O'Leary largely responsible for Grand Forks' rebuilding and recovery. When confronted with the claims of her critics, she was genuinely stunned.

"There was criticism for giving them too much power, and criticism for not giving them enough power," Owens said. "I was caught between them, the council, and the public. I had to build a little box." Ensconced in her rickety box, and isolated on a rising tide of discontent, Owens was oblivious to the approaching flood swell.

Like Curt Stofferahn, Robert and Mary Kweit have found Grand Forks to be an instructive, if familiar, case study. The couple has co-authored four books on citizen participation, urban politics, research methods, and public budgeting. The aftermath of the 1997 flood provided them an array of controversies and political puzzles; but as with Stofferahn, there was a problem. The researchers were too close to their subject.

"Almost all these people are friends of ours," Robert Kweit said. "And they all have a case." What he meant was that John O'Leary had a case against Pat Owens, and Pat Owens had a viable defense; that Ken Vein had a legitimate complaint against the city council, and that the city council could claim to merely be doing its job; that National Weather Service officials were justified in feeling targeted by the *Grand Forks Herald,* and

the *Herald* had every right to pursue the story of the botched crest prediction; that it was reasonable that Pat Owens was upset by the unrealis-
tic expectations of her constituents, and that her constituents couldn't help
but feel disappointed in the scant information coming out of City Hall to
edify them about the processes of recovery. The problem, Robert Kweit
said, was sorting it all out without losing your friends. The Kweits weren't
the only ones with that problem.

12 *Disaster Democracy*

Pat Owens' modest split-level house on Thirteenth Avenue was the object of some controversy in the weeks following the flood, when it was clear that she had not suffered as much damage as she had claimed in an emotionally charged press conference held during evacuations. Three years later, all the black shutters of this home were tightly closed, as if the house itself were trying to shut out the fusillade of criticism.

Inside that house in the early spring of 2000, Pat Owens was planning her re-election campaign. Immediately after the flood, when the "little giant" was performing miracles in Washington, she could not have received bad press had she asked for it.

Even Eliot Glassheim gave Owens credit for her performance: "The federal money we got was the result of two things: the spectacular fire that made the national news, and Pat Owens." With this kind of success, re-election would have seemed a foregone conclusion, and if the Grand Forks mayoral election had been held within a few months after the floodwaters receded, Pat Owens would certainly have won handily. But the mood of the city had fundamentally shifted. Owens had been warned by a number of ex-mayors from cities around the country that that she would soon be made a target.

While she was trying to untangle herself from the Amazon.com controversy, two men were setting their sights on unseating her: Eliot Glassheim and Mike Brown.

Eliot Glassheim was a familiar face in Grand Forks, having served on the city council for eighteen years. He was a policy analyst with the Northern Great Plains Initiative for Rural Development in Crookston, Minnesota. Everyone knew his bookstore had been damaged in the flood and wouldn't reopen until August of that year. Glassheim had a slight stoop, a shock of dark hair, and thick glasses. Despite a tendency to be acerbic and gloomy, he was known as a fair, intelligent, forthright man who, in his many years in North Dakota politics, possessed some savvy about how things worked up here. He was also known as a staunch supporter of the city council's actions, and as a man rather resistant to change.

"People don't bring me their complaints because they know I'm a defender of the city," Glassheim said. "This sense of just wanting change, no matter what the change is, that discouraged me; I don't like change much." He had narrowly survived what he termed the "French Revolution" council elections of 1998, in which many members lost their seats to newcomers. He felt marginalized by the strident, self-interested voices now at the council table with him. He had been voted off a committee he had chaired for nearly eighteen years; many of the neophytes had treated him with what he considered disrespect and, sometimes, contempt. Glassheim was seen as part of the old guard. "My past was all dried up," Glassheim said. "I had no future." He was looking for an opening, and saw one in the 2000 Grand Forks mayoral election.

It would not be completely accurate to say that no one knew who Michael Brown was prior to his surprise entry into the field of candidates. He was a popular obstetrician/gynecologist at Altru Health System in town and had served as an Air Force missile launch control officer when a young man. At forty-nine, Brown had a warm, open face and seemed steady and understated. Yet he had never held political office, nor had he expressed any interest in politics, so his entry into the mayoral race was inevitably seen as an opportunity for discontented Grand Forks citizens to lodge their complaints by voting for the protest candidate. Brown was Everyman. His campaign would use the old "Mr. Smith Goes to Washington" hook; he didn't really want to get involved in this mess, but he was so deeply and personally offended by the slop-job the city was doing that he couldn't stand idly by. But perhaps the jewel in Mike Brown's campaigning crown was the fact that he had lost his home in the dike alignment, though his home was undamaged by the flood. It was the ultimate sacrifice.

Pat Owens chose not to advertise on television, focusing instead on billboards and direct mailing. She and her campaign staff put together a brochure that included an open letter to the city of Grand Forks and an outline of her "priorities" for the city ("A Safe Community," "A Stable Community," "A Comfortable Community," and "Government Restructuring"). It also included a page-and-a-half-long list of the awards, citations, and memberships Owens had been given while mayor.

Even before the river had completely fallen back between the banks, the awards had started coming. She was named America's Mayor by HUD secretary Andrew Cuomo, one of the Most Fascinating Women of '97 by the *Ladies Home Journal*, 1998 Municipal Leader of the Year by *American City and County* magazine. She collected leadership awards from the Salvation Army, the U.S. Coast Guard, the U.S. Army, and the Veterans of Foreign Wars, among others.

While drawing attention to her leadership awards might normally be an effective political weapon, in this changed landscape, the weapon was useless. Worse, it was seized by her opponents and turned against her. Implicit in their criticism was the feeling that while Pat Owens had been out there accepting awards and giving speeches, her city had suffered. That as her shelves grew crowded with plaques and trophies, something fundamental had changed in the social landscape of Grand Forks, and that she had ignored it, or worse, had taken advantage of it. Many accused her of attaching herself to the city's wound like a leech, and growing fat off its leaking blood. So when she listed her honors and awards as evidence of her competence, many read it as a reminder of her absence and her hunger for the spotlight.

The election promised to be interesting. Most people believed Owens would win, but her critics hoped the race would be close enough that it could serve as a kind of reprimand.

The *Grand Forks Herald* would play a critical role in the city's 2000 mayoral election. As one of the few sources of local news and information for Grand Forks voters, the *Herald* could influence the outcome of any election. Ex-city councilman Duane Hafner had been disappointed by the *Herald's* coverage of the city's recovery efforts. He felt the paper should have been used as a tool to boost the city's sagging spirits—and that it should have presented itself as such, or at the very least as the city's friend. He was dismayed by what he felt was the paper's shift in focus and tenor.

"There was a point, I'd say four or five months into the recovery, when they turned," he said. When Hafner was asked by a reporter why the city was pouring so much federal money into rebuilding downtown, he told the paper: "We have no choice," by which he meant that HUD and FEMA guidelines severely limited the city's choices. The paper "knew full well what our constraints were," Hafner said. "What I think is disturbing is that many of the reporters that reported didn't say those things." What the reporters didn't seem to say, and what the council members had hoped they would, was that Grand Forks decision makers were in fact somewhat hamstrung by the federal guidelines that dictated what they could and could not do with the grants, what parts of downtown had to be rebuilt, what projects could not be funded with the HUD and FEMA money, and what was considered economically feasible and what was not. Instead of conveying this complexity, Hafner believed the *Herald* seemed to lay all the blame on the council and the mayor.

Never before had the city council been under such scrutiny. Accustomed to seeing the *Herald*'s City Hall beat reporter sitting in the near-empty chambers on Monday nights for years, council members and city officials now found themselves the target of pointed questions and, eventually, accusations. Where's the money? Why did you drop one and a quarter million on a piece of undeveloped land and not tell your constituents what it was for? What really happened in that closed-door meeting with Amazon? What are Ken Vein's real motives? Why wasn't John O'Leary fired? Suddenly the City Hall beat seemed to have become one intense, perpetual investigation. The *Herald* had become a star. Its performance during the flood had drawn admiring attention and the ultimate decoration from the journalism establishment: a Pulitzer—albeit for service, not for reporting. Still, it was a major-league paper in a minor-league town. The *Herald* began practicing a brand of "community journalism" in which "holding the community together"—the way the Pulitzer committee described the *Herald*'s 1997 achievement—meant performing surgery, taking it apart first it see what was going wrong. But now many city council members thought the *Herald* had failed to complete the second part of the operation—putting the community back together again.

Tom Dennis, the *Herald*'s opinion editor, disagreed. He had come to the paper in November of 1997 from Wilkes-Barre, Pennsylvania, after spending eight years as a columnist and reporter for the *Duluth News Tribune* in Minnesota. A Rhode Island native and a graduate of Columbia University's School of Journalism, Dennis spent his summers in Minnesota and came to feel an affinity for small midwestern towns like Grand Forks. But when he rolled into town in November 1997, he was entering a city that was under a great deal of stress, sinking in a federal fund quagmire, and still mourning.

"The *Herald* realized in no uncertain terms that its fortunes were completely linked to the fortunes of Grand Forks," Dennis said. "If anything, I think the greater danger would be a newspaper in that situation would become too much of a booster of civic projects. It's counterintuitive to think a paper would try to hurt progress in a town." But what if it were unintentional? What if, as Dennis said, a newspaper found itself in a situation in which "all the reporters had their homes flooded, and there was no standing back for an impartial or critical or cynical observation"?

Pat Owens felt editor-in-chief Mike Jacobs was responsible for what she perceived as a negative change in the *Herald*'s tone. As the 2000 election neared, the relationship between the mayor and the paper's editor would turn adversarial.

"He changed, you know," Owens said of Jacobs.

In June, the *Grand Forks Herald* invited each of the mayoral candidates into its offices for separate interviews with the paper's editorial board. Owens' interview was especially important to her campaign since she had chosen not to advertise much; it was her big chance to do a little self-promotion and to reemphasize her service to the city in the past three years. Before the interview, Owens sat down and jotted down some talking points and then typed up a kind of platform statement that she planned to review point by point. When she arrived for the interview, she asked Jacobs if she could pass out copies of her platform statement to those present. "Give them to Tom," Owens remembers Jacobs saying, without looking at one. The *Herald*'s entire editorial board sat across the table from Owens, including Tom Dennis and Mike Jacobs. Suddenly, Owens says, Jacobs pounded his fist on the table and shouted: "Why didn't you fire the SOB?" The SOB was John O'Leary.

"I should have walked out," Owens said later. "And that thought passed my mind. But I thought 'I'll lose this election if I do that, and I want to win.'" As Owens described it, she sat there, stupefied by Jacobs' abrasive opening, then Jacobs leaned across the table and asked her again, sharply: "Why didn't you fire John O'Leary?"

"What do you mean, why didn't I fire him?" Owens said.

"He was wrong," Jacobs said. Owens paused, uncertain and confused. Owens recalled the gist of her response: "Well, I couldn't fire him even if I wanted to; you don't fire a person in civil service without due cause. It didn't even enter my mind. This was a complicated project. Look, all people make mistakes. We don't know if he was wrong. Amazon made a business decision." Jacobs asked Owens a third time why she didn't fire O'Leary because, as Tom Dennis later put it, "she was not really answering the question." Owens was, indeed, fumbling. She was completely taken aback by Jacobs' question. Finally she said about the Amazon deal: "Sure, maybe if we were to go back over it there would have been changes. As long as I worked for the city, the mayor wasn't ever really involved in any of those things. John did the best he could with what he had."

With that, Jacobs backed off, but Owens was worried. The interview was going badly, and she was furious with Jacobs. "It was a cross-examination," she said later. Tom Dennis, on the other hand, felt that Owens' discomfort was of the sort a "public official would ordinarily feel when a newsperson asks an inconvenient question. It was maybe not the way interviews always happened in North Dakota, and I like North Dakota for this reason, this element called 'North Dakota nice.' People, on balance, are friendly and even suppress anger to a fault, almost. But for a couple of moments it was like *Sixty Minutes*."

When Owens picked up the paper the next morning, she found a front-page headline that read: "Owens calls Amazon.com plan flawed."

Owens wasn't the only one who picked up the *Herald* that morning and put it down furious. If the *Herald* was accurate, John O'Leary had been betrayed. He read that his project had been called "flawed" and read that he had not kept Owens informed of the proceedings when she had actually sat in on a number of EDC meetings in which the project was discussed. City council president Doug Carpenter, who along with O'Leary had led the charge to bring Amazon to Grand Forks, was angry too. He wrote a scathing letter to the *Herald*, which published it immediately.

"This letter is not to rehash the pros and cons of the Amazon.com proposal . . . but to demand a public apology by Mayor Owens to John O'Leary," Carpenter wrote. He went on to cite three relevant meetings at which Pat Owens had been present. "It is inappropriate for the mayor to publicly blame a department head for not keeping her informed when the record clearly shows that he did. If it were true that the mayor was not informed, she should have reprimanded him privately or fired him and dealt with the repercussions and not have publicly tried (months afterward) to destroy the reputation of a man who has done many good things for the people of Grand Forks."

Carpenter was Eliot Glassheim's campaign manager. His main contention—that Owens had been kept well-informed of the Amazon dealings—was accurate.

Despite Carpenter's letter, Owens stood by her comments publicly, but privately she wondered how the Amazon meetings could have her slipped her mind.

"There was no way you could remember everything," Owens said later. "I was working twenty-hour days; too few people doing too much work. I just couldn't remember everything. It was not humanly possible."

A few days later, Mike Jacobs wrote an editorial noting that Owens was "intimidated" by his questions. Owens felt she couldn't let Jacobs' editorial slide by without a response. In a Texas hotel room on June 6, she sat on a king-sized bed to write a letter to the editor, countering his charges that she had mishandled what could have been the largest economic development project in Grand Forks history. Owens was attending, as it happened, an economic development conference—she was the only mayor in the country invited to present at the conference. She decided to take a mild tack, and suggested that the 2000 mayoral race should steer clear of negativity. She could not resist, however, bringing up the *Herald* interview.

"In a recent interview with the editorial board at the *Herald*, I was not intimidated by Mike Jacobs (as he alluded to in the Sunday *Herald*) but rather taken aback by his demeanor and questions to the Amazon project and one specific employee," Owens wrote. "Instead of going over my reasons for running and my future plans that I handed to the editorial board in writing as a guideline setting my goals, it was turned into a very negative political interview." She added that it was "inappropriate to use one (or any) employee as a political sacrifice in this campaign. I refuse to let that happen. My employees always have been treated with respect and dignity on all matters before me."

The *Herald* ran Owens' editorial. It also ran a front-page story about comments the mayor had made about the newspaper on a radio talk show: "Owens attacks *Herald*," the headline read. The article began: "Grand

Forks Mayor Pat Owens issued an attack on the *Herald* Tuesday for the way it treated her during a May 30 candidate interview." Other headlines were equally troubling for the mayor. "Owens defensive in second debate" was the headline over an article about the second mayoral debate held at council chambers. In that debate, Glassheim declared himself "deeply offended" by Owens' alleged statements about John O'Leary and the Amazon deal, telling her she was picking open old scabs. Owens felt stuck; she had tried to distance herself from these "scabs," but the *Herald* had insisted on picking at them.

Glassheim's interview with Jacobs went much more smoothly than Owens' had. "Jacobs and I have known each other for years," Glassheim said later. "So he treats me with some respect. We like each other, and I think he knows I'm a straight shooter, if not as much of a political player as he likes. Jacobs was low key, alert, wry, mildly exploratory. But he likes excitement. He likes repartee."

On June 8, 2000, five days before the vote, the *Herald* editorial board convened to decide which candidate the paper would endorse. It was clear there was no chance Pat Owens was going to win the *Herald's* endorsement this election year.

"The majority felt that it was a little bit along the lines of Winston Churchill," Tom Dennis said. "She had been an exceptional wartime leader and had done great things for the city through the flood, but that now there seemed to be a series of bad calls or projects that—however well intentioned—did not work. It was kind of a reluctant decision, even on the majority side on the board because Pat really is a nice person and everybody here respected her an awful lot, and didn't want to hurt her feelings. That 'North Dakota nice' extends even to hard-bitten newspaper men and women." Mike Jacob's editorial the next day was shrewd, the work of a talented editorialist.

"You haven't been a bad mayor," Jacobs wrote. "But there's a problem, Mayor. We are ready to move away from the flood and from our status as flood victims. . . . you seem to be caught up in the victim mentality."

When *St. Paul Pioneer Press* columnist Nick Coleman visited the city a year after the flood, he saw a town still in mourning. But he also saw a mayor who was trying to encourage her constituents to move on. "To me," Owens had told Coleman, "it seems like the flood happened a long, long time ago. But any time the river comes up now, it gets people nervous. We can't dwell on our fears, though, because that will ruin our health. We have to grieve and be angry and so forth, but life is short."

Despite what Mike Jacobs said in his editorials, Grand Forks was still a victim. As long as empty lots filled with debris and crushed brick remained on Third Street, Grand Forks was still going to be staring the 1997 flood straight in the face. As long as city council members were charged with allocating FEMA and HUD flood recovery funds, they were still, technically, flood victims. As long as there were homes in the footprint of the new dike that had not yet been bought out, and as long as the people living in those homes resisted the city's attempts to do so, Grand Forks was still suffering from the flood. And as long people were divided into the "flood victim" and "getting over it" camps, it was obvious that the city of Grand Forks was still suffering what Curt Stofferahn had called "flood angst."

What was, perhaps, most difficult for Pat Owens to swallow was the criticism that she talked too much about the flood during her campaign when, as a first-time politician whose first term had been interrupted nine months in by a disaster, it was her record. She was being asked, in essence, *not* to run on her record, to reintroduce herself to the city of Grand Forks as if she had not actually been around during the flood or the recovery. She was a souvenir of the flood that no one wanted to look at anymore.

"There was a backlash against Pat because people were going through hell and thought they could go to Pat and make it better," Robert Kweit said. "And in so many ways she did. But two or three years later when they still had problems, Mommy didn't fix it."

"Because I was a female and because I had respect for people and listened to everyone, people thought I was trying to 'please everyone,'" Owens said. "That was not it at all. I relied heavily on the people who were trained, who had the expertise to explain things to me. No mayor, or anyone else, can have expertise in every area. I was just trying to get all the information." Owens had just discovered the danger in consensus building.

"I think she created a great public impression that she was in control by the way she rallied people to evacuate, saying 'Get out of those buildings, those buildings are not what you are; you need to save yourself,'" Professor Mary Kweit said. "And she had somehow communicated to people that she would be able to handle the recovery similarly. But recovery is so much messier than rallying people in a sense of urgency. I think the expectations were too high for anyone to have been successful."

If Pat Owens was caught in a trap of contradictory expectations, Kelly Straub, for one, had no sympathy.

"I think if you are going to be a woman in politics and you are going to hold the highest position, say, in a city, then you know what, lady? You better grow some nuts and look at these bigwigs and say, 'Look, this is wrong; You can't do this to the people.' What just killed her was to step forward and say 'This is what John O'Leary wants and this is what I want: now, what do the people say?'"

At times, however, it all could seem like too much for Owens to handle; even her bruised urban development director was worried for her. John O'Leary confided in Eliot Glassheim.

"Towards the end, O'Leary said to me in a seemingly sympathetic way that he was afraid she was going to crack," Glassheim recalled. "It was near the end of the election and she would just lose it and would just talk and talk and talk. He said to me at least twice in a month and a half, 'Gee, you know, I'm afraid she's going to have a breakdown.'"

"I thought I was going to lose my mind," Owens said. "I'm not kidding you."

In October 1997, Pat Owens told an interviewer from the University of North Dakota's flood oral history project that her father had taught her two important lessons. One was "You will never fail if you work hard. The other: "If you're always honest, you never have to backtrack."

Mike Brown, whom the *Herald* endorsed, was faceless. He had no name, no platform, no clear-cut ideas other than generic and nebulous promises for change ("We must provide those services that keep our city a place in which people want to live, not a place people want to leave"). That no one knew him, that he was an outsider, meant that Brown had a real chance in the 2000 mayoral race.

"You had a virtual unknown running that could be anything that people made him out to be," Curt Stofferahn said. "A white knight, this amorphous, indistinguishable person who had no prior experience—all the visions of what they wanted could be projected on to him."

Eliot Glassheim, meanwhile, was no white knight. Although a normally modest, even self-deprecating man, he had moments of ill-timed bluster. "I've been mayor for the last month," he told the *Herald* editorial board during his interview. No one but Glassheim knew what that meant, and even he seemed to be pondering it when the *Herald*'s photographer snapped the picture that would accompany the article: Glassheim, appearing deep in thought, holds his chin in his left hand, his index finger over his mouth, and directs his dark gaze just over the camera lens, presumably towards the windows that are reflected in his glasses. He was, however, likely thinking about something far different, something completely honest. "I just don't have visionary or leadership or imaginative powers to hold out a notion of where we're going," as he would later put it.

On June 10, three days before the election, nearly a third of Grand Forks voters surveyed by the *Herald* were undecided. Owens was in a precarious lead, with Mike Brown in second place.

"A month ago I think everyone would have said that Pat had a lock," Robert Kweit told the *Herald*. "But there's been an awful lot of noise out there." The next day the *Herald* gave the candidates one last chance to state their platforms. Owens, having nothing to plumb from her record but the flood, noted her commitment to the city's recovery and her role in developing public and private partnerships. Glassheim offered another peculiar statement, saying that the people of Grand Forks want from their government "both stability and change." Mike Brown utilized a catchword that had become, perhaps, the most uttered word in Grand Forks since the flood hit: accountability. Now it seemed to suggest that Brown knew who the bad guys were, and would call them to account. The word had become a kind of political amulet; anyone in a position to be heard in Grand Forks was likely to use it. The concept caught on. At city council meetings, the word was wielded often.

"I ran on accountability," Doug Christensen, a new city council member, would say at a council meeting a few months after the 2000 election. A few minutes later at the same meeting, city auditor John Schmisek would say: "Someone should be accountable. Are we going to make anyone accountable?" Christensen again: "I'm concerned about accountability."

Accountability is defined by Webster as "an obligation or willingness to accept responsibility, or to account, for one's actions." Its contextual example: "public officials lacking accountability." Yet in Grand Forks, the word was now used as a synonym for blame. Communities recovering from disaster have few sources of comfort. Everything is in disarray and there is no one to hold responsible. Nothing is scarier than chaos. The concept of accountability is a linchpin in an ordered world. To placate an anxious constituency, city leaders promised to "hold someone accountable."

The day before the election, the *Herald* reported that "throughout Grand Forks, a general interest in Brown, if not a pledge to vote for him, appeared to predominate among citizens." But *Herald* reporter Dan Curry wrote of one female Grand Forks voter who was planning to vote for Pat Owens because of Owens' passion for the city, "not," Curry wrote, "because they're both women." Owens still couldn't seem to escape gender; while it was an advantage in her first campaign against Moine Gates, it seemed now just one of a host of liabilities.

"I still, in my heart and mind, say that part of it is, in this part of the country . . ." Owens trailed off. "Well, I was the first woman mayor and I was fine and I was an 'inspirational' mayor but when it came time to go forward then they felt they wanted someone"—she paused—"different."

On June 13, the polls opened in Grand Forks at seven in the morning. When they closed thirteen hours later, Pat Owens was out of a job and Mike Brown had just been hired.

13 *After the Flood*

On June 27, 2000, Pat Owens, Ken Vein, Lisa Hedin, and other city and Corps officials gathered near the banks of the Red River. Owens placed her silver shovel halfway into the gravel near the Riverside Park dam and posed for pictures. The next day her first and last mayoral term would officially end. In the two weeks following her defeat, she was presented with even more awards from organizations outside of Grand Forks, even from the city just across the bridge. The city of East Grand Forks gave Owens a ceremonial key to her hometown. North Dakota's mythical navy, created by former governor William Guy in the 1960s to honor those who display unusual skill at managing state water resources, made Owens a member. FEMA offered Owens a job traveling across the country to disaster-affected towns and offering guidance, which she accepted. The Corps' $360 million dike construction project, finally approved by the city of Grand Forks, was slated to begin the next day, and would take an estimated four years to complete. Pat Owens would not stick around to see it finished.

It could sometimes seem that each day to which the people of Grand Forks awoke was really just part of one Joycean day—one that dawned the day the Red River broke through the dikes in 1997, a day that is still unfolding, filled with considerable pain, and with considerable hope.

Jim and Mary Lien moved into their new house after accepting the city's buyout offer in January 1998. They deliberately built their new home outside the Grand Forks city limits, on a lonely, poorly lit two-lane county road. From the outside, their elegant white split-level house seems the perfect home, with its generous lawn and its two-car garage. Inside, too, it seems ideal: spotless plush white carpet, roomy kitchen, vaulted ceilings.

But the Liens can't help but think about their demolished home on East Elmwood, the one that had fewer than ten years left on its mortgage. Jim, who is sixty, anticipated retiring in five years. Now he has a twenty-seven-year mortgage.

"That's what I resent," Mary said. "I resent being this age, and being as calculated as we were, as educated as we were, and how well we had things planned out. And now . . . ," she trailed off. "I mean, our parents could stay in their home. We were hoping for the same." The Liens anticipate having to move out of their new house when Jim retires, perhaps just as the antiseptic aura of the newly built house is shading into a feeling of home.

"We're starting to get memories in this home," Mary said, "and now I am starting to get attached to the home. I don't know if I'm going to want to leave when we have to." Mary laughed. "And it's no big deal; I know a home is a material thing . . . but if you can have only one 'thing,' shouldn't it be a home? It's going to be hard for me to move again," she said. "That might be my demise."

On a chilly day in September 2000, Kelly Straub and her children drove down to the old house in Lincoln Drive, rolled up their sleeves, and dug nearly two thousand bricks out of the hardened mud surrounding her home. Kelly had just won the buyout she had been demanding for more than three years.

"I'll be darned if I didn't get everything. I got the $25,000, got to keep my insurance money; I got it all." Because her home had been in the footprint of the proposed dike, the city said it needed to acquire her property before starting the project; this was not exactly correct. The dike could have been constructed with Kelly's home in the floodplain, and once it had been built, and Kelly had found herself on the wet side of the dike, the city wouldn't have had any obligation to purchase her home. It could have, finally, condemned it, and let the federal government deal with her. So the buyout of Kelly's home—the concession to her demands—could be seen as an act of generosity or, perhaps, penance. Most likely, though, it was a way of getting a thorn out of their side.

Kelly and her children piled the bricks into the back of their car and drove to the family's new home on Eighteenth Avenue. Over the next week, they placed each brick from their old home into the earth surrounding their new home, creating a garden terrace in the backyard. Kelly's new baby often draws on those bricks with colored chalk: big, blooming flowers. She, of course, never knew the home on Maple, may never understand what it had meant to her mother and her sisters and brother.

"I am very proud of what I did," Kelly said. "I may not have changed the world, I may not have gotten everything I wanted out of this, but I've got my dignity. Now I'm a mom with four kids and a $101,000 loan."

"Do I hold a grudge? I don't forget, but I'm not holding a grudge."

Leon Osborne, despite an ongoing effort to mend his fractured relationship with the National Weather Service, still winces when talking about the 1997 flood. Just when he thought he might be through with it, along came the NSP trial. In August 2000, eight insurance companies and three real estate firms sued Northern States Power for nearly thirty million dollars, alleging the electric company was negligent in not turning off the power quickly enough to downtown Grand Forks during the 1997 flood, thereby causing the downtown fire. Osborne was called to testify about the internal flood forecast from his Regional Weather Information Center, and when transcripts of his testimony reached the National Weather Service offices, they opened old wounds. Osborne said he had heard secondhand that the National Weather Service thought he and the RWIC were "overstepping their bounds." (Eventually, a jury returned a verdict in NSP's favor.)

"The whole point with the litigation that took place was that everyone wanted to blame the National Weather Service for all the problems that we had," Osborne said. "We can't. We all have to accept a measure of responsibility. The problem is, is the National Weather Service accepting their measure?"

Osborne has now ventured into the private sector, co-founding Meridian Environmental Technology, a Grand Forks company that offers custom, site-specific weather forecasting and analysis. Similar to Osborne's UND-based operation, Meridian reaps in the private sector what the RWIC still sows in the public sector. In addition to manning the RWIC and Meridian, Osborne serves as a contractor for the city of Grand Forks during flood season, sitting in on the Department of Emergency Management's conference calls with the National Weather Service. Osborne's RWIC program is still a kind of feeder program for the National Weather Service, training future meteorologists.

"We're still mending the relationship, is probably the safe way to put it," Osborne said. "They probably recognize that in the future, if I don't agree with their numbers, I won't be quiet."

Eliot Glassheim remained on the Grand Forks city council after losing the mayoral election in 2000. He is also the assistant minority leader in the North Dakota House of Representatives. Still a bookseller, he now does business over the Internet. He watches the city evolve with the critical eye of a longtime citizen who hasn't lost his outsider's perspective.

"It's a mixed bag. Downtown looks good, the buildings are fixed, the old mall that most disliked is gone, some businesses are wonderful and doing well. But there's an awful lot of unfilled office space.The town square is great, it's being used, regular Saturday farmers market draws people, young bands are now playing Wednesday nights, but business simply isn't flocking there as hoped."

"They say many times a person can go back one year from a cancer diagnosis and find a traumatic stress," Peg Rogers said. One year from the date of the Grand Forks evacuations, she was diagnosed with breast cancer. "I have no family history of cancer. I guess the flood affected our lives more than we would like." After completing chemotherapy, Peg has been in remission for four years. "I plan to beat this." Since the flood, Peg has watched three of her kids graduate from high school, and is still busy with a teenager and a six-year-old. Tim still works for the telephone company he helped save during the flood, U.S. West—now renamed Qwest.

Ken Vein, Grand Forks city engineer during the flood and the nearly four years of recovery, now works in the private sector, for Altru Health System.

"Having experienced what we had, I needed a break. We lived and breathed flood recovery for four years," he said. "We've corrected a lot of past sins—building in the flood plain, for example. There were vast improvements in the infrastructure after the flood. We could've gone into a shell and said 'Poor me.' But we continuously looked to the future and stayed on track. These events are life changing; they certainly are educational; they are things you wouldn't wish on anybody else. But I am thankful for the experience." Vein hopes to take some time off to drive across the country on his motorcycle, alone.

John O'Leary left Grand Forks in 2000 to take a job with HUD's Portland, Oregon office. He declined to be interviewed for this book.

Although Mike Anderson had returned to Grand Forks many times since the 1997 flood, he had never brought his son, and now he wanted to show him something important. They drove along the crumbling roads of Lincoln Drive, where even Kelly Straub's home has now been demolished, and imagined the Red spilling over the top of the dike, imagined people running up the street toward Almonte and Euclid Avenues, clutching photo albums to their chests, looking over their shoulders for a last glimpse of their homes.

"You think about what used to be there, and what has taken place with all these people," Anderson said. "It drives it all home, what you're doing here."

After showing his son the vanished riverside neighborhood, Mike Anderson drove to the Sorlie Bridge and pulled into the parking lot of the Blue Moose Bar and Restaurant. He first led his son to a small aluminum shack just off the bridge, on the East Grand Forks bank of the Red. The USGS Stream Gauging Station is built on a knoll high above the river. Anderson remembered laughing at Wendy Pearson, the young service hydrologist at the Grand Forks office in early 1997, when she told him that she had placed a backup gauge at an elevation of 54 feet.

"We're covered," she told Anderson. He laughed and said, "Gee, I hope so." Now, years later, Anderson keeps a photograph of that gauge, barely peeking out from above a 54-foot-deep Red River, on the wall of his office.

As father and son stood on the Sorlie Bridge, they looked at the slender, deceptive river threading quietly between the two towns below them. "So," Anderson said to his son, "the water got to the top of this staff gauge." He pointed to a silver box hanging with a wire weight from the bottom of the bridge.

"Wow," his son said, a little too indifferently for Anderson's taste.

"Well, if you can't visualize that," Anderson said, and reached into his pocket to pull out the picture of the drowned USGS river gauge. His son looked at the photograph, then at the river, at the photograph again, then at his father and said, "My God, Dad."

Ex-mayor Pat Owens—most people still call her Mayor Pat—was packing boxes and closing on her house when the Red began its spring rise in 2001. Owens and her husband Bobby had decided to move to an Ocala, Florida house near their son. In the summer of 2003, Owens resigned from FEMA in order to have time to work one on one with disaster victims in Florida.

But Pat Owens was shattered by her defeat. It was unfathomable, a great betrayal.

"It's like being pregnant, and carrying the baby for nine months, and going through the pain and labor and then, after it's born, somebody else wants to take it and run with it," Owens said. She surrounded herself, after the election, with the mementos of her term. A framed photograph of a sad-eyed, gray-haired President Bill Clinton with his arm around the ex-mayor hung in one room of her home. A photo album filled with shiny press photographs, more proof of Owens' efforts for the city, was kept in her bedroom.

"Like my daughter said, 'When you look in the mirror, what do you think?'" Owens said. "I said I put my heart and soul into the community. We made some bad decisions, and maybe some that weren't so good." Owens still tries, almost obsessively, to make sense of it.

"They said that I was a victim of my own success," she said. "I always accepted my awards on behalf of my people. I said 'I was the leader but I was working on a team.' But I think there were a lot of people who resented that. They thought I was living off the sore of the people." Owens' eyes filled with tears. "You know, that's the only thing . . . because it was tough."

"She wanted to be good," her opponent in the 2000 mayoral election, Eliot Glassheim said. "She wanted to be perfect, so she told herself stories." To Pat Owens, the story was this simple: farm girl becomes first female mayor, leads city through flood and fire, rebuilds city, is not reelected. There is no nuance, there are no paradoxes, except for the final cruel irony of the election. Days before leaving Grand Forks for Florida, Owens told a reporter: "As long as I lived here, it was going to be part of my daily life.

I think I need to recover a bit." The city of Grand Forks was a souvenir of the flood that Pat Owens didn't want to look at anymore.

Now, more than seven years after the flood, Grand Forks has become a town of superstores, monuments, and greenways. The city is healthy, even if downtown is still quiet and, but for a few exceptions, largely vacant. The economic locus of the city is now unquestionably just off the interstate, where Super Target, Menards, Best Buy, and Old Navy occupy the land John O'Leary bought for Amazon in 1999. These chain stores mean jobs. They indicate economic interest and confidence in Grand Forks. But now, these years later, it's clear the flood also took away some of the city's identity, with these large superstores popping up like mushrooms after a rainstorm. It's something that may have been bound to happen anyway, but the flood helped it along.

A memorial to the flood stands outside the striking new *Herald* building, on the old site of the Security Building. It has been engineered with the precision of a Corps draftsman: the U.S. flag atop the memorial flies at 54.35 feet, the height of the Red when it crested in 1997; the flag of the city of Grand Forks flies at 28 feet, the river's official flood-stage level; the height of the monument itself is 98.6 inches, the amount of snow the city received that winter. It is built with bricks from homes that had to be demolished. And it is ringed with photographs from the flood, including one of Pat Owens. Someone has defaced it.

Kelly Straub's home has finally been removed from the Lincoln Park floodplain. At the entrance of the greenway, a sign reads "Future Lincoln Drive Park." Now, instead of homes and driveways, Lincoln Drive contains a playground, park buildings, a Frisbee golf course, and a dog run. Down near the river, where the Corps is building the new dike, massive piles of boulders line the banks. Some people return to Lincoln Drive once a week to visit the former site of their homes.

In the biography of this city, the flood was not the concluding chapter; it was, instead, its turning point. What comes next is up to the author— the residents of Grand Forks, North Dakota.

Notes

1. THE WAY WINTER ENDS

4 autumn moisture level in Grand Forks was more than twice. . . : NWS, "Current Soil Moisture."

4 "We've already had a month . . .": *Grand Forks Herald, Come Hell and High Water,* p. 11.

6 "You say it's going to snow . . .": Gregory Gust, interview by the author, January 5, 2001.

8 "We've never seen this much water . . .": North Dakota Museum of Art Oral History Project (hereafter NDMA-OHP), Wendy Pearson, interview by Kimberly K. Porter, January 8, 1998, tape recording and transcript, p. 9.

8 "Above normal soil moisture . . .": NWS, "February 13 Narrative Flood Outlook."

9 "You'd look over the people . . .": Michael Anderson and Steve Buan, interview by the author, December 27, 2001.

10 "I can tell you right now . . .": ibid.

11 "They're going to see more water . . .": Associated Press, "Forecasters Warn."

11 "This situation is the most . . .": Von Sternberg, "Spring Forecast for State."

11 "If we should get into a . . .": Meryhew, "Spring Flooding Forecast."

11 "We hope that residents . . .": FEMA Press Release, February 15, 1997.

12 "Slater looks over his shoulder . . .": Professor Leon Osborne Jr., interview by the author, January 4, 2002.

14 "If we needed something . . .": Michael Anderson and Buan, interview.

15 "In years past . . .": Nelson, "Fighting a Flood."

16 "Technology has become . . .": ibid.

16 "The snow cover in the Wahpeton-Breckenridge area . . .": U.S. Army Corps of Engineers, Flood Reconnaissance Report, March 29, 1997.

17 "Farm lady said . . .": U.S. Army Corps of Engineers, Flood Reconnaissance Report, March 31, 1997.

17 "hungry-looking" coyote: NWS, *Central Region Highlights,* "Typical Mid-January Co-op Station Visit in North Dakota," [February, 1997].

18 "On the left-hand side of the equation . . .": Osborne, interview, 2002.

19 "I don't have to . . .": ibid.

19 "Yeah, there was some subjectivity . . .": ibid.

19 "We were trying to be very respectful . . .": ibid.

20 "elected to go it alone.": NWS, "News Clip Analysis."

20 "These could be the highest floods . . .": Knutson, "Spring Floods."

20 "have been depositing snow all winter . . .": Williams, "Midwest Gets Warning."

20 "The highest floods in 150 years . . .": ibid.

20 "Friday predicted . . .": Knutson, "Spring Floods."

20 "Spring flooding could . . .": Allen, "Large Areas."

20 "Flood alert puts . . .": Associated Press, "Flood Alert."

20 "NWS says major . . .": Associated Press, "NWS Says."

21 "He said, 'Out on the street' . . .": Pearson, NDMA-OHP interview, p. 21.

2. RIVER TOWN

26 "his children": Robinson, *History of North Dakota*, 29.

26 "You are now our children . . .": ibid., 241.

31 "We all have warm blood . . .": NDMA-OHP, Pat Owens, interview by Jim McKenzie, October 1, 1997, tape recording and transcript, p. 34.

32 "I thought it was a virtual slap in the face": Bob Brooks, interview by the author, August 19, 2000.

32 "The tension between Pat and the Chamber . . .":Mary and Robert Kweit, interview by the author, October 9, 2001.

33 "I believe I am a very good consensus builder . . .": *Grand Forks Herald*, "Communication Key, Gates Says," May 15, 1996.

33 "Over the years . . .": *Grand Forks Herald*, "Is Gender an Issue? Answer Depends on Who You Ask," May 15, 1996.

33 "You've got to be able to operate . . .": *Grand Forks Herald*, "Gates: Owens Feeling Stressed," May 15, 1996.

33 "Pat is a nice lady . . .": ibid.

33 "You gotta run . . .": Pat Owens, interview by the author, January 4, 2001.

3. WATERSICK

35 "The Red is a different animal": Michael Anderson and Buan, interview.

36 "Is that data correct? . . .": ibid.

37 "current rotation of high water": ibid.

37 "fry-pan": Braatz, "Spring of 1997 Record Flooding on the Red River of the North."

37 "They had to decide . . .": Lynn Kennedy, interview by the author, January 5, 2001.

39 "Since the outlook process . . .": U.S. Department of Commerce, "Service Assessment."

39 "We were saying yes . . .": Osborne, interview, 2002.

42 "when everything kind of went into . . .": Michael Anderson and Buan, interview.

43 One farmer told . . .: Noreen O. Schwein, NWS internal memo, April 16, 1997. Freedom of Information Act (hereafter FOIA) document.

44 "The blizzard came . . .": Michael Anderson and Buan, interview.

44 "On Tuesday, April 8, Lou Bennett . . .": Bennett, "Input for Disaster."

45 "There seemed to be an unspoken fear . . .": Peg Rogers, personal correspondence with author, February 21, 2001.

45 "Emotion will kill you . . .": Ken Vein, interview by the author, January 3, 2002.

46 "I had faith in the National Weather Service . . .": Ken Vein, interview by the author, May 7, 2001.

49 saving the Canadian government billions . . .: Government of Canada, "National Mitigation Policy."

49 "are better prepared . . .": *Grand Forks Herald*, April 2, 1997.

50 "We've been here before . . .": Terry Bjerke, interview by the author, November 14, 2000.

51 "Grand Forks called . . .": U.S. Army Corps of Engineers, Flood Reconnaissance Report, April 11, 1997.

51 "The Corps increased the releases . . .": North Dakota National Guard, Situation Report.

52 "never seen water do this.": Pearson, NDMA-OHP interview, p. 22.

4. RED RIVER RISING

53 "Have any of these people . . .": Rogers, personal correspondence, February 21, 2001.

54 "a pivotal day.": Braatz, "Spring of 1997 Record Flooding on the Red River of the North."

57 "all water in sight": Isaac Cline, *Storms, Floods and Sunshine* (New Orleans: Pelican Publishing, 1945), 124, quoted in Barry, *Rising Tide*, 183.

57 "I keep my emotions within . . .": Nance, "Vein Refuses."

57 "We were approaching . . .": Vein, interview, May 7, 2001.

58 "The numbers sometimes change . . .": *Grand Forks Herald*, "Deluge of Rumors."

58 "I vaguely remember . . .": Michael Anderson and Buan, interview.

58 "Don't answer any more phone calls . . .": Osborne, interview, 2002.

60 apply rhodamine dye . . .: White, personal correspondence, October 29, 2001.

60 "Obviously we know . . .": Michael Anderson and Buan, interview.

61 "It's like ballistics on a Howitzer shot . . .": ibid.

62 "providing there are no surprises.": *Grand Forks Herald*, "Coulee Diversion."

63 "Intuition told me what was happening.": Owens, NDMA-OHP interview, 1997, p. 8.

63 "Jim, I think I need to tell . . .": ibid., p. 8–9.

63 "I hope most of you . . .": Owens, interview, January 4, 2001.

64 "Do not make up rumors . . .": Jacobs, "Let's Pull Together."

64 "Will the river crest at 53 feet? . . .": *Grand Forks Herald*, "5 Vital Flood Questions."

64 "My level of confidence is high . . .": ibid.

65 "I am asking people not to panic . . .": Hertzel, "First a Drip."

66 "Do I get the title . . .": NDMA-OHP, Howard Swanson, interview by Kimberly K. Porter, February 18, 1999, tape recording and transcript, p. 4.

66 "All residents please evacuate . . .": Foss, "Hundreds Flee."

66 "You can't go in there . . .": Rogers, personal correspondence, February 21, 2001.

67 "I just had a feeling that . . .": Foss, "Hundreds Flee."

71 "I tracked it to check . . .": Patrick Foley, personal correspondence with the author, January 22, 2002.

71 "offered no clear insights": Browning and Shaffer, "Their Level Best."

72 "The St. Paul District recognizes . . .": U.S. Army Corps of Engineers, "1997 Flood Fight."

72 something "odd" about it . . .: Browning and Shaffer, "Their Level Best."

72 "could kind of see the writing on the wall": Window, "It Was Unbelievable."

73 "There were spots . . .": Dale Dobesh, personal correspondence with the author, March 2, 2002.

74 "I felt so helpless . . .": Rogers, personal correspondence, February 21, 2001.

74 "We felt that the current forecast . . .": Michael Anderson, personal correspondence with the author, February 27, 2002.

75 "We realized there was . . . ": Vein, interview, May 7, 2001.

75 "Things really went to hell . . .": Michael Anderson and Buan, interview.

75 "I think that up until that day . . .": ibid.

76 "It just started to come and come . . .": ibid.

78 He asked a National Guard major . . . : Browning and Shaffer, "Their Level Best."

78 "It's all over, Mike . . .": Michael Anderson and Buan, interview.

5. FLOOD AND FIRE

79 "Mayor, . . . you gotta come back.": Owens, interview, January 4, 2001.

79 "We've lost it . . .": ibid.

80 "The dikes are failing . . .": ibid.

80 "It was impossible . . .": Vein, interview, May 7, 2001.

81 "I don't know how you describe it . . .": John Burke, interview by the author, January 3, 2001.

81 Down on the dikes . . .: *Grand Forks Herald, Come Hell and High Water,* p. 32.

81 "to stop these waters . . .": McCallum, "Losing Lincoln Drive."

82 "to convey urgency": U.S. Army Corps of Engineers, "1997 Flood Fight."

82 "I remember this call very vividly . . .": Michael Anderson, personal correspondence.

82 "The corner of the dike . . .": Jim and Mary Lien, home video.

83 "You'd go pick up people . . .": Burke, interview.

84 "We had already moved . . .": NDMA-OHP, Leon Osborne Jr., interview by "Jan," summer 1998, tape

recording and transcript, p. 4.

85 "communicate a certain degree . . .": U.S. Army Corps of Engineers, "1997 Flood Fight."

85 "a fifty-five foot crest value . . .": NWS, "Chronology of 1997 Flood."

85 "How are things going . . .": Michael Anderson and Buan, interview.

86 "as urged . . . by all . . .": U.S. Army Corps of Engineers, "1997 Flood Fight."

86 "We're just playing catch-up . . .": Michael Anderson and Buan, interview.

87 "Hey, Father . . .": Father William Sherman, interview by the author, May 31, 2001.

87 "Father, . . . you better say something encouraging . . .": ibid.

88 "I noticed that my oldest son . . .": Rogers, personal correspondence, February 21, 2001.

88 "And I said . . .": Howard Swanson, NDMA-OHP interview, p. 21.

89 "I knew I probably should . . .": Glassheim, *Voices from the Flood,* 8.

90 "The faces on the people . . .": Osborne, NDMA-OHP interview, 1998, p. 5.

91 "We're going in . . .": Don Shelby, interview by the author, January 20, 2001.

92 "I could smell the smoke . . .": Howard Swanson, NDMA-OHP interview, p. 35.

92 "I felt like a fist hit me . . .": Owens, interview, January 4, 2001.

93 "As soon as I walked outside . . .": Rex Sorgatz, interview by the author July 30, 2001.

94 "I couldn't help but feel . . .": Dobesh, personal correspondence.

95 "God, it's like Vietnam.": Brooks, interview.

95 "the *big* helicopter crew": Dobesh, personal correspondence.

96 "no news was good news.": Peg

Rogers, personal correspondence with the author, April 14, 2001.

96 "We noticed a house burning . . .": Dobesh, personal correspondence.

98 "Walk away from those homes . . .": Fedor, "Mayor Inspires GF."

98 "Mayor Pat Owens lost . . .": Associated Press, Region Briefs.

98 "People need to stick with me . . .": Fedor, "Mayor Inspires GF."

98 "You wouldn't want to be a freshman . . .": Lee, "Volunteers Scramble."

99 "I hate to even say this . . .": Ryan Bakken, "Waterfront Advances."

99 "He would spend the rest of his time . . .": Osborne, NDMA-OHP interview, 1998, p. 6.

99 "Whenever these people would call . . .": ibid., p. 9.

99 "I think he recognized . . .": ibid., p. 7.

100 "As we started down I-29 . . .": Rogers, personal correspondence, April 14, 2001.

6. DEVASTATION

102 "I never thought . . .": Monte Paulsen, "A Heart Destroyed," *Grand Forks Herald,* April 21, 1997.

103 "eleven million pounds . . .": North Dakota Department of Agriculture press release, August 4, 1997.

104 "We knew we were going to win . . .": de Sam Lazaro, "Hell and High Water."

104 "They missed it . . .": Coleman and Wangstad, "Officials Rap Agency."

105 "Boy, that's got to be . . .": ibid.

105 "I don't care if they are upset . . .": ibid.

105 "I don't know, Ed . . .": Sorgatz, "Driven Out."

106 "Lights were out everywhere . . .": Sorgatz, interview, July 30, 2001.

106 "Dear Ian . . .": Sorgatz, "Driven Out."

106 Floodwaters from the Mississippi . . . : Larson, "The Great USA Flood."

106 "Oh my God . . .": Howard Swanson, NDMA-OHP interview, p. 88.

107 "I thought that I had bad reception . . .": White House, "Remarks by the President."

107 "First of all . . .": ibid.

107 "My greatest worry . . .": ibid.

109 "The hardest part . . .": ibid.

109 "The fifty-six–year-old . . .": de Sam Lazaro, "Flood Aftermath."

110 "In a crisis like this . . .": ibid.

110 "Some people would just tear at you . . .": Owens, interview, January 4, 2001.

111 "I just kept saying we will . . .": ibid.

111 "The National Weather Service did not predict. . .": Ljung and Pynn, "Flood Insurance," 175.

113 "carpetbaggers": Howard Swanson, NDMA-OHP interview, p. 90.

115 "it's an absolute fishbowl . . .": Mary Lien, interview by the author, August 3, 2001.

117 "out on the boulevard . . .": Rogers, personal correspondence, April 14, 2001.

118 "You turn on South Washington . . .": Osborne, NDMA-OHP interview, 1998, p. 11.

119 "It was so hard to take anything . . .": Rogers, personal correspondence, April 14, 2001.

119 "Do you hear what I'm hearing? . . .": Curt Stofferahn, interview by the author, August 21, 2000.

119 "We were doing very well . . .": Owens, interview, January 4, 2001.

120 "We like democracy with . . .": Stofferahn, interview, August 21, 2000.

122 "Pat Owens, I need to talk to you . . .": Owens, NDMA-OHP interview, 1997, p. 12.

122 "I was, at one point, surprised . . .": Howard Swanson, NDMA-OHP interview, p. 61.

123 By December, North Dakota disaster victims . . . : Federal Emergency Management Agency (FEMA), "Task Force Report."

123 "Please sir . . .": Steve Stark, opinion page, *Fargo Forum*, April 22, 1997.

7. ANGELS AND DEVILS

127 "I'm not blaming anybody at this point . . .": Nance, "Vein Refuses."

128 "officials were worried . . .": Associated Press, Region Briefs.

128 "Hydrology 101": Michael Anderson and Buan, interview.

128 "We tried to bring it . . .": ibid.

128 "It's an act of God . . .": Coleman and Wangstad, "Officials Rap Agency."

128 "This was very personal . . .": ibid.

128 "It was dynamic for a month and a half . . .": Michael Anderson and Buan, interview.

129 "If there had been more time . . .": ibid.

129 "except for the people at the National Weather Service.": Pat Neuman, NWS internal e-mail, April 18, 1998. FOIA document.

129 "The Monday morning quarterbacking . . .": Lee Larson, NWS internal e-mail, April 24, 1997. FOIA document.

129 "computer model": Black, "Lessons Learned."

129 "For many, loss is turning to anger . . .": Avila, "Great Flood Mistake?"

130 "pleading guilty, with explanation . . .":ibid.

130 "concede[d] forecasters . . .": ibid."

130 "I can appreciate the consternation . . .": Richards, NWS internal e-mail, April 27, 1997. FOIA document.

131 "well beyond any operational . . .": Sec. William Daley to Sen. Kent Conrad, n.d. [May 1997]. NWS, FOIA document.

131 "I'm very concerned . . .": Sen. Kent Conrad to Sec. William Daley, April 30, 1997. NWS, FOIA document.

132 "as early as six weeks . . .": Sec. William Daley to Sen. Kent Conrad, n.d. [May 1997]. NWS, FOIA document.

132 "We had a reporter from NBC . . .": Osborne, NDMA-OHP interview, 1998, p. 12.

132 "Finger-pointing has begun . . .": Randee Exler, NWS internal e-mail, April 24, 1997. FOIA document.

132 "NBC called this afternoon . . .": unidentified NWS employee, internal e-mail, April 25, 1997. FOIA document.

133 "I'm angry. . .": Julia Prodis, "N.D. Flood Evacuees Visit Homes," Associated Press/*Washington Post*, April 25, 1997.

134 "You didn't get water . . .": Owens, NDMA-OHP interview, 1997, p. 11.

134 "He rolled over and said . . .": Rogers, personal correspondence, April 14, 2001.

135 "Look Mom . . .": Morten G. Ender and others, "Graffiti on the Great Plains," 150.

135 "You grind out forecasts . . .": Michael Anderson and Buan, interview.

135 "six shingles up . . .": Kelly Straub, interview by the author, May 27, 2001.

136 "It looks like a war zone . . .": Amanda Covarrubias, "Angel of Grand Forks Turns Out to Be McDonald's Heiress," Associated Press, May 20, 1997.

137 "She looked at me and said . . .": Owens, NDMA-OHP interview, 1997, p. 44–45.

137 "a beautiful woman . . .": Liz Fedor, "Donor of $15 Million Sees Devastation, Says 'It Looks Like a War Zone with No Bodies,'" *Grand*

Forks Herald, May 19, 1997.

137 "She didn't want a lot of red tape . . .": Howard Swanson, NDMA-OHP interview, p. 74.

137 "The donor wanted us to make . . .": ibid., p. 76

137 "So we just started writing checks. . .": ibid., p. 77

137 didn't have the heart.: Sorgatz, "Driven Out."

138 "If only the poorest of the poor . . .": Eliot Glassheim, interview by the author, June 26, 2001.

138 "We're finding people's . . ." Ryan Bakken, "Angel Fund: $10 Million and Rising," *Grand Forks Herald*, May 6, 1997.

139 "What improvements are necessary . . .": International Red River Basin Task Force, "Fact Sheet" (International Study of Flooding in the Red River Basin), November 19, 1997.[12]

140 "He said, 'A hundred million . . .'": Pat Owens, interview by the author, October 24, 2001.

140 "Her presentation of the situation moved people.": Ward, "The Natural."

140 "I'm not a politician . . .": de Sam Lazaro, "Flood Aftermath."

141 "In every big disaster . . .": Ward, "The Natural."

141 "I remember sitting down . . .": Owens, interview, October 24, 2001.

141 "I've never seen Stevens . . .": Black, "Owens' Legacy."

142 "Sister Adelaide taught me . . .": Ward, "The Natural."

142 "Grand Forks Mayor Pat Owens . . .": Reeves, "Grand Forks Mayor."

142 In an article in *American City and County* . . . : Ward, "The Natural."

142 "I would come home and sit down . . .": ibid.

143 "unfocused": Owens, NDMA-OHP interview, 1997, p. 16.

143 "I do not like being treated . . .": ibid.

143 "People said this to me . . .": Glassheim, interview.

143 "People would say 'Pat . . .' ": Associated Press, "Former Grand Forks Mayor Watches As Flooding Returns," April 16, 2001.

143 "We don't want to talk about . . .": Owens, NDMA-OHP interview, 1997, p. 47.

144 "We were in hopes . . .": Kwame Holman, "Sandbagged," transcript, Lehrer News Hour, June 5, 1997.

144 "FEMA's not doing its job . . .": ibid.

145 Among other things she learned . . .: NWS, Zevin debrief, April 23, 1997. FOIA document.

145 "I'm not denying . . .": Vein, interview, January 3, 2002.

146 "It's right at the tips of . . .": Fedor, "Council Offers."

146 "We can't bite the hand . . .": ibid.

146 "Monday, I had my insurance guy . . .": de Sam Lazaro, "High and Dry?"

146 "You have money sitting. . .": ibid.

146 "We need to meet this week . . .": ibid.

147 "When our crew met them . . .": Dobesh, personal correspondence.

148 "Don't, don't, don't . . .": Ryan Bakken and Mark Silva, "Angel's Wings Registered to Kroc." *Grand Forks Herald*, May 19, 1997.

148 "Sunday night, when we knew . . .": Doug Grow, "*Grand Forks Herald* Back to Being an Ink-Stained Wretch," *Minneapolis Star Tribune*, May 21, 1997.

148 "I think there are times when . . .": Liz Fedor and Mark Silva, "Flood of Complaints Follows Newspaper's Disclosure of Donor," *Grand Forks Herald*, May 20, 1997.

149 "How did this do that?": Ryan Bakken, "Residents Blast *Herald*

for Identifying Angel," *Grand Forks Herald*, May 20, 1997.

149 "If she really wanted to remain anonymous...": Mike Jacobs, "Four Lessons of Newspapering... Come Hell and High Water," remarks to the American Society of Newspaper Editors, Poynter Institute, April 2001.

149 "You all have encountered a stressor.": Sandy Turner of Managed Health Network, Inc. (San Rafael, CA) by fax to Edward Johnson, June 2, 1997. FOIA document.

149 "making a whole town disappear.": Michael Anderson and Buan, interview.

149 "An $800 Million Oversight.": Paulsen, "$800 Million Oversight."

150 "As with most articles in the *Grand Forks Herald*...": Richard Pomerleau, personal correspondence with the author, March 4, 2002.

151 "That's the problem with people...": Gust, interview.

151 "the inability to get realistic...": Paulsen, "$800 Million Oversight."

151 "They talk about lack of interagency...": Kennedy, interview.

152 "You open the front door...": ibid.

154 "People were a little shell-shocked...": Roger Pielke Jr., interview by the author, June 28, 2001.

154 "We've got a lot of emotion...": Prodis, "Flooded Town."

154 "It was very intense...": Pielke, interview.

8. THE VALUE OF HOME

156 "Never once...": Osborne, interview, 2002.

156 "It's hard to imagine anything...": Ryan Bakken, "Crest Rumor Fell Short," *Grand Forks Herald*, August 27, 2000.

157 "It was very interesting...": Osborne, interview, 2002.

157 "There was tremendous friction...": ibid.

157 "Nobody ever said to us...": Michael Anderson and Buan, interview.

158 "To say that Wonsik's staff...": Jacobs, "More Disappointment."

158 "It's been passed...": Owens, interview, January 4, 2001.

158 "Mr. President?...": Owens, interview, October 24, 2001.

158 "A farm girl.": Owens, NDMA-OHP interview, 1997, p. 28.

159 "sustained action that...": FEMA, "Reducing Risk Through Mitigation." Posted in 2002 at http://www.fema.gov/fima/.

158 "The flood dug the hole...": Straub, interview.

160 "We had moved nine times...": ibid.

161 "I wasn't doing it...": ibid.

161 "The whole city's devastated...": ibid.

162 "I said, 'You know what...'": ibid.

163 "After weeks of privation...": *New Orleans Time-Democrat*, March 29, 1882, quoted in Mark Twain, *Life on the Mississippi*.

164 "Nobody wanted to do it...": Art Bakken, interview by the author, July 4, 2001.

164 "tough Norwegian": Sam Martinson, interview, August 3, 2001.

165 "A lot of people think...": McCallum, "Losing Lincoln Drive."

167 "We were made to feel...": Fedor, "GF Couple Loses Appeal."

167 an inflated housing market meant that the average price of a home...: Erin Burt and Catherine Siskos, "After the Flood," *Kiplinger's Personal Finance*, April 2001.

167 "so important": Lien, interview.

168 "We are not going to allow...": ibid.

168 "It's more than I would...": ibid.

168 "I would sit in the meetings...":

Duane Hafner, interview by the author, May 28, 2001.

168 "It seemed that a home . . .": Rogers, personal correspondence, April 14, 2001.

169 "People only hear what they want . . .": Art Bakken, interview.

169 "compassion and humanism.": Burt and Siskos, "After the Flood."

169 "We experienced being alone . . .": Lien, interview.

9. THE MISTAKE

171 "act of God": Lehrer NewsHour, "Act of God," quoting Frank Richards.

171 "But okay, . . . what do you do . . .": Michael Anderson and Buan, interview.

172 "extrapolation of the rating curve . . .": NWS, Central Region, NCRFC, "Q&As for Red of the North," e-mail. FOIA document.

172 "The Red River drops a foot . . .": Michael Anderson and Buan, interview.

173 "It didn't follow that same curve . . .": ibid.

173 "The NCRFC uses a logarithmic . . .": Braatz, "Spring of 1997 Record Flooding on the Red River of the North."

174 "They didn't deal in worst-case . . .": Kennedy, interview.

175 "come to suggest that there were . . .": McPhee, *Control of Nature*, 11.

176 "Well, that's bogus . . .": Gust, interview.

177 "The Corps rating curve could have . . .": Lisa Hedin, interview by the author, May 29, 2001.

177 "It is possible to use . . .": U.S. Department of Commerce, "Service Assessment."

177 "We always prepare for the worst . . .": Mark Angeles, "Predicting the Flood," *Grand Forks Herald*, May 12, 1997.

177 "The more numbers you get into the mix . . .": ibid.

178 "seamless suite of user-friendly products.": NWS, "AHPS Implementation."

178 "I was the forecaster that put . . .": Michael Anderson and Buan, interview.

178 "single value, best estimate": NWS, "Memorandum for Record."

178 "They're looking for a number . . .": Michael Anderson and Buan, interview.

178 "They don't like it because . . .": Daniel Luna, interview by the author, December 27, 2001.

179 "Their idea that the model would . . .": Pielke, interview.

179 "I have argued in many settings . . .": ibid.

179 "What part of 'record flooding' . . .": Gust, interview.

180 "there was needed neither a prophetic . . .": Annual Report of the Chief of Engineers for 1926, p. 16, quoted in Barry, *Rising Tide*.

180 "Good for whose morale . . .": Osborne, interview, 2002.

180 "In a weird sort of way . . .": de Sam Lazaro, "Hell and High Water."

181 "Disappointment, not anger . . .": Jacobs, "Disappointment, Not Anger."

182 "You wonder if the National Weather Service . . .": *Grand Forks Herald*, May 10, 1997.

182 "True, there is dismay . . .": Jacobs, "Ethical Scavenging."

182 "Col. J. M. Wonsik is too defensive . . .": Jacobs, "More Disappointment."

183 "get in some rehearsal time . . .": Patrick Slattery, internal e-mail, NWS, January 6, 1998. FOIA document.

183 "the most vehement critic . . .": Patrick Slattery, "Memorandum for

the Record: Visit with the *Grand Forks Herald* Editorial Board," January 16, 1998. FOIA document.

183 "I remember a fairly straightforward . . .": Tom Dennis, interview by the author, January 30, 2002.

184 "the only one of the *Herald* group . . .": ibid.

184 "sustained and informative coverage . . .": Pulitzer Board, Citations.

10. TO REBUILD A CITY YOU MUST TAKE IT APART

186 "Part of it was just . . .": Hedin, interview.

186 "The fact that anyone . . .": Vein, interview, January 3, 2002.

187 "In Europe they save everything . . .": ibid.

188 "Our city has been through three . . .": Fedor, "Council Offers."

189 "allow us to stay closer to the river": ibid.

189 "It's very hard for us to come in . . .": Hedin, interview.

190 "impersonal, a question of science . . .": Barry, *Rising Tide*, 62.

190 "We were vulnerable . . .": Ken Vein, interview by the author, May 28, 2001.

191 "It didn't make our team all that much happier . . .": Hedin, interview.

191 He later said he wanted to buy some time . . . : Vein, interview, May 28, 2001.

191 "People thought Ken was . . .": Owens, interview, October 24, 2001.

192 "I'm sincerely sorry . . .": Liz Fedor, "Consultant to Return to Grand Forks," *Grand Forks Herald*, August 4, 1998.

192 "We'd worked well together . . .": ibid.

192 "It kind of wears you out . . .": Hedin, interview.

193 "provide the National economy . . .": National Oceanic and Atmospheric Administration, "National Disaster Reduction Initiative," February 1999. Posted at http://www.outlook.noaa.gov/floods98/ndri.htm.

193 "Like a watery ghost . . .": Nick Coleman, "A Year Later, Mourning Isn't Over," *St. Paul Pioneer Press*, April 19, 1998.

195 "My husband wants to get it over with . . .": ibid.

195 "They didn't know what I was . . .": Straub, interview.

196 "bullying residents into selling . . .": Chris Bjorke, "Critic of City Believes Recovery Still a Long Way Off," *Grand Forks Herald*, April 19, 1998.

196 "We just wanted to get back on our feet . . .": Straub, interview.

196 "the thorn in the side . . .": Bjorke, "Critic of City."

196 "I got key chains that said . . .": ibid.

197 "The first one scared the bejesus . . .": ibid.

198 "I couldn't find anything . . .": Stofferahn, interview, August 21, 2000.

198 "Private builders weren't interested . . .": Pat Owens, interview by the author, August 16, 2000.

199 "cracker-box houses.": Stofferahn, interview, August 21, 2000.

199 "Where I live now . . .": ibid.

199 "Everyone was saying this was going . . .": Stofferahn, interview, August 21, 2000.

201 "brilliant": Hafner, interview.

201 "creative": Glassheim, interview.

201 "innovative": Vein, interview, May 28, 2001.

201 "instrumental in bringing Grand Forks back": Owens, interview, October 24, 2001.

201 "a history of transgressions": Bjerke, interview.

201 "This all took place without . . .":
Brooks, interview.

202 "Doug Carpenter opened the doors
. . .": Hafner, interview.

202 "We're trying to do a deal . . .":
Glassheim, interview.

202 "And he said to them . . .": Hafner,
interview.

202 "if we're going to spend a lot of
money . . .": Reha, "Grand Forks
Looks."

203 "Some people didn't like Amazon
coming in . . .": Glassheim, interview.

203 "value of the facility as collateral":
Black, "Lack of Profit."

203 "Someone unknown to me . . .":
ibid.

203 "I want to see economic development . . .": Brooks, interview.

203 "The relationships didn't build . . .":
Owens, interview, August 16, 2000.

203 "He said, 'He doesn't know how to
do this stuff.'": Brooks, interview.

203 "He would say 'I sent her memos
. . .'": Hafner, interview.

204 "O'Leary said he briefed her . . .":
Glassheim, interview.

204 "Essentially, . . . [the city of Grand
Forks] . . .": Ian Swanson, "Ama-
zon.not.now."

205 "unusual for the state to be kept
outside . . .": Ian Swanson, "Task
Force to Interview."

205 "We *were* running loose . . .": Vein,
interview, January 3, 2002.

205 "I didn't feel it was appropriate . . .":
Owens, interview, January 4, 2001.

205 "doesn't return his phone calls": Ian
Swanson, "Task Force."

206 "babysit a city.": ibid.

206 "She never defended the Amazon
deal . . .": Glassheim, interview.

206 "not to place blame for the Amazon
project.": Ian Swanson, "Improve
Communication."

206 "I don't mind not getting credit

. . .": Vein, interview, May 28, 2001.

207 "There were times . . .": Owens, interview, October 24, 2001.

207 "opportunity to comment . . .": U.S.
Department of the Interior, *National Register of Historic Places.*

208 "We worked very closely . . .":
Hedin, interview, May 29, 2001.

208 "Historic requirements did take
away . . .": Vein, interview, May 28,
2001.

209 "We were told that in order . . .":
Owens, interview, August 16, 2000.

209 "Downtowns are where towns . . .":
Rolene R. Schliesman, personal
correspondence.

210 "A city has to have a downtown
. . .": Pat Owens, interview by the
author, October 24, 2001.

210 "Before the flood . . .": Brooks, interview.

210 "a pitiful gesture . . .": Jacobs, *Death
and Life,* 5.

210 "Whether Armilla . . .": Calvino, *Invisible Cities,* 49.

11. FLOOD ANGST

211 "at most, two generations . . .": Stofferahn, "Ten Reasons."

212 "loyal members of the . . .": Robinson, *History of North Dakota,* 289.

212 "We are left with the residue . . .":
Sherman, interview.

212 "Ian, please come back . . .": Sorgatz, "Driven Out."

213 "There's no one in Grand Forks
. . .": Sorgatz, interview, August 1,
2001.

214 "We told Mom . . .": Peg Rogers,
personal correspondence with author, April 29, 2001.

214 "What do you think about . . .":
Glassheim, *Voices from the Flood,*
100–101.

215 "We've heard victims had to
. . .": WCCO-TV/wcco.com, "Flood
Caused Domestic Abuse."

215 "I'll buy you a new pencil . . .": Straub, interview.

215 "My mother always told me . . .": Stofferahn, interview by the author, August 19, 2000.

216 "I think that anyone who went through this . . .": ibid.

217 "evil. . . . You know what Pat Owens was? . . .": Straub, interview.

217 "They forgot that we were one of their citizens.": Art Bakken, interview.

217 "You mean humiliated? . . .": Stofferahn, interview, August 21, 2000.

218 "We have a strong mayor . . .": Vein, interview, May 28, 2001.

218 "Grand Forks government is weak mayor . . .": Hafner, interview.

218 "weak mayor/strong council . . .": Kweit, *Guide to Grand Forks.*

218 "The effectiveness of a mayor . . .": ibid.

218 "Consensus building will be vital . . .": Haga, "Next Time, Stronger."

219 "ability to be a coalition builder . . .": de Sam Lazaro, "Flood Aftermath."

219 "You'll never come to an agreement . . .": Vein, interview, May 28, 2001.

220 "intensely involved in all aspects . . .": Associated Press, "Mayor Said Job."

220 "He recalls one late-night meeting . . .": ibid.

220 "I love her like a sister . . .": Hafner, interview.

221 "There was criticism for giving them . . .": Owens, interview, October 24, 2001.

221 "Almost all these people are friends of ours . . .": Mary and Robert Kweit, interview by the author, October 9, 2001.

12. DISASTER DEMOCRACY

223 "The federal money we got was the result . . .": Glassheim, interview.

224 "People don't bring me their complaints . . .": ibid.

225 "There was a point, I'd say . . .": Hafner, interview.

227 "The *Herald* realized in no . . .": Dennis, interview.

227 "He changed, you know": Owens, interview, October 24, 2001.

227 "Give them to Tom . . .": ibid.

227 "I should have walked out . . .": ibid.

228 "She was not really answering . . .": Dennis, interview.

228 "Sure, maybe if we were . . .": Owens, interview, October 24, 2001.

228 "It was a cross-examination.": ibid.

228 "public official would ordinarily feel . . .": Dennis, interview.

228 "This letter is not to rehash . . .": Doug Carpenter, "Mayor's Amazon Timeline Contains Errors," *Grand Forks Herald* mailbag/editorial, June 2, 2000.

229 "There was no way you could remember everything . . .": Owens, interview, October 24, 2001.

229 "In a recent interview with the editorial board . . .": Owens, "Don't Let Negativity."

229 "Grand Forks Mayor Pat Owens issued an attack . . .": Sam Black, "Owens Attacks *Herald*," *Grand Forks Herald,* June 7, 2000.

230 "Owens defensive in second debate": Sam Black, "Owens Defensive in Second Debate," *Grand Forks Herald,* June 2, 2000.

230 "deeply offended": ibid.

230 "Jacobs and I have known each other for years . . .": Eliot Glassheim, personal correspondence with the author, February 12, 2002.

230 "The majority felt it was . . .": Dennis, interview.

230 "You haven't been a bad mayor . . .": Jacobs, "A Letter to the Mayor."

230 "To me, it seems like the flood . . .": Coleman, "Grand Forks Uneasy."

231 "There was a backlash against Pat. . .": Mary and Robert Kweit, interview.

231 "Because I was a female . . .": Owens, interview, October 24, 2001.

231 "I think she created a great public impression . . .": Mary and Robert Kweit, interview.

232 "I think if you are going to be a woman . . .": Straub, interview.

232 "Towards the end, O'Leary said . . .": Glassheim, interview.

232 "I thought I was going to lose . . .": Owens, interview, October 24, 2001.

232 "You will never fail if you work hard . . .": Owens, NDMA-OHP interview, 1997, p. 7.

232 "We must provide those services . . .": Grand Forks Herald, "Candidates Give Their Reasons."

232 "You had a virtual unknown running . . .": Stofferahn, interview, August 21, 2000.

232 "I've been mayor for the last month . . .": Sam Black, "Glassheim: Lead-ership Needed," Grand Forks Herald, June 3, 2000.

233 "I just don't have visionary or leadership . . .": Glassheim, personal correspondence.

233 "A month ago, I think everyone . . .": Ian Swanson, "Too Close to Call."

233 "both stability and change.": Grand Forks Herald, "Candidates Give Their Reasons."

233 "I ran on accountability.": Grand Forks City Council Meeting, August 21, 2000.

233 "Someone should be accountable . . .": ibid.

234 "throughout Grand Forks . . .": Dan Curry, "Mayoral Vote a Lively Topic in GF," Grand Forks Herald, June 12, 2000.

234 "I still, in my heart and mind . . .": Owens, interview, January 4, 2001.

13. AFTER THE FLOOD

All quotes are from interviews conducted by author.

Selected Bibliography

BOOKS

Barry, John M. *Rising Tide*. New York: Simon & Schuster, 2000.

Bluemle, Mary E. *Guide to the Geology of Northeastern North Dakota*. Bismarck: North Dakota Geological Survey, 1972.

Calvino, Italo. *Invisible Cities*. Translated by William Weaver. New York: Harcourt, Inc., 1974.

Dynes, R.R., B. de Marchi, and C. Pelanda, eds. *Sociology of Disasters: Contribution of Sociology to Disaster Research*. Milan: ISA Research Committee on Disasters/Franco Angeli, 1987.

Glassheim, Eliot, ed. *Voices from the Flood: An Oral History of the 1997 Flood of the Red River of the North*. Grand Forks, ND: North Dakota Museum of Art, 1999.

Grand Forks Herald. A Pictorial History of the Community of Grand Forks. Grand Forks, ND: Quebecor Books, 1999.

———. *Come Hell and High Water: The Incredible Story of the 1997 Red River Flood*. Grand Forks, ND: *Grand Forks Herald*, 1997.

Jacobs, Jane. *The Death and Life of Great American Cities*. New York: Random House, 1961.

LeFever, Julie A., John P. Bluemle, and Ryan P. Waldkirch. *Flooding in the Grand Forks–East Grand Forks North Dakota and Minnesota Area*. Educational Series 25. Bismarck, ND: North Dakota Geological Survey, 1999.

McPhee, John. *The Control of Nature*. New York: Farrar, Straus, and Giroux, 1989.

Perec, Georges. *Species of Spaces and Other Pieces*. Translated by John Sturrock. New York: Penguin, 1974.

Pielke, Roger A. Jr. "Flood Impacts on Society: Damaging Floods as a Framework for Assessment." In *Floods*, edited by D. J. Parker, p. 133–55. London and New York: Routledge Press, 2000.

Prince, Samuel H. *Catastrophe and Social Change*. New York: Columbia University Press, 1925.

Robinson, Elwyn B. *The History of North Dakota*. Lincoln, NE: University of Nebraska Press, 1966.

Turner, Ralph. *Manmade Disasters*. London: Wykeham, 1978.

Twain, Mark. *Life on the Mississippi*. New York: Penguin Books, 1883.

Upham, Warren. *The Glacial Lake Agassiz*. USGS monograph 25. Washington, DC: United States Government Printing Office, 1896.

ARTICLES AND PAPERS

Allen, Vicki. "Large Areas of U.S. Face Spring Flooding Threat." *Reuters North America,* March 18, 1997.

Angeles, Mark. "Experts: Choose Hell Instead of High Water." *Grand Forks Herald,* May 14, 1997.

Associated Press. "Flood Alert Puts Focus on N.D." *Bismarck Tribune,* March 19, 1997.

———. "Forecasters Warn of Widespread Floods." *Washington Post,* March 19, 1997.

———. "Mayor Said Job Was Easier When Town Was Underwater." *Hannibal Courier-Post,* April 16, 1998.

———. "NWS Says Major Flood Is Probable." *Wahpeton Daily News,* March 19, 1997.

———. Region Briefs. *Fargo Forum,* April 22, 1997.

Avila, Jim. "Was There a Great Flood Mistake?" Transcript. NBC News, April 24, 1997.

Bakken, Ryan. "Waterfront Advances to the West, South." *Grand Forks Herald,* April 21, 1997.

Bales, Roger, Holly C. Hartman, and Soroosh Sorooshan. "Weather, Climate, and Hydrologic Forecasting for the Southwest United States." CLIMAS Report Series CL2-99. Tucson, AZ: University of Arizona, February 1999.

Barkun, M. "Disaster in History." *Mass Emergencies* 2, no. 4 (1977): 219–31.

Black, Sam. "Lack of Profit Concerns Banks." *Grand Forks Herald,* January 6, 2000.

———. "Lessons Learned: NWS Uses '97 Flood Experience to Improve Communication." *Grand Forks Herald,* March 14, 1999.

———. "Owens Calls Amazon.com Plan Flawed." *Grand Forks Herald,* May 31, 2000.

———. "Owens' Legacy." *Grand Forks Herald,* June 25, 2000.

Braatz, Dean T. "Spring of 1997 Record Flooding on the Red River of the North: Emphasis on Grand Forks–East Grand Forks." National Hydrologic Warning Council ALERT Transmission. Summer 1997.

Bradbury, Randy. "A Blow of Historic Proportions." *Grand Forks Herald,* May 11, 1997.

Brokaw, Chet. "Rapid City, S.D., Learned Lessons from '72 Flood." Associated Press / *St. Paul Pioneer Press,* June 8, 1997.

Browning, Dan, and David Shaffer. "Their Level Best." *St. Paul Pioneer Press,* May 18, 1997.

Bussman, Michael D., Blake A. Evans, H. Katherine O'Neill, and D. Kimberly Strandberg. "Psychological Distress during the Red River Flood: Predictive Utility of the Conservation of Resources Model." *Applied Behavioral Science Review* 7, no. 2 (1999): 159–69.

Byerly, Radford Jr., Dale Jamieson, Roger A. Pielke Jr., and Daniel Sarewitz. "Prediction in the Earth Sciences and Environmental Policy Making." *EOS Transactions* (American Geophysical Union) 80, no. 28 (July 1999): 309–313.

Byerly, Radford Jr., Roger A. Pielke Jr., and Daniel Sarewitz. "Prediction: A Process, Not a Product." *Geotimes* (April 1999): 29–31.

Castaneda, Carol. "Flood Evacuees Return Home, but Just to Look." *USA Today,* April 25, 1997.

Changnon, Stanley A., Kenneth E. Kunkel, and Roger A. Pielke Jr. "Temporal Fluctuations in Weather and Climate Extremes that Cause Economic and Human Health Impacts: A Review." *Bulletin of the American Meteorological Society* 80, no. 6 (June 1999): 1077–98.

Coleman, Nick. "Grand Forks Uneasy

About Marking Flood." *St. Paul Pioneer Press,* April 15, 1998.

Coleman, Nick, and Wayne Wangstad. "Officials Rap Agency for Flawed Forecast." *St. Paul Pioneer Press,* April 24, 1997.

de Sam Lazaro, Fred. "Flood Aftermath." Transcript. Lehrer NewsHour, April 30, 1997.

——. "Grand Forks: High and Dry?" Transcript. Lehrer NewsHour, May 26, 1997.

——. "Hell and High Water: Spring Siege." Transcript. Lehrer NewsHour, April 22, 1997.

DeVillers, Greg, and Wayne Nelson. "Hundreds Allowed to Check Homes." *Grand Forks Herald,* April 25, 1997.

Dodds, David. "Babinchak Yields Seat." *Grand Forks Herald,* January 17, 2001.

——. "O'Leary Questioned First by Task Force." *Grand Forks Herald,* January 28, 2000.

Downton, Mary W., and Roger A. Pielke Jr. "Precipitation and Damaging Floods: Trends in the United States, 1932–1997." *Journal of Climate* (American Meteorological Society) 13 (October 2000): 3625–37.

Ender, Morten G., Carol A. Hagen, Clifford O. Hagen Jr., and Kathleen A. Tiemann. "Graffiti on the Great Plains: A Social Reaction to the Red River Valley Flood of 1997." *Applied Behavioral Science Review* 7, no. 2 (1999): 145–58.

Fedor, Liz. "Council Offers Few Answers." *Grand Forks Herald,* May 14, 1997.

——. "GF Couple Loses Appeal to Increase Their Home Buyout Price." *Grand Forks Herald,* January 6, 1998.

——. "Mayor Inspires GF as Dad, 92, Evacuates Farm." *Grand Forks Herald,* April 21, 1997.

Findley, L. R. "Soaked, Burned and Salvaged." *Architecture Magazine* (March 1998): 49–53.

Foss, Steve. "A Rift Runs Through It." *Grand Forks Herald,* January 11, 1998.

——. "Hundreds Flee Lincoln Drive Area." *Grand Forks Herald,* April 18, 1997.

Foster, David. "Weather Service Says Prediction Impossible." Associated Press, April 27, 1997.

Grand Forks Herald. "Answers to 5 Vital Flood Questions." April 17, 1997.

——. "Candidates Give Their Reasons for Your Vote." June 11, 2000.

——. "Coulee Diversion Diverts Worry." April 17, 1997.

Haga, Chuck. "Gone Is the Stuff of Many Lives." *Minneapolis Star Tribune,* April 27, 1997.

——. "Next Time, Stronger." *Minneapolis Star Tribune,* April 27, 1997.

Hertzel, Laurie. "First A Drip, Then a Trickle—Then Disaster." *Minneapolis Star Tribune,* April 27, 1997.

Jacobs, Mike. "A Letter to the Mayor" *Grand Forks Herald,* June 9, 2000.

——. "Congress Will Help—But Not Right Away: Politics Will Work Out Controversy About Flood Relief." *Grand Forks Herald,* May 10, 1997.

——. "Disappointment, Not Anger, Is Emotion of the Hour" *Grand Forks Herald,* May 5, 1997.

——. "Ethical Scavenging—It Can Be Done." *Grand Forks Herald,* May 6, 1997.

——. "Let's Pull Together Now." *Grand Forks Herald,* April 17, 1997.

——. "More Disappointment from Army Corps." *Grand Forks Herald,* May 30, 1997.

Knutson, Lawrence L. "Spring Floods." Associated Press, March 19, 1997.

Kweit, Robert W., Ph.D. "A Guide to Grand Forks City Government." Grand Forks: University of North Dakota Bureau of Governmental Affairs, 1998.

Larson, Lee W. "The Great USA Flood of

1993." Silver Spring, MD: National Oceanic and Atmospheric Administration (NOAA), Hydrologic Research Laboratory, 1996.

Lee, Stephen J. "Volunteers Scramble to Save Select Editions for University Library." *Grand Forks Herald*, April 21, 1997.

Lehrer NewsHour. "Act of God." Transcript (roundtable discussion). April 21, 1997.

Ljung, Greta M., and Ronald Pynn. "Flood Insurance: A Survey of Grand Forks, North Dakota, Homeowners." *Applied Behavioral Science Review* 7, no. 2 (1999): 171–80.

McCallum, Laura. "Losing Lincoln Drive." Transcript. Minnesota Public Radio, December 30, 1997.

Meryhew, Richard. "Spring Flooding Forecast Largely the Same." *Minneapolis Star Tribune*, March 15, 1997.

Nance, Kevin. "Vein Refuses to Give In." *Grand Forks Herald*, April 21, 1997.

Nelson, Tim. "Fighting a Flood." *St. Paul Pioneer Press*, in the *Grand Forks Herald*, April 17, 1997.

Owens, Patricia. "Don't Let Negativity Ruin the Campaign." *Grand Forks Herald*, June 7, 2000.

Parris, Geov. "Leaving Las Seattle." *Seattle Weekly*, August 10–16, 2000.

Paulsen, Monte. "An $800 Million Oversight." *Grand Forks Herald*, May 4, 1997.

Pielke, Roger A. Jr. "Nine Fallacies of Floods." *Climatic Change* 42 (1999): 413–38.

———. "Who Decides?: Forecasts and Responsibilities in the 1997 Red River Flood." *Applied Behavioral Science Review* 7, no. 2 (1999): 83–101.

Prodis, Julia. "Flooded Town Angry at Officials." Associated Press / *Washington Post*, April 23, 1997.

———. "N.D. Flood Evacuees Visit Homes." Associated Press / *Washington Post*, April 25, 1997.

Reeves, Tracey E. "Grand Forks Mayor to Be Profiled on NBC News." *St. Paul Pioneer Press*, May 9, 1997.

———. "Victims 'Begging for Help,' Mayors Say." *St. Paul Pioneer Press*, May 8, 1997.

Reha, Bob. "Grand Forks Looks for a Place in the Amazon (.com) Jungle." Transcript. Minnesota Public Radio, January 13, 2000.

Robertson, Kent A. "Can Small-City Downtowns Remain Viable? A National Study of Development Issues and Strategies." *Journal of the American Planning Association* 65, no. 3 (Summer, 1999): 270–84.

Sorgatz, Rex. "Driven Out by Water and Flame, Will Young People Return to Grand Forks?" *High Plains Reader* (Fargo, ND). Reprinted by *Grand Forks Herald*, May 12, 1997.

Stevens, William K. "When Scientific Predictions Are so Good They're Bad." *The New York Times*, September 29, 1998, p. 6.

Stofferahn, Curt. "Ten Reasons Why Urban North Dakota Ought to be Concerned about Rural North Dakota." From "The Changing Face of Agriculture," Prairie Public Radio. Posted at http://www.prairiepublic.org/features/changing/reasons.htm.

Swanson, Ian. "Amazon.not.now." *Grand Forks Herald*, January 21, 2000.

———. "The Flood of 1997: Can We Learn Anything From 1979?" *High Plains Reader* (Fargo, ND), March 1997.

———. "Improve Communication." *Grand Forks Herald*, February 9, 2000.

———. "Task force." *Grand Forks Herald*, January 23, 2000.

———. "Task force to Interview GF Officials Today." *Grand Forks Herald*, January 27, 2000.

———. "Tax Talk Dominates." *Grand Forks Herald*, June 4, 2000.

———. "Too Close to Call." *Grand Forks Herald,* June 10, 2000.

Von Sternberg, Bob. "Spring Forecast for State: Sloppy and Wet, with Lots of Near-Record Flooding." *Minneapolis Star Tribune,* March 1, 1997.

Ward, Janet. "The Natural: Grand Forks' Pat Owens: Municipal Leader of the Year." *American City and County,* November 1998, p. 60–66.

WCCO-TV/wcco.com. "Flood Caused Domestic Abuse Increase." Posted on March 4, 1998.

Williams, Jack. "Midwest Gets Warning for Spring Floods. *USA Today,* March 19, 1997.

Window, John. "It Was Unbelievable." *Minneapolis Star Tribune,* April 27, 1997.

DOCUMENTS

Bennett, Lou. "Input for Disaster Survey Team." Weather Service Office, Fargo, ND. Freedom of Information Act (FOIA) document.

Columbia University, Graduate School of Journalism. Pulitzer Board, Citations, 1998. http://www.pulitzer.org/year/1998/public-service/.

Federal Emergency Management Agency (FEMA). "Task Force Report on Upper Midwest Long-Term Recovery." December 13, 1997.

Government of Canada. Office of Critical Infrastructure Protection and Emergency Preparedness (OCIPEP). "A National Mitigation Policy: Findings from National Consultations on Canada's Preparedness for Disasters." Institute for Catastrophic Loss Reduction, Toronto. December 1998.

Manitoba Department of Conservation, Programs Division, Water Branch. "Facts and Figures about the Flood of the Century." 2000. http://www.gov.mb.ca/conservation/watres/spring.html.

National Weather Service. "1997 Red River Post Flood Community Meetings Report." October 6, 1997.

———. "Chronology of 1997 Flood Outlooks and Forecasting Activities for the East Grand Forks Forecast Point." May 1997.

———. "Memorandum for Record: Red River Valley Post Flood Meetings." September 22, 1997. FOIA document.

———. "News Clip Analysis: Spring Hydrologic Outlook News Conference." March 18, 1997. FOIA document.

National Weather Service. Bismarck Weather Forecast Office. "Current Soil Moisture and Snow Conditions 1997 (North Dakota & NW Minnesota)." January 1997.

National Weather Service. NCRFC/ Grand Forks Weather Forecast Office. "February 13 Narrative Flood Outlook for the Red River of the North." February 1997.

National Weather Service. Office of Hydrology. "AHPS Implementation for the Red River of the North at the North Central River Forecast Center." November 1997.

———. "Requested Text Regarding AHPS Implementation." Fax from John J. Ingram, Ph.D., PE, to Senator Kent Conrad. April 25, 1997. FOIA document.

The Natural Hazards Center. 1998 Hazards Research and Applications Workshop. "Session Summary S98-12." University of Colorado, Boulder. August 28, 1998.

North Dakota Division of Emergency Management. Situation Reports for Incident No. 97-015. 1997. http://www.state.nd.us/dem/current.html.

North Dakota Museum of Art Oral History Project (NDMA-OHP). Selected transcripts. Interviewers: Kimberly K. Porter, Ph.D., Eliot Glassheim, Ph.D., Jim McKenzie, and Marcia Harris. Department of Special Collections, Chester Fritz Library, University of North Dakota, Grand Forks.

North Dakota National Guard. Situation Report 22, Incident 97-015. April 16, 1997.

North Dakota State Water Commission. *The Floods of 1997: A Special Report.* June 1997.

U.S. Army Corps of Engineers. "Emergency Operations Situation Reports for Event Red River of the North and Minnesota River Spring Flood of 1997." 1997.

U.S. Army Corps of Engineers. St. Paul District. "1997 Flood Fight at Grand Forks, N.D.: Chronology of Related Flood Forecast." May 6, 1997.

———. Flood Reconnaissance Reports. Richard Pomerleau and Terry Zien. 1997.

U. S. Code. National Historic Preservation Act of 1966, as amended (U.S.C. 470 et seq.), Section 106. Posted at http://www2.cr.nps.gov/laws/NHPA1966.htm.

U.S. Department of Commerce. National Oceanic and Atmospheric Administration (NOAA). "Service Assessment and Hydraulic Analysis: Red River of the North 1997 Floods." National Weather Service. Silver Spring, Maryland. August 1998.

U.S. Department of Housing and Urban Development (HUD). Office of Community Planning and Development. "Relocation Assistance to Persons Displaced from Their Homes." HUD-1044-CPD. December 1999. http://www.hud.gov/offices/cpd.

White House. Office of the Press Secretary. "Remarks by the President in Briefing on Flood Damage by Local Officials." Transcript. April 22, 1997.

Acknowledgements

This story of the 1997 Red River of the North flood is incomplete. The flooding also devastated another city, just across the Red River from Grand Forks, and its story of recovery is much different from that of its sister. East Grand Forks, a much smaller community, has a story to tell. I hope someone tells it.

In addition, many heroes in the flood fight of 1997 remain unsung: city engineers and emergency managers up and down the Red River valley who designed flood protection systems that worked, small-town mayors who rallied their constituents during an extremely tough flood season, countless United States Geological Survey employees who risked their lives to collect river data during the flooding, Corps engineers and National Weather Service employees who were preoccupied by the Red River for months before the flood, and then haunted by it for years afterward, mental health workers who had to help piece together thousands of broken lives; and, perhaps most importantly, those ordinary citizens whose lives were irrevocably changed by what happened in the Red River Valley in 1997. There are thousands of stories that deserve to be heard. Luckily, the University of North Dakota has compiled an oral history, excerpts of which have been published in *Voices from the Flood*.

The events portrayed in this book are drawn from interviews I conducted, newspaper accounts, personal accounts, photographs, and the North Dakota Museum of Art Oral History Project (NDMA-OHP); from National Weather Service, NOAA, and Department of Commerce documents, most secured through a Freedom of Information Act (FOIA) request; and from U.S. Army Corps of Engineers documents and countless other notes, letters, court documents, city codes, and federal disaster relief documents. Various other materials I collected from individuals, newspapers, libraries, government agencies, and other sources during interviews and research.

All quotes, including those collected from my interviews, are appropriately cited in the backmatter, as are all research materials and other resources. All of the National Weather Service e-mails and internal correspondence quoted come from the more than two thousand documents received from a Freedom of Information Act request.

A number of people made this project possible. I would like to thank a few of them. Kimberly Porter, Ph.D. and Eliot Glassheim, Ph.D., along with everyone involved in the North Dakota Museum of Art Oral History Project, for their help and generosity. Patricia Owens, for allowing me to probe still open wounds, despite a number of family difficulties that arose soon after she left Grand Forks. Ken Vein, who was gracious enough to grant me a number of interviews about a difficult subject. Duane Hafner, Terry Bjerke, Bob Brooks, Art Bakken and Sam Martinson for their candor and generosity of time. Lisa Hedin from the Corps of Engineers who, despite controversy and a busy schedule, spoke with me at length about Grand Forks. Richard Pomerleau, from the Corps of Engineers, who so kindly offered time and valuable materials. Jim and Mary Lien (who were kind enough to tell me I was "cleaning their wound," not adding salt to it), Kelly Straub, Peg Rogers, and John Burke, for their openness, sincerity, and willingness to rehash a traumatic time in their lives. Dr. Roger Pielke, Jr., for helping me understand the sociology of science, and to Curt Stofferahn, Ph.D., for helping me understand the sociology of disaster and of the city of Grand Forks. Rex Sorgatz, for his time, generosity with print sources, and friendship. Alf Warkentin from Manitoba's Water Branch for spending a great of time helping me understand Manitoba's approach to hydrologic forecasting. Professors Robert and Mary Kweit from the University of North Dakota, for sharing their thoughts on the Grand Forks political landscape following the flood.

Piecing together the National Weather Service's story was the most difficult task I faced when crafting this narrative. I am indebted to Michael Ravnitzky, who donated his time and expertise in assisting me with Freedom of Information Act requests, and is responsible for securing the documents needed to produce an accurate account of the National Weather

Service's activities. Without Michael's help I would not have been able to tell this story.

Thanks also go to National Weather Service employees from the Grand Forks office: Gregory Gust, Lynn Kennedy, and Michael Lukes, for speaking with me at length and answering endless follow-up questions. I would like to express my deep gratitude to Michael Anderson, Steve Buan, and Daniel Luna at the North Central River Forecast Center for spending an entire afternoon reviewing their activities, thoughts, and motivations during the 1997 flooding.

I am thankful to my amazing agent, Doug Stewart, for his enthusiasm and advice. I also owe thanks to Wendy Sherman for seeing the potential in the story of Grand Forks. Thanks to Greg Britton of Borealis Books for publishing this book and for believing in it. I am indebted to my smart, sensitive editor, Ann Regan, for making this a better book, and to Mindy Keskinen, a wonderful copyeditor with sharp eyes and great literary sensibility. Thank you also to Kevin Morrissey for all he's done for this book.

Thank you to my sisters, Lacy and Delta, for their love and support. I owe a great debt to Starr Sage for always being there. I will always be grateful to Ken Siman.

My mother, Barbara, kept me company on many of my trips to Grand Forks, even asking a few questions of her own in my interviews with Kelly Straub. I'm thankful for her encouragement and her support, and for her friendship.

And finally, I am deeply grateful to my father, Don, for helping me to understand that the only way to tell the story is to talk to the people who lived it. He is my journalistic touchstone and I have aspired to treat my subjects with the same respect and insight with which he treats his own. This book is for him.

Red River Rising was designed and set in type by Will Powers at the Minnesota Historical Society Press. The typeface is Miller, designed by Matthew Carter. Printed by Maple Press, York, Pennsylvania.